D0423462

Carl Becker

Carl Becker

Carl Becker

Carl

Becker

A Biographical Study in American Intellectual History

by
BURLEIGH TAYLOR WILKINS

Published jointly by

The M.I.T. Press
MASSACHUSETTS INSTITUTE OF TECHNOLOGY

and

Harvard University Press

Cambridge, Massachusetts

1961

To My Mother and Father

Foreword

SINCE HIS DEATH in 1945, Carl Becker has become the subject of a lively and sometimes critical curiosity among scholars. George Sabine, Leo Gershoy, Charlotte Smith, Cushing Strout, David Noble, and others have written articles or books concerning some aspect of his thought, usually his ideas about historiography. I have long felt that such a restricted approach to Becker, however interesting and fruitful its results, might in time create a distorted image of Becker and lead future generations to neglect other dimensions of his thought. I have, therefore, attempted to restore the balance somewhat by writing an "intellectual biography" of Becker, which is based upon a study of all his published works as well as upon a careful scrutiny of the Becker Papers at Cornell University.

By relating his "thoughts" to his "environment" and by tracing the development — and the interconnections — of his ideas about history, philosophy, politics, religion, and literature, I have tried to see Becker "whole" while at the same time discriminating between the major and the minor aspects of his work. In studying the "influence" of men such as Frederick Jackson Turner, James Harvey Robinson, and Woodrow Wilson upon Becker, I have sought to avoid that mechanistic and sometimes comical treatment of "influence" that Becker himself deplored in intellectual history. Although I have sometimes pointed out weaknesses in Becker's works or ventured an occasional criticism of his ideas, this volume is offered mainly as an exercise in historical understanding. Readers will, of course, see that I do not share Becker's relativism; but on the other hand they will find that I do not accept that contempt for "useful" history which is currently fashionable. For a perhaps utopian picture of a useful history that might "work" because it is true and for no other reason, as well as for a more detailed criticism of some of the ideas common in Becker's time, the reader may want to consult my "Pragmatism as a Theory of Historical Knowledge," in the July, 1959, *American Historical Review.*

I wish to thank Corpus Christi College, Cambridge, England, for a Donaldson Research Studentship and the Southern Fellowships Fund for a fellowship that helped to make this book possible. I also wish to thank Mrs. Harold Goffigon, Mrs. Ruth Dubois, and the secretarial staff of the Humanities Department at the Massachusetts Institute of Technology for having typed the original manuscript of this book. Finally I must express my indebtedness to George B. Wynne, Richard Watson, Harold T. Parker, A. M. Schlesinger, Jr., Thomas LeDuc, and Phil Snyder for the encouragement they have given me, either in this particular work, or at some point in my studies.

BURLEIGH TAYLOR WILKINS

Cambridge, Massachusetts
August, 1960

Contents

"He thinks I am an unprejudiced
observer and will tell him the
exact truth. Now what am I to say?"

HENRY ADAMS, *Esther*

Chapter I

The Origins of Carl Becker: An Introduction

THE DIFFICULTIES of explaining American history in terms of great families are well known, so much so that I hesitate to begin a book with such a commonplace. In political history it is a truism that the Byrds, Lees, and Adamses, fascinating as they are, do not provide an adequate point of reference around which to organize events. In intellectual history the comparative unimportance of great families is even more evident, for after we have mentioned the Adamses, again, and the Jameses, there is an embarrassing silence. It may, of course, be wise for future historians to remember that Reinhold Niebuhr has a brother named Richard; and we cannot well forget, however much we should like to, that Increase Mather had a son named Cotton. When, however, we speak of the comparative unimportance of the "great-family principle" in American intellectual history, it is logical to inquire: Comparative to what? If we mean comparative to political history in the United States, then there is only a difference of degree and not of kind. But if we mean comparative to the history of intellectual activity in Britain, for instance, the word *comparative* clearly assumes a wider significance.

We have had in America no equivalent of the Stephen family, described by Noel Annan in his recent biography of Leslie Stephen;[1] nor have we had such patrons as the sometimes patronizing Monckton Milnes. Instead, we have had individuals who spring up from what often seems a barren soil, without unusual family stimuli or beneficent patrons to take them in hand. We have certainly had the high moral purpose of evangelical Protestantism that appears to have informed the spirit of the Stephens and their equivalents even after the articles of faith had been lost; but, after the demise of Transcendentalism, it has been too diffusely spread over too wide an area to explain any concentrated unit of creative effort.

[1] *Leslie Stephen, His Thought and Character in Relation to His Time* (Cambridge, Massachusetts, 1952).

1

Still at the end of the nineteenth century the evangelical spirit remained much in evidence, for instance, in the writings of critics of the apparent amorality of business enterprise. As often as not, however, the evangelical mood was sidetracked into a reactionary defense of the rural, Anglo-Saxon supremacy of a bygone day; recent historiography has illustrated the essentially backward-looking mentality of many of the reformers in the last days of the nineteenth century.[2] On a more elevated level, even a casual reading of a work such as William Dean Howells' *The Rise of Silas Lapham*[3] will show that the final moral rise of Silas Lapham (and his economic fall) came from his clinging to the simple and, by the author's own terms, largely obsolete ethics of a previous era.

My mention of Howells by way of illustration is deliberate, for he comes from the same general geographic region as the subject of this biography, and he symbolizes the best of the first genuine literary talent that burst forth in amazing profusion from the Middle Border. An analysis of the *Zeitgeist* of the area west of the Alleghenies lies beyond my present intent — here I must respectfully refer the reader to Carl Becker's spirited essay on "Kansas."[4] I do, however, think it wise to call attention to what might be termed the "Mid-Western Myth," according to which that portion of the United States is held to be highly original. The notion that freshness, and a fresh start, are essential to creative effort influenced a host of American writers, especially Mid-Westerners, for a considerable length of time — writers ranging in talent from William Dean Howells and Sherwood Anderson to Zona Gale and Zane Grey. Furthermore, the "Mid-Western Myth" is an idea that died hard, perhaps because it was so useful. When, for example, A. N. Whitehead in the 1930's would occasionally tire of the blasé Harvard student, he would recall that the University of Chicago had seemed to him a veritable Athens, and he would find momentary relief in thinking of the freshness and promise of the Mid-West.[5]

Later in this study, I shall try to explain what Carl Becker and his great teacher, Frederick Jackson Turner, thought of this "Mid-Western Myth" and to explore the ways in which this myth entered into Beck-

[2] An intelligent summary of recent studies in the field, as well as a stimulating interpretation of the reaction to industrialization in terms of "status revolution," is found in Richard Hofstadter's *The Age of Reform, From Bryan to F.D.R.* (New York, 1955), especially 60-212.

[3] Boston, 1886.

[4] In *Essays in American History, dedicated to Frederick Jackson Turner*, edited by Guy Stanton Ford (New York, 1910). Reprinted in *Everyman His Own Historian: Essays on History and Politics* (New York, 1935), 1-28.

[5] Lucien Price, *The Dialogues of A. N. Whitehead* (Boston, 1954), 56, 62, 70-71.

er's consciousness. What I am doing at present, however, is in keeping with Carl Becker's dictum that "it is obviously desirable, first of all, to define one's presuppositions."[6] Becker also cautioned that "as historians we cannot find causes; we can only observe events and note their correlation,"[7] or that at least we must remember that the "causes" of phenomena are "implicit in the phenomena themselves."[8] It is far too early to quarrel with Becker when I have yet to record his birth, but it is my presupposition, as against Becker's, in this case, that the historian *can* find causes, whether or not they are "implicit" in phenomena. It would, I think, be futile to have a "frame of reference" (the phrase is Charles Beard's, but the idea is equally Carl Becker's) or a point around which to organize events, if the frame of reference didn't serve to connect events in some way, causal or otherwise, more strongly than any observation (which can lead nowhere) or any correlation (which can be a matter of chance).

My first two chapters will be used to examine the available evidence concerning the youth of Carl Becker, and many of my observations will refer to something outside of Becker — to his family, to the politics and religion of his family, and to the college and the universities that he attended. Obviously much of Becker's development was an internal affair — as what development is not? — and cannot be reconstructed, let alone explained. By now it may also be clear that, while Becker was a historian or a thinker about history, I am predisposed to regard his talent as being essentially of the "creative" sort. However private his development and however creative his talent, Becker, like the rest of us, was earth-bound to a considerable extent. While his creative processes cannot be reproduced, the historian can discern at what points he touches earth and can suggest what points should be regarded as the sources (as distinct from the contents) of some of his thoughts. What then is the historian to make of the son of an Iowa dirt farmer who wrote, as Charlotte Watkins Smith has aptly said, with "the urbanity of a Lord Chesterfield and the pithiness of a Benjamin Franklin"?[9]

True, Carl Becker's father prospered and moved to a town where he acquired during the course of his lifetime a library of over one hundred books, but for a talented son from such a background it is a long way to a reputation ranking, in some respects, near that of Francis Parkman

[6] *Progress and Power* (Stanford, California, 1936), 6.
[7] *Ibid.*, 21.
[8] *Ibid.*, ix.
[9] *Carl Becker: On History and the Climate of Opinion* (Ithaca, New York, 1956), 132.

and Henry Adams. Perhaps it was somewhat easier in Becker's day, but today in his eastward trek to fame he might encounter the formidable Peter Viereck. Witness Viereck's awesome declaration of Eastern exclusiveness:

> I intend to talk of nothing except hogs to the next Iowan who arrives at Grand Central reading the *New Yorker* and who tells me in a voice of urbane banter, "I am a bittersweet observer of life's little ironies. Why have you no feeling for nuance?"[10]

Despite Carl Becker's reputation for irony and nuance, one cannot imagine him as Professor Viereck's Iowan. Professor Viereck, I suspect, would have been left waiting for other trains, and other Iowans to pounce upon. But the question of how to explain the kind of talent that Becker had, and its reception, remains.

As the first biographer of Carl Becker, I feel a duty — at times it is an escape — to record more than I explain, but where I do explain, I shall explain a great deal by reference to the rôle of the university in Becker's life. I would suggest that American higher education has done for American intellectual life, if not for her political life, services analogous to those rendered by Oxford and Cambridge to Britain; here the friendships were formed, the apostles gathered. I would point to the obvious: that Carl Becker spent most of his life and all of his adult years at universities, and that several of these institutions were in the vanguard of the revolution that was transforming our colleges from boys' schools into universities.

Also, I would in the course of this study deplore the myth that because Carl Becker was not a campus politician or a jovial extrovert, he was by necessity the exact opposite of these things, an unusually shy man *all* his life, a "loner" because of his sensitivity and frequent bouts of illness. Too much has been made of Becker's "tragic view of life,"[11] and not enough of the less sensational features of his thought and life. A man with a devoted wife and family, who could number among his friends Frederick Jackson Turner, Wallace Notestein, William E. Dodd, Charles A. Beard, Harold J. Laski, and Felix Frankfurter, to name only a few of the more eminent, ought not to be called lonely, without qualification. If friendships such as these be the fruits of introversion, then perhaps we would do well to cultivate such a limitation in ourselves. Also, it is clear that Becker's friends, as a whole,

---

[10] *Shame and Glory of the Intellectuals* (Boston, 1953), 67.
[11] Charlotte Watkins Smith, *Carl Becker: On History and the Climate of Opinion* (Ithaca, New York, 1956), 32.

had no especially tragic view of life and that many were incurable optimists. One theme, and one of the constant sources of this biography, might be called "Carl Becker and His Friends."

Finally, in order not to obscure the uniqueness of Carl Becker, I would call attention to a side of his character that made him in his intellectual and personal relations what might be called a "countervailing force," that is to say, a man who leaned by temperament just a little in the opposite direction from whatever was being championed at the time. I do not mean to make him out to be a chameleon — he wasn't — or a man greatly out of harmony with his times or contemporaries. I simply mean that among optimists, he would play pessimist; among pessimists, he would hold out hope. Among reformers, he would point to the limitations of human effort; among conservatives, he would point to the limits of the status quo. Among "New Historians" and among "old historians" he would always call attention to the merits of the opposite school. He would be a "countervailing force" — I use this phrase in the sense in which it was employed before the days of David Riesman[12] — sometimes out of playful perversity, but more often he would be a countervailing force from the conviction that it is the better part of wisdom and charity to recognize, with Oliver Wendell Holmes, that "truth is only the system of one's limitations."[13] However doubtful this may be for a sound theory of knowledge, it makes a sound principle for understanding the mind of Carl Becker.

I must, however, take first things first, and it is an assumption of biography that the family is first, if only in point of time. "It is a limitation of moderate men," Becker once wrote, "to be much governed by observable facts. . . ."[14] And I am constrained to admit that the observable facts about Becker's family are few. Of the external events of their lives enough is known to fit them into a social pattern, the familiar pattern of westward expansion. As individuals in their own right, they appear only enough to tantalize.

"My paternal great-grandfather could not speak anything but German; my father could not speak anything but English,"[15] Carl Becker wrote in recollection of his family, and he went on to add that his father had no quality that would have marked him as other than Eng-

---

[12] For Riesman's use of the "countervailing force" concept, see his *Individualism Reconsidered* (Glencoe, Illinois, 1954), 1-54, where the role of conviction in a man's decision "to countervail" is dangerously minimized.
[13] Becker, *Progress and Power*, 14.
[14] *The Eve of the Revolution* (New Haven, Connecticut, 1918), 191.
[15] *The United States: An Experiment in Democracy* (New York, 1920), 239.

lish in origin. Becker's brief memories of his family appeared in his
The United States: An Experiment in Democracy, published in 1920,
a book whose value today stems more from what it tells us of Becker
than from what it tells of the United States. Usually Becker was reticent about himself and his family, proceeding upon the urbane assumption that he at least was of little consequence, so that he seldom came
between the reader and his story in the sense of autobiography. The
exception to this rule occurred in a section of Becker's book devoted
to the problems of Americanization, where he used his family background to illustrate the point of view from which he had as a child
witnessed the Americanization of others, of a German family that had
settled on a farm next to his father's in Iowa and that underwent the
same transformation the Beckers had experienced several generations
before.

On the paternal side, Becker's ancestors were of German and Dutch
origin and had arrived in New York state "probably," Becker surmised,
in the eighteenth century. On his mother's side, Becker thought his
ancestry was a mixture of English and Irish immigrants who had come
to New York he knew not when. In fact, since the name Sarvay seems
French rather than English or Irish, Becker may have been even more
in ignorance than he recognized. On the whole, Becker's recollections
are as sketchy as those of most Americans. In Becker's case exactitude
as to his origins was made even more difficult because his family had
not seen fit to remain forever in New York.

The decision to leave New York had been made by Becker's father,
Charles Dewitt Becker, a veteran of three years' service in the Union
Army during the Civil War and a man capable, by all accounts, of
abiding by his decisions. He decided, according to his son, "like thousands of others, to abandon the state of his birth in order to acquire
much better land at a much lower price in the new West."[16] Becker
did not exempt his father's conduct from the economic interpretation
that he would sometimes offer of the behavior of other individuals,
especially that of the early American settlers.[17] The desire of Becker's
father to acquire "better" land does, however, put his economic motive
on a level different from that of the land speculator; in fact he seems to
have been a man bent on self-improvement in several directions, a kind
of Puritan transplanted to the near frontier. First Becker's father went
to Illinois and from there to Iowa. In Iowa he purchased a farm of

[16] *Ibid.*
[17] *The Beginnings of the American People* (New York, 1915), *passim.*

eighty acres at a cost of about eight dollars an acre,[18] and there his westward migration ended.

The decision of Charles Becker to leave Carthage, New York, was made in the year 1867. On February 18, 1868, he married Almeda Sarvay. She had been born of "well to do parents," who had given her, as her daughter Jessie was to recall, a "good education." To judge by the size of his land purchase in Iowa, Charles Becker could scarcely have been considered well to do; and in this discrepancy between the Sarvay and Becker families there lies a possible explanation of Becker's desire to go West. His daughter has recorded the fact that the parents of Charles Becker were "poor people" and that his formal education had of necessity ceased when he was twelve years old. She hastened to add that he was self-educated: "Had you met him in later years you would have been sure from his manner of speaking and from his appearance that he was a college graduate."[19] Unfortunately Charles Becker's in-laws had not met him in his later years, and his decision to join the westward migration may have sprung from his wanting to be independent and to prove his real worth more quickly.

Charles Becker realized both of these intentions, if such they were, in Black Hawk County, Iowa. His daughter Jessie used nearly the same phrase as his son had in describing the intentions of her parents: "to acquire much better land at a lower price." She remembered, however, that her father had purchased two hundred and forty acres of land — which he had, but not all at once. She remembered, correctly, that their land was "as good land as could be found." Apparently this was a matter of family pride: Carl Becker, too, remembered its being "as good farm land as there is any where to be found."[20]

On this two hundred and forty acre farm, four children were born to Charles and Almeda Becker. Carl Becker was born on September 7, 1873, and was christened Lotus Carl Becker, a name he later changed to Carl L. Becker, partly because no one in college could remember "Lotus," and partly because of the somnolent qualities it suggested.[21] Carl Becker was second in seniority among three sisters: Mary, the eldest, Ann, and Jessie. Of the three sisters Mary became a housewife, had one son, and died at the age of forty-three. Ann was a school

[18] *The United States: An Experiment in Democracy*, 240.
[19] Jessie Becker to Phil L. Snyder, Waterloo, Iowa, November 24, 1955.
[20] *The United States: An Experiment in Democracy*, 240.
[21] Carl Becker to George Lincoln Burr, Minneapolis, Minnesota, February 25, 1917. The George Lincoln Burr Papers, Regional History Archives, Cornell University, Ithaca, New York.

teacher until ill health forced her to resign; she too died at an early age. Jessie worked for thirty years in the office of the Clerk of the District Court in Waterloo, Iowa, where she advanced from stenographer to head deputy in charge of probate work for Black Hawk County. She is still living.

Richard Hofstadter began his *The Age of Reform* with what may well become a classic sentence: "The United States was born in the country and has moved to the city."[22] When Carl Becker was eleven years old, the Becker family rented out its farm and moved to Waterloo, Iowa, fifteen miles away. The year was 1884, and Waterloo was not yet a city. It was, however, a fast-growing town with a population of over five thousand, and the scene of considerable commercial and industrial activity. A flour mill had been erected in 1865, and this was followed in rapid succession by a wool mill, a pickle factory, an agricultural implement factory, a packing company — for Professor Viereck's hogs — and a brewery. By the end of the 1880's there were twenty-five factories in operation in Waterloo, and schemes for new railroads flourished, although there were already two railroads in operation.[23]

Opportunities for speculation were rife, but for the "retired" Charles Becker there were other, less selfish opportunities, for Waterloo was also the county seat of Black Hawk County. Black Hawk County had been named, according to legend, by the famous Lieutenant Zebulon Pike, who had surveyed that part of Iowa and had in the process met Chief Black Hawk himself. The area was rich in Indian lore, but now most of the Indians were gone. In their place were some highly energetic business men and farmers of strong nationalist convictions. One out of every twelve citizens of Black Hawk County had served in the Union Army:[24] the veteran Charles Becker was among friends. He became active in Republican politics (which were *the* politics in Waterloo), as well as in the Masonic lodge. For these activities he was in time rewarded with positions of public trust. He served on the Waterloo school board and on the county board of supervisors;[25] also, he was elected County Recorder, a position he held for ten years.[26] There is, however, ample evidence that the Beckers had no need for

---

[22] *Op. cit.*, 23.

[23] *History of Blackhawk County, Iowa and Its People,* John G. Hartman, Supervising Editor (Chicago, 1915), I, 395-403, 355-379.

[24] *Ibid.*, 165-209.

[25] Jessie Becker to Phil L. Snyder, Waterloo, Iowa, November 24, 1955.

[26] Bruce Gates to Phil L. Snyder, West Palm Beach, Florida, January 10, 1956. Gates is Becker's nephew by his sister Mary.

the honorarium from this office, that they had a prosperous living derived from the rental of their farm.[27]

Since Charles Becker had been in the Mid-West less than two decades before he and his family were able to "retire" to Waterloo, the extent of his success is readily apparent. Equally apparent is the fact that Charles Becker's "retirement" to the town seems only to have brought out hitherto latent talents for public affairs. The details of how he became one of the mainstays of the Masonic and the Republican orders and of the public school system are lost; but it is known that he was one member of the school board who never allowed his own education to flag, or the education of his family to fall into neglect. Of his children only Carl attended college, but the girls who stayed at home were "all well read."[28] Little is known of Mary, but Ann was sufficiently educated to teach school, and Jessie was always an avid reader of her brother's books and articles.[29] On the level of material things Charles Becker was able to provide his family with a large, comfortable house on Randolph Street, conveniently located next door to the Methodist parsonage[30] and near the Methodist Church, which the Beckers attended regularly.

Charles Becker had, presumably, achieved a synthesis of physical and spiritual well-being. The frontier or the near-frontier had served, as Carl Becker's teacher Turner might have explained it, as a release for any discontent that Charles Becker may have felt with the circumstances of his life in the East. In turn the critics of Turner's "safety-valve theory" might explain that the town of Waterloo then served as a reverse kind of safety-valve releasing tensions caused by the Beckers' discontent with rural living. If in Charles Becker's case there was any such discontent, it could not have been economic in origin. The winds of Populism and radicalism swept by, not through, the house on Randolph Street. Like the Mid-Western father of another distinguished future historian, Charles A. Beard, Charles Becker was an economic conservative and individualist; but he would not have been at ease in the company of the free-thinking Indiana farmer William Beard, nor would he have encouraged his son in any eccentricities — a trip to Hull House in Chicago, for instance, or graduate study and reform activities in England. The house on Randolph Street was in short a place for

[27] *The United States: An Experiment in Democracy*, 242.

[28] Bruce Gates to Phil L. Snyder, West Palm Beach, Florida, January 10, 1956.

[29] There are numerous, undated letters from Jessie Becker to Carl Becker in the Becker Papers commenting briefly but approvingly on her brother's works. The approval did not extend to his politics, or to his loss of religious convictions.

[30] Judge Phillip Elliott to Carl Becker, Flint, Michigan, September 25, 1942.

moderation and security, but not for romance or revolution, whose proper place was in books, which is where Carl Becker eventually found them.

Carl Becker was, for the most part, never a child of rebellion; he shared with his father a willingness to abide by the rules of the game. There was a certain economy in the father, an absence of loose ends and extravagance, that was to reappear in the son. There were commitment and direction in the lives of both, generally towards specific goals of an unspectacular sort. Carl Becker has often, with good reason, been regarded as a pragmatist in his philosophical orientation.[31] On the practical level — where pragmatism is often considered to belong — both father and son might be called conservative pragmatists: people who chose to live carefully without any attempt at "conspicuous consumption," and who were never unaware of the intimate connection between thinking and eating. Or, as the son later expressed it: "Reason, we suspect, is a function of the animal organism. . . ."[32] In describing the character of his father, Carl Becker struck just the right note when he returned from Charles Becker's funeral in 1919. "He was an old man," Carl Becker wrote, "who had lived a good life, had got much [of] what he wanted by dint of hard labor, was much respected and much mourned and left his affairs just as he would have done if he could have foreseen his death. On the whole, therefore, it was a good end, and there is nothing to regret."[33]

Nothing to regret in retrospect, little to regret while his father had lived. The father had only wanted his son to lead a good life, to be a Republican, and perhaps a lawyer.[34] Carl Becker would choose to lead a good life, although there would be a divergence between the good life as defined by a Methodist father and as defined by a son who would in time come to be known as a "twentieth century *philosophe*."[35] As far as being a Republican was concerned, however, this was a habit

[31] Merle Curti, Review of Becker's *Everyman His Own Historian*, *American Historical Review*, XLI (October, 1935), 116-118.

George H. Sabine, Preface to Becker's *Freedom and Responsibility in the American Way of Life* (New York, 1955), xvii, xxvi.

George H. Sabine to the author, Ithaca, New York, November 14, 1956. Becker, writes Sabine, is a "good example" of the impingement of pragmatism upon a "sensitive historian."

[32] *New Liberties for Old* (New Haven, Connecticut, 1941), 93.

[33] Carl Becker to William E. Dodd, Ithaca, New York, December 2, 1919.

[34] Becker, "Wild Thoughts Notebook," April 8, 1895. The "Notebook" was kept by Becker during part of his student days at the University of Wisconsin. Dated entries are from January, 1894, to May, 1895, but there are a score or so undated entries, some of which appear to be of later date.

[35] Obituary of Carl L. Becker, *American Historical Review*, L (July, 1945), 885.

that Carl Becker kept for some time: people's politics are to a large extent a matter of habit, a conviction that Carl Becker and Frederick Jackson Turner would share.[36] In the "Wild Thoughts Notebook" of his undergraduate days, Carl Becker made the following entry: "There is a list of great men in the history of the U. S. who have been fortunate enough to be honored with a refusal of the presidency" — the first of these was Alexander Hamilton; the second, James G. Blaine.[37] Where Blaine had failed, William McKinley succeeded; and Becker in the campaign of 1896 had the pleasure of hearing McKinley speak in Madison, Wisconsin.[38] That fall Becker cast his first vote in a presidential election. "I helped to save the country (I was young then)," he later recalled, "by voting for 'sound' money."[39]

Becker men were expected to vote the straight Republican ticket, whether against maverick free-silver Democrats or conservative gold-standard ones; and when the vote was given to the women Jessie would vote Republican, too. Evidence of this strong Republican feeling turned up, about every four years, in letters from Jessie to Carl for as long as he lived.[40] Carl, however, chose to be an independent as he grew older. "I don't believe he was either a republican or democrat," Jessie admitted after his death, "and if he voted at all voted for the man he thought most capable. My father said he did too, but I remember hearing him say that the best man always seemed to be on the Republican ticket."[41] One wonders what Charles Becker would have thought of a son who would some day cast protest votes for two Socialist Presidential candidates, Eugene Debs and Norman Thomas.[42]

[36] We are, according to Becker, attached to our political institutions because they have worked well, because we have experienced nothing else, "because they are sustained by instinctive emotional responses and unconscious habitual ways of behaving." (*Freedom and Responsibility in the American Way of Life*, 21.)

"Probably the mass of voters inherit their party and their political affiliation. Habit rather than reasoning is the fundamental factor in determining political affiliation of the mass of voters." (Turner, *The Significance of Sections in American History* (New York, 1932), 48.)

[37] "Wild Thoughts Notebook," (no date, probably 1895 or 1896).

[38] Carl Becker to William E. Dodd, Ithaca, New York (no date, probably mid-1920's.) The exact date of McKinley's visit is unknown, but Becker appears to have remembered correctly that McKinley did speak in Madison in 1896.

[39] "The Modern Leviathan," *Everyman His Own Historian*, 88.

[40] "But you always did lean toward the Democrats. Shame on you with your father such a strong Republican." Jessie Becker to Carl Becker, Waterloo, Iowa (1940).

[41] Jessie Becker to Phil L. Snyder, Waterloo, Iowa, December 4, 1955.

[42] Carl Becker claimed to have voted for Eugene Debs in 1920 "not because he was a Socialist, but because he was in jail." ("The Modern Leviathan," *Everyman His Own Historian*, 88.) Debs got 900,000 votes that year while serving a sentence in the Atlanta Federal Penitentiary for violating the Sedition Act; but it is not cer-

Politics and the study of law aside — and Carl Becker was willing to put the study of law aside forever — there were other, more immediate differences between father and son. There was a difference in temperament. The father was "stern," "aristocratic" in bearing; the mother — fortunately — was "mild, patient, kindly." The son resembled the mother in "looks and disposition," a cousin was to recall. "He was a quiet studious boy and got along with people very nicely. I think he was the silver lining in his mother's life. . . ."[43] The mother was a good Methodist, and there is every indication that the son tried to be, even after he had left home and gone to the University of Wisconsin. There was, however, one early difficulty: the mother (and father) believed in observing the Sabbath strictly, which meant attending church and not attending baseball games. Becker's passion for the latter greatly exceeded his tolerance for the former,[44] and he remained all his life, with just a shade of defiance, a lover of ball games.

---

tain that Becker remembered correctly how he had voted in the election which put the Republican candidate William G. Harding into office. See Carl Becker to William E. Dodd, Ithaca, New York, October 25, 1920. In this letter, he said that his sympathies were "instinctively" with the Democratic candidate, James Cox. "I shall be glad if he wins, although my intelligence tells me it is a case of Tweedle and Dum."

For Becker's Thomas vote, see Carl Becker to William E. Dodd, Ithaca, New York, November 29, 1932. "Are you one of the 3,000,000 people who voted for Roosevelt in the belief that you were voting for T. R.? I voted for Thomas because I knew he couldn't be elected. I wouldn't want to be in any way responsible for the people that run things at Washington." Dodd received many such letters; Becker seems always to have written Dodd when his own sense of public responsibility ebbed. Dodd would write painfully earnest replies beseeching Becker not to lose faith.

Generally, except in times of crisis, Becker wore a mask of indifference and disdain toward practical politics and never played even a minor role in a presidential election. Despite his commitment to the idea of "pragmatic" history, he would not surrender his detachment, save in wartime, for involvement in national affairs. He preferred theory to practice, and he might be called an "armchair pragmatist" in this matter of politics. Also, despite his commitment to liberal democracy, he preferred to appear above the parties and factions that he believed essential to the healthy functioning of democracy. In other words, he believed in what others were doing, but he refused to do it with them. As to *why* others were doing what they did, he pretended to wear a mask of cynicism or indifference. Certainly politicians were not politicians simply to insure the success of liberal democracy. Often Becker's "mask" was the predominant reality, as he tired easily of public-office seekers. For these reasons I have found it impossible in many cases to reconstruct his actual voting record. Evidence indicates, however, that he must have voted for Wilson at least once, and for Franklin Roosevelt possibly in 1936, probably in 1940 and 1944. But, as his "protest" votes for Debs and Thomas suggest, he was not a party man; and he delighted in appearing unpredictable.

[43] Mrs. W. G. Henning to Phil L. Snyder, Waterloo, Iowa, December 28, 1955.
[44] *Ibid.*

In 1916 in reviewing the *Autobiography* of Charles Francis Adams, Carl Becker would emphasize how Adams was haunted to the end by the "terrible New England conscience" even after he had ceased attending church. With evident personal relish, Becker quoted Adams on the subject of church-going: " 'Then came the going to church! Lord! that going to church!' That is a good style because, to one who has ever felt the oppression of the Puritan Sunday, the ejaculation leaves nothing to be desired."[45]

The detachment of Becker the professor of history from Methodism in Iowa was not apparent in the "Wild Thoughts Notebook" of Becker the undergraduate. It was a long road, largely obscured now, to Becker's cry to a friend in 1928: "if Methodism is slowly dying in Iowa there is hope for the world."[46] While the road to detachment may have been long, there is no evidence that it was especially painful. If Becker ever had a "religious experience" or a "religious crisis" of any intensity, he kept it to himself.

Where church attendance was concerned, there is the possibility that church-going may have influenced Becker *away* from the good life as defined for him by his family. This possibility centers in part upon a sermon preached by the Reverend Van Ness in Waterloo while Becker was a boy, a sermon in which Voltaire and atheism were attacked so vigorously that Becker began, as soon as he could, to read books about the horrible Voltaire. Becker, as he later recalled, was disappointed to learn that Voltaire was less than an atheist, but pleased to discover that he mattered more in the wide world than the "very popular" Reverend Van Ness. Perhaps the anecdote is true, in which case it reveals the first seed from which Becker's interest in French culture may have flowered. Becker's memory of the sermon, many years afterwards, was still vivid, "chiefly because the words 'atheist' and 'Voltaire' unlike such words as 'Solomon' and 'sanctification' were altogether novel, so that the passionate eloquence of the preacher invested them with horrific and engaging connotations."[47]

Heresy may be born, it seems, at a baseball game, and nurtured on a sermon denouncing Voltaire. Had Becker's disposition been stern like his father's instead of kind like his mother's, his biography might at this point become the story of adolescent rebellion; instead there is peace and tranquility. The love of learning and the love of religion,

---

[45] *Political Science Quarterly*, XXXI (December, 1916), 611.

[46] Carl Becker to E. R. B. Willis, Cornell University librarian, Waterloo, Iowa, June 13, 1928.

[47] *American Historical Review*, XXXIII (July, 1928), 883-885.

which, according to Frederick Jackson Turner,[48] the pioneers carried westward with them, had not yet come into opposition in the mind of Carl Becker.

Where learning is concerned, there is evidence of some precocity on Becker's part. According to his sister Jessie, Carl Becker's brilliance came, not from his well-educated mother, but from his self-educated father, and it was noticeable at an early age. When the Beckers moved from the country to Waterloo, Carl Becker was, at the age of eleven, placed in a class above boys his own age despite the fact that he had come from an inferior rural school. Becker, however, appears to have tired, momentarily, of his precocity and to have experienced a period of indifference to learning, at the time he entered high school. One morning, according to legend, he was expelled from school for a minor incident involving playing cards. He came home to report with pleasure to his mother "no more school for me"; but after lunch his father sent him back to school with a note to the school superintendent. The contents of the note remain a mystery, but Carl Becker's expulsion was terminated with almost indecent haste on the part of the superintendent.[49]

Both Becker's sister and his cousin, Mrs. W. G. Henning, remember another abortive rebellion on Becker's part; and this episode, it is thought, had as much to do with the problems of living with three sisters as with those involving inconstant superintendents. Carl Becker, after his family had moved to Waterloo, went back to the country every summer to live on the farm of Mrs. Henning's parents. There were four male cousins, as well as hired hands on that farm; and here Becker could be a man among men. One summer he wrote to his father that he had chosen to remain on the farm and not to return to school that fall; his father, aware perhaps of his responsibilities as a member of the school board, drove the fifteen miles to the farm and returned with his son.[50]

For the most part, however, the son caused no trouble. He learned to ice skate; he had a girl friend. He resigned himself to education, and it is suggested that when Mrs. Annie S. Newman became principal of the West Side High School Becker decided irrevocably in favor of

[48] "The Children of the Pioneers," *The Significance of Sections in American History*, 256-259.

[49] Jessie Becker to Phil L. Snyder, Waterloo, Iowa, November 24, 1955.

[50] *Ibid.* Also, Mrs. W. G. Henning to Phil L. Snyder, Waterloo, Iowa, December 28, 1955.

learning. In an essay called "The Art of Writing," Becker recalled toward the end of his life how some one in high school had taught him "much about good literature, and something about the rudiments of good grammar."[51] In the manuscript copy of this essay Becker crossed out the word *principal* and put *teacher* in its place; but probably Mrs. Newman was both. By the time Becker was graduated from high school, the new superintendent was able to inform Charles Becker that his son had been "by far the best student in school and we'll hear from him some day."[52]

The "we'll hear from him some day" was as vague as it was flattering. Carl Becker remembered, many years later, that he had decided at the age of eleven to be a writer, and that by the time he entered the university, "having read a great deal but nothing systematically," he was "more determined than ever to be a writer, preferably a writer of novels."[53] Perhaps the recollection was stronger than the reality had been. Becker did, however, remember enough to provide a delightful story of how his literary aspirations had begun. Their beginning was due, not to the Reverend Van Ness, but to something quite disreputable, a weekly journal of adventure, western, and detective stories entitled *Saturday Night*. Becker bought his first copy at the age of eleven — obviously a seminal year in his life —, but when he asked his mother for five cents to buy the next issue, he ran afoul the distinction (common enough among Puritans or near-Puritans) between good and bad literature. The distinction was made at the expense of *Saturday Night*, which his mother, "never brutal till then," refused to help support. Becker failed to communicate to her his excitement over the stories and "the magic in the garish title, blackly spread across the page, something in the feel and smell of the cheap, soft, dampish paper — that had the essential glamor of romance." Even if he could no longer buy *Saturday Night*, he resolved to become "an author, a writer of stories for *Saturday Night*."[54]

The more "normal" reaction would surely have been for the boy to want to relive the exploits of the heroes of *Saturday Night*. To choose to write means, to some extent, to choose to live vicariously, an unusual decision for a boy of eleven. Even this was too heady a wine — at least, there is no evidence that the decision was acted upon in the near

---

[51] An address given at Smith College sometime in the spring of 1942 and printed for the first time in *Detachment and the Writing of History: Essays and Letters of Carl L. Becker*, Phil L. Snyder, ed., (Ithaca, New York, 1958), 121-144.
[52] Jessie Becker to Phil L. Snyder, Waterloo, Iowa, November 24, 1955.
[53] "The Art of Writing," *Detachment and the Writing of History*, 124.
[54] *Ibid.*, 122.

future — and the boy was reduced to reading in the public library of Waterloo. Greek mythology and Eric the Red. But one day he discovered *Anna Karenina* and took it home to read by "the light of the kerosene lamp, sitting in the old tall-backed, padded rocking chair," with his feet on the fender of the base burner. "Not knowing that it was good literature," Becker remembered, "I found it interesting. This is pretty good, I thought; nearly if not quite as good as the stories in *Saturday Night*. It was the first critical literary judgment I ever pronounced." Becker resolved to become a writer of novels: "The novels I would write would be good literature" — he had capitulated to the good by the time he had finished high school — "as good as Anna Karenina, or even, if fortune was favorable, as good as Ben Hur or the Last Days of Pompeii."[55]

The story is delightful, parts of it are probably true. From this and other evidence Dr. Smith concludes that Becker "wanted always and overwhelmingly to be a good writer."[56] So it may have been, or so it may have seemed in retrospect. But the author has discovered that Becker in his freshman year in college was a candidate for the Bachelor of Science degree and that he planned to major in one of the natural sciences.[57] Of course, science and *Anna Karenina* need not be mutually exclusive, but they usually suggest different modes of thought. It seems probable that Becker, like so many others, did not have quite the singleness of purpose in his youth that he later remembered having had. He had usually a passion for literature, but passion comes and goes; and although he never mentioned it in later life, Becker had wanted for at least one year in his life to be a scientist more than a novelist, or a historian.

That year was 1892-93, when Becker was a freshman at Cornell College in Mount Vernon, Iowa, a Methodist college not far from Waterloo. Today Cornell College has an enrollment of over seven hundred students and a chapter of Phi Beta Kappa.[58] In 1892, although it had been in existence since 1853, it was, however, still largely an act of piety. It owed its origin to the zeal of a Methodist circuit rider, the Reverend George B. Bowman; its first President had been Samuel

---

[55] *Ibid.*, 122-124.

[56] Smith, *op. cit.*, 133. Dr. Smith has successfully refuted Professor Sabine's judgment that "Becker's historical curiosity apparently carried with it little desire to impart what he found." (Preface to *Freedom and Responsibility in the American Way of Life*, xii.) She has done so, however, by leaning to the opposite extreme of accepting uncritically "The Art of Writing" in all its parts.

[57] Evlyn N. Fisher, Registrar of Cornell College, to the author, Mount Vernon, Iowa, February 21, 1957 and March 18, 1957.

[58] *Cornell College Bulletin*, LVII (February 27, 1956).

Fellows, a graduate of DePauw University, another Methodist-affiliated college (which was, incidentally, to become the first alma mater of Charles A. Beard).[59] In short, Cornell College was another monument to the pioneer's enthusiasm for religion and education; the only trouble was that the number of monuments made it impossible for any single denomination to rally to the support of any one college. Thus the Methodist Church in Iowa helped to sponsor four or five colleges simultaneously, a procedure followed by most denominations from Ohio westward. Struggling denominational colleges, judged, as Guy Stanton Ford has observed, by the number of preachers they can produce,[60] can be dismal things, especially when the piety far exceeds the purse. There is evidence that this is how Cornell College struck Carl Becker.

The transcript of his year at Cornell College shows a large number of false starts on his part. One finds him taking, and dropping, during the fall quarter courses in Freshman Engineering and astronomy; and taking, and dropping, again, the course in engineering during the winter term, during which time he also managed to drop a course in German and a course in Christian Evidences, the latter being a required course.[61] In depicting Becker's career at Cornell College, Guy Stanton Ford, a student of Frederick Jackson Turner's who was to become a lifelong friend and admirer of Becker's, writes, "He stayed but one year, leaving before he might be faced with courses in Butler's *Analogy of Natural and Revealed Religion* and Paley's *Natural Theology*."[62] Apparently Becker faced Butler and Paley before leaving Cornell College, since these authors were then standard in most courses in Christian Evidences.

Becker, of course, did not do badly in every respect at Cornell College. His grades in Essays ranged from 43 to 95, and his work in Greek, Latin, Algebra, and Trigonometry was generally in the 80's and 90's.[63] Whether Becker would have returned to Cornell College, and to Butler and Paley, for his sophomore year is not known. The letters he sent home each week were not preserved, and never in the letters or publications of his adult days did he mention Cornell College. Members of his family recall, however, that his year at Cornell was marred by a painful

[59] Marjorie Medary, "The History of Cornell College," *The Palimpsest*, XXXIV (April, 1953), 145-152.

[60] "Carl Lotus Becker," *American Philosophical Society Year Book 1945*, 340.

[61] Record of Carl Lotus Becker, 1892-1893, at Cornell College.

[62] Ford, "Carl Lotus Becker," *American Philosophical Yearbook 1945*, 340.

[63] Record of Carl Lotus Becker, 1892-1893, at Cornell College.

event: the death from typhoid fever during the academic year of a cousin, Leonard Sarvay, who had attended Cornell with Becker. Leonard Sarvay was the son of Becker's uncle and namesake Lotus Sarvay, who had followed the Beckers to Iowa from New York in 1869. First the Sarvays had farmed next to the Beckers; then they had moved to town, buying the house on the other side of Beckers'. Carl and Leonard had been as inseparable as Almeda Sarvay Becker and Lotus Sarvay apparently were; Leonard had been involved with Carl in the affair of the playing cards in high school and had shared his love of baseball. Relatives remember that Carl's shock at Leonard's death was profound. Jessie Becker listed it as one reason why Carl "refused" to go back to Cornell College. The other reason she gave was that he wanted to go to a university,[64] but another may have been his not wanting to encounter Christian Evidences again.

[64] Jessie Becker to Phil L. Snyder, Waterloo, Iowa, November 24, 1955. Also, Mrs. W. G. Henning to Phil L. Snyder, Waterloo, Iowa, December 28, 1955.

Chapter II

The Character and Sensibility of Carl Becker as an Undergraduate: His "Wild Thoughts Notebook"

THERE IS no evidence that Becker's refusal to return to Cornell College was taken badly by his father, who must, however, have regretted the loss of a year. No credit was given by the University of Wisconsin for Becker's work at Cornell. By taking a heavier work load and by attending summer sessions, Becker was, however, able to complete the four year undergraduate program in three years. He was also able to avoid the academic errors of his year at Cornell. In shifting from the natural sciences to the liberal arts he showed a better understanding of what his aptitudes were, and by his senior year he succeeded in becoming what he had been in high school: an A student.[1]

If Becker had arrived at Cornell College during an unexciting period in its academic growth, he had no such misfortune at the University of Wisconsin. He arrived there, as he was later to arrive at Columbia University, at a time of strategic importance in the development of that institution from a college into a university. Dr. Smith has stated: "Probably no more stimulating atmosphere could have been found at any American university in the 1890's than that at the growing University of Wisconsin."[2] Of all the colleges and universities with which Becker was associated as either a student or a teacher, the University of Wisconsin mattered the most, I think, certainly in the formative sense. Later he might in his maturity find a more congenial atmosphere at Cornell University in Ithaca, New York, but the virtues of Becker's that would be applauded at Cornell University were first cultivated at Wisconsin.

Becker arrived at Wisconsin as a twenty-year-old freshman; he remained there for five years, three years as an undergraduate, two years as a graduate student. At Wisconsin he met two of the four most important teachers to influence his development: Charles Homer Haskins

[1] Record of Carl Lotus Becker, 1893-1896, at the University of Wisconsin.
[2] *Op. cit.*, 6.

19

and Frederick Jackson Turner; the other two, H. L. Osgood and James Harvey Robinson, he would meet later at Columbia. Under the stimulus principally of Turner, Becker chose to be not a scientist or a novelist, although his dream of writing novels flourished again for a time at Wisconsin, but a historian; and he would eventually return to take his Ph.D. in history from Wisconsin. At the University Becker acquired a measure of self-confidence, much needed after his year at Cornell College. He chose a career not as a lawyer, as his father had wished, but as a teacher of history, and he worked with conscientious effort toward that end. He also solved, in fundamentals at least, the question of what to do about religious fundamentalism; his solution was honest and direct — he would resign from the Methodist Church. And he did all these things with an absence of any further false starts and without excess. Clearly, if any man is ever influenced by anything outside himself, Becker was influenced by the University of Wisconsin; and if my use of the word *influence* has been a bit too easy, perhaps I might be allowed to put my case negatively, in the words of Carl Becker: "we can't count on people *not learning* from experience."[3]

The experiences of Carl Becker at Wisconsin were myriad, and at last — in comparison with the limited evidence available for his childhood and adolescence — so are the documents that tell of them. For the first time I encounter, as Becker's biographer, what Becker himself came to regard as the central problem in historical writing: how to combine an analysis of experience, leading, one hopes, to certain generalizations, with the narrative method by means of which one hopes to make these unwieldy generalizations move through time.[4] This suggests a further problem: does dissection for the purpose of analysis alter what is being analyzed? It was in large measure from these two problems that Becker's famous reflections on historical method would originate. Like it or not, authors do dissect and select and arrange, regardless of whether these operations deserve the emphasis Becker later placed upon them; and here I have chosen to make what may be a very arbitrary distinction between Becker personally and Becker professionally. I have chosen first to look at Becker personally, as he is revealed in his "Wild Thoughts Notebook," and then in the next chapter to look at him professionally, mainly in relation to his master, Frederick Jackson Turner. The order is perhaps misleading, for the

[3] Carl Becker to Louis Gottschalk, Ithaca, New York, September 3, 1944.
[4] Becker, "Frederick Jackson Turner," *American Masters of the Social Sciences,* Howard Odum, ed., (New York, 1927). Reprinted in *Everyman His Own Historian,* 229.

most important event in Becker's personal life at Wisconsin is that he decided to become professional, that he saw, as Edward Gibbon had expressed it, the use of grafting his "private consequence on the importance of a great professional body, the benefits of those firm connections which are cemented by hope and interest, by gratitude and emulation, by the mutual exchange of services and favors."[5]

Carl Becker kept his "Wild Thoughts Notebook," with care at least, for only one year and five months of his five years' residence in Madison, Wisconsin; the "Notebook" is, however, indispensable for those who would understand the growth of Becker's character and sensibility. For the first time Becker speaks of himself, not through the haze of the anecdotal and highly polished recollections of later life, but in terms of what he has just now seen or felt. The "Notebook" entries are in Becker's crabbed undergraduate handwriting, which did not become much clearer as he grew older. Although for the first time in his life Becker was living entirely apart from his family, the "Notebook" is not filled with thoughts — or deeds — that would seem in any way wild to readers addicted to the novels of Francoise Sagan. The entries are sometimes searching and mature, but they are not bold or cynical; they have their full share of aphorisms that do not quite come off, as well as the pointless observations to be expected of an undergraduate. As things in themselves the entries are of dubious value; as guides to the nature of young Carl Becker, now removed forever from Uncle Lotus on the one side and the Methodist minister on the other, they are more than we could reasonably hope for.

Dr. Smith in her study of Becker has chronicled briefly how the "Wild Thoughts Notebook" reveals Becker's retreat from the "comfort of certainty" in things religious;[6] but, although hers is primarily a study in historiography, she has not seen fit to stress the fact that Becker's skepticism about religion is the pivotal point in a progression — or retrogression — towards skepticism concerning all claims to absolute certainty, whether made by clergymen, philosophers, or historians. Had Becker died during the 1930's when he was in his sixties instead of at the end of World War Two, his biography would be a study in disenchantment; as it is, Becker's is a story in which skepticism alternates with faith. From the time of his leaving the University of Wisconsin onward, however, whatever faith Becker was to feel would be of a secular nature while his skepticism would be aimed at all theories of

[5] *Memoirs of My Life and Writing* (London, 1891), 154.
[6] *Op. cit.*, 11-13.

knowledge that permit judgments of probable relationships of facts or judgments about values to masquerade as absolutes.

Before considering the "Wild Thoughts Notebook" in this connection, I should like to jump ahead a bit — to the time when a matured Becker was writing his essays, "What Are Historical Facts?" and "On Historical Evidence," and when he was delivering his famous Presidential speech before the American Historical Association, "Everyman His Own Historian." The starting point of Becker's "skepticism" or "historical relativism," it is clear from even a casual reading of these essays, had always to do with the question of testimony, of why we should believe something simply because witnesses testify to its truth. How should we act when witnesses disagree, or when their experience is so contrary to our own? On the question of miracles, should we follow Hume or DeMaistre — can testimony ever establish that a miracle occurred in violation of all the known "laws of nature"?[7] There is, I believe, a connection between Becker's later concern as a professional historian with the problems of testimony and his earlier religious difficulties. Certainly there is a strong parallel, and his conclusions in both cases are strikingly similar.

In some primitive Protestant sects, it is still a habit for members "to testify" as to their religious experiences; I doubt that Becker as an Iowan Methodist was unaware of this practice, since it sometimes creeps into the best of churches. And all churches rest ultimately upon such testimony. The question is simply whether such testimony is held to be mainly historical or whether we refuse to confine miracles and other religious experiences to the Bible and to a select group of past occurrences officially recognized by a given church. On the question of evidence then, what should be said? Becker writing in 1938 on miracles was quite direct: "The vital point here is not testimony but the disposition of people to accept testimony as establishing this or that kind of event."[8] The vital point was no longer the truth or falsity of

[7] "What Are Historical Facts?" A paper read before the forty-first annual meeting of the American Historical Association at Rochester, New York, December, 1926. *The Western Political Quarterly*, VIII (September, 1955). Reprinted in *Detachment and the Writing of History*, 41-64.

"On Historical Evidence," manuscript read by Becker before "The Circle" at Cornell University, November 19, 1937, and at Princeton, March 31, 1938, and revised during the war period. "Everyman His Own Historian," *American Historical Review*, XXXVII (January, 1932). Reprinted in *Everyman His Own Historian*, 233-255.

[8] Review of Ernest C. Mossner, *Bishop Butler and the Age of Reason*, *American Historical Review*, XLIII (October, 1938), 117.

evidence, but something behind the evidence — the implication being that the question now fell within the province of psychology or the sociology of knowledge.

Becker's final position on what he called the "Christian story" was, to say the least, highly detached. Bishop Butler and his kind, he wrote, had had their day. Their day hadn't been a long one because the disposition of people to accept miracles was much altered by the Age of Reason. People came to look upon the Christian story as a myth and to examine its premises with detachment, "That is to say," Becker added, "with a prejudice against them. So examined the whole structure collapsed." Clearly it had collapsed in Becker's mind, for he concluded with Hume's ironical remark that to be a philosophic skeptic is, in a man of letters, the "first and most essential step towards being a sound, believing Christian."[9]

Becker, having taken the first step, never took the second. His disposition to accept miracles and other Christian tenets had been too much altered by his own "Age of Reason," which had begun in earnest at the University of Wisconsin and which was confirmed subsequently by his studies of the eighteenth century *philosophes*. In his "Wild Thoughts Notebook" there is an undated entry, probably from 1895: "I cannot understand why all miracle believing Christians are not Christian scientists." As he grew older, Becker extended his skepticism concerning the divine origins of miracles to the divine origins of Christian values. In 1940, in reviewing a book by a deeply religious historian, Henry Osborn Taylor, Becker would advise that it might "be read with profit by all those who accept the author's values, even if they do not find any origin for them that transcends the human mind."[10] This inability of Becker's to find the hand of God in history would get him into difficulties occasionally, with reviewers or readers who would detect, or think they had detected, a note of irreligiosity in his writings. Becker would, however, almost never strike an arrogant or dogmatic note in his disbelief in the supernatural, which may have offended the dogmatic believer even more. He simply affirmed that he was unaware of any divine plan for human beings and voiced the suspicion that the universe was indifferent to mankind, including Carl Becker. Sometimes there were mock heroics of a quiet, literary sort associated with Becker's skepticism: man alone, an accident of nature,

[9] *Ibid.*, 117-118.

[10] Review of Henry Osborn Taylor, *A Historian's Creed, American Historical Review,* XLV (April, 1940), 591.

struggling heroically with nature, against overwhelming odds, but struggling still, et cetera.[11]

Generally, however, Becker's attitude was a tolerant one; in temper it resembled that of Thomas Jefferson and Benjamin Franklin, whom he much admired but not to the extent of following them in their deism. Dr. Smith speaks of Becker's "semi-deistic" ideas as an undergraduate,[12] but I find no evidence of this except for one entry in the "Notebook," which is quoted by Dr. Smith. In this passage Becker records Tolstoy's definition of religion as "man's relation to the universe." Becker's only response was to think "that is about equivalent to saying that it is his relation to God."[13] But that could be pantheism, or almost anything — it is not even clear that Becker assented to this definition.

We are forced, I think, to content ourselves without any exact definition or even chronicle of Becker's changing metaphysics, just as Becker had to content himself with the limits of human understanding as explicated by Hume. It is, however, possible to chronicle Becker's skepticism about one Christian tenet, that of Original Sin, and to understand that Becker's skepticism on this point grew strong because of the attraction of a rival faith; in place of the Christian idea of Original Sin, Becker put something like a moderate version of the Wisconsin "Progressive" idea of Perfectibility. On January 20, 1894, Becker recorded his feelings about the poem "Eugene Aram." His reaction to Eugene Aram's placing the blame upon Cain for his own murderous impulses was one of disdain. Why, Becker wondered, should Cain be the "dumping ground for all the guilt of murderers in every generation as Adam was for the Sin of the world?"[14] The university student suggested a more adult theory of responsibility; namely, that people blame themselves for their own follies and spend less time on Adam's.

There can be no question that the longer Becker thought about religion, the more subjectivist his conclusions tended to become; the undergraduate was working toward the modern's conception of religion as that which concerns a man in his spare time. In March, 1894, Becker defined religion as that "secret part" of man's soul "which is never revealed to mortal man and which is known to himself and God alone." The same entry includes the following bit of comparative

---

[11] See, for example, his *The Heavenly City of the Eighteenth Century Philosophers* (New Haven, 1932), 1-28, and his "Progress" in *Encyclopedia of the Social Sciences*, XII, 495-499.

[12] *Op. cit.*, 11.

[13] "Wild Thoughts Notebook," March 5, 1894.

[14] *Ibid.*, January 20, 1894.

religions, which, however bland, suggests that in Becker's case a form of religious relativism antedates his well-known historical relativism: "Christianity is one attempt to formulate religion."[15]

Of one thing Becker was certain: "Every man has a religion. It may be good or it may perhaps be bad, but it's no man's business but his own." In 1894, Becker, however, was still attending church, and he was still reasonably certain that religion was good. "A man's religion is the best there is of him." At that time, Becker's conception of religion remained sufficiently objective for him to say what the church should be, and his categorical imperatives were in part those of the Social Gospel. "The province of the church is educational and charitable. . . . The church that isn't in the world and *of* the world amounts to nothing." The province of the church, however, wasn't reformatory, according to Becker; and here his thought was less in harmony with the Social Gospel and more in keeping with the traditions of individualism and self-help. "A man can reform himself but none can do it for him. . . . Don't try to reform men, it can't be done." There was, however, a note of optimism: "Feed a starving man and he will desire to reform if he is wicked. Educate him and he will know how to do it." Above all else, don't *tell* him he's wicked. He knows that, and if you persist in being critical, you break the only tie, "that of sympathy," which binds you to him. Let us teach by example, and act by charity, Becker seemed to be saying. Let us reform not by coercion, but by indirection. Above all, "Reform yourself."[16]

Meanwhile the undergraduate Becker was seeing in the town life of Madison behavior that would tend to dampen optimism of the hardiest kind. His "Notebook" contains descriptions of old men sitting aimlessly in cheap hotels, of drunks wandering about the streets, and of derelict families. A man can reform himself, perhaps; but what about his environment, and what if, after all, some of his evil is hereditary? Concerning a young Madison man arrested for falsifying bank reports, Becker speculated, "How much (if he is guilty) of such tendency has he inherited?"[17]

As the year 1894 drew to a close, Becker seems to have given less and less thought to questions of religion. Instead of worrying about the relation of the church to morality and character, his attention appears to have shifted somewhat. His principal concern now had to do, in an amateurish way, with the relation of the artist to his subject-matter.

[15] *Ibid.*, March 5, 1894.
[16] *Ibid.*
[17] *Ibid.*, March 14, 1894.

In the "Notebook" there are a number of character sketches, crude efforts at reporting commonplace experiences, and a draft of a passably good short story — the story of a homely youth in love with an actress visiting Madison.[18] More will be said shortly about the "sensibility" of Carl Becker and his "artistic" efforts, but first it is necessary to conclude this account of Becker's youthful ideas on religion as expressed in his "Notebook." "It is my idea," he wrote with an air of finality, "that people should teach children how to act and let them believe as they please rather than teach them what to believe and let them act as they please. Less religion and more manners would increase the value of many 'very good' people."[19]

Becker's new emphasis upon manners instead of metaphysics is apparent in several other entries. He noted, for instance, that the people who would go to hear a quartet in a Methodist church were not as cultured as those who would attend the same performance in the Madison Opera House; and he interpreted this as a reflection not upon cultured people but upon the Methodist church. The provincial was catching on to the social distinctions of Wisconsin's capital city. Even in the university library Becker noted the peculiarities of the Christian as represented by "a very peculiar individual" who looked "somewhat idiotic. . . . He never reads anything but commentaries on books of the Bible. And he has the air of reading these as a sense of duty."[20]

What kept Becker from dropping over into an extreme intolerance of religion remains largely a mystery; probably some saving grace of character or family loyalty helped him keep his disdain private until his differences had congealed into indifference. But there was also the power of a negative example: the audiences that attended with Becker some of the lectures given by Robert Ingersoll in Madison in 1895. Ingersoll's position was simple; as he succinctly informed another citizen of Waterloo, Iowa, he was "a believer in the natural. The supernatural does not and cannot exist. I reject all religions based on the miraculous — the supernatural. . . ."[21] In two of his books, *The Heavenly City of the Eighteenth Century Philosophers* and *The Declaration of Independence,* Becker would raise pointed questions as to what is natural. In 1895 he had pointed remarks to make about Ingersoll's

---

[18] *Ibid.,* March 24, 1894. The story of "stubborn conceited ignorant useless harmless uninteresting mistaken foolish Billy" has a Ring Lardner quality to it.

[19] *Ibid.,* August 14, 1894.

[20] *Ibid.,* October 25, October 4, 1894.

[21] Robert G. Ingersoll to Mrs. J. E. Oliver of Waterloo, Iowa, April 3, 1895. *The Letters of Robert G. Ingersoll,* Eva Ingersoll Wakefield, ed. (New York, 1951), 338.

audience — they were fanatics, and Becker abhorred fanatics. This abhorrence would be carried over into his adult years, when as a historian he chose to minimize the importance of the dogmas that were involved in partisan disputes. In his *The Eve of the Revolution*, it would not be constitutional theory but the psychology of agitators and mobs that would interest him; in *The Heavenly City* he would underplay the abstract differences between Christians and *philosophes* and underscore their emotional affinities. Becker's conclusion concerning the fanaticism of Mr. Ingersoll's admirers was one of fatigue — "a man who disbelieves the Bible because most people believe it makes me tired" — and of disgust — "nothing is so disgusting as a man who don't [sic] know anything except that he doesn't believe in Bible."[22] So Becker's position ultimately became a countervailing one: he would countervail in his mind against militant believer and militant atheist alike, but he would never forget that "Every man has a religion."

From the conviction that every man has a religion, however much religions may differ in content, it was an easy step to the conclusion that, since no religion is demonstrably true, all religions or philosophies of the good life are somehow equal. Varying according to circumstances and "climates of opinion" (a favorite phrase of Becker's), such religions could best be examined historically, with some measure of "detachment." In Becker's case detachment could involve irony or sympathy. Sympathy can become pity, and pity can become a form of contempt; ordinarily, however, Becker avoided this pitfall. Throughout his life he adhered stubbornly to the belief that historical study is more profitable than philosophical analysis. History was, to Becker's mind, more subtle than the law of contradiction. Although Becker held fast to one either-or distinction — the traditional empiricist one between judgments of fact and judgments of value[23] — he undermined even this by emphasizing the determining influence that unverifiable judgments of value have upon our judgments of fact.[24] Becker himself was never without his judgments of value: what ex-Methodist could be? His urbane admission of not being able to prove his judg-

---

[22] "Wild Thoughts Notebook," January 9, 1894.

[23] See his *Progress and Power, passim,* and especially his *New Liberties for Old,* 13, where he stresses the difference between "value judgments" and judgments about "matter-of-fact."

[24] This is a basic theme in Becker's historiography from the time of his "Detachment and the Writing of History," *Atlantic Monthly,* CVI (October, 1910). Reprinted in *Detachment and the Writing of History,* 3-28. It runs through all his writings and the extent to which it is inconsistent with his empiricism will be discussed later.

ments of value would, however, sometimes annoy both believer and naturalist. Professor Ralph Barton Perry was later to put the case against Becker's extreme tolerance or relativism as follows:

> It is a pity that Professor Becker should seem fit to adhere to the School of the Paretics, and strengthen the cult of those half-philosophers who disseminate the confused belief that one conception of 'the good life' is as good as another, for it is clear that he has not only candor and learning but moral convictions that are supported by his experience and reflection.[25]

There would be occasions when Becker's bemused, Olympian detachment would disappear. When, for instance, Becker would support American participation in the two World Wars of the twentieth century, his candor and conviction would be evident, almost to the point of evangelical ardor. Running through even the most detached of Becker's reflections there would be evidence of a concern with morals; in fact, a casual reader of the "Notebook" might exclaim that here was an undergraduate born to be a moralist. At Wisconsin Becker moralized about the manners of believers and nonbelievers. He moralized also at the expense of students whose energy and certainty as to their goals in life exceeded, he thought, their capacity for thought. Even a student riding a bicycle without using his hands aroused Becker's ire. "A snob," Becker called him, "flaunting his abilities before the public" — to be pitied "for the limitations of his intellect."[26]

It is possible that Becker's preoccupation with the manners of others may have come from an insecurity about his own. There is no evidence that Becker, before attending the University of Wisconsin, had been much of a "loner"; but from his years at Wisconsin date many of the legends concerning his aloneness and his stand-offish attitude. Perhaps the death of his cousin Leonard the year before his arrival at Wisconsin had predisposed Becker against intimacy. Then, too, upon his arrival he had been found to be unfit material for a social fraternity; there is evidence that he was black-balled.[27] At some time in his life before he reached Cornell University, Becker did, however, acquire some attributes of sociability. He learned to relax among friends, to drink moderately and to smoke immoderately, and to be nearly expert

---

[25] Review of Becker's *New Liberties for Old, Yale Review*, XXI (December, 1941), 411.
[26] "Wild Thoughts Notebook," October 6, 1894.
[27] Ford, *op. cit.*, 341.

at billiards.[28] Perhaps, from the nature of these attainments, they may be dated from his student days at Wisconsin; but at least during his first year or so at Wisconsin Becker had of necessity to go it alone. "Motto, Abstain and Buy Books," he wrote in his "Notebook."[29] Another motto *might* have been "Live vicariously through books and the observation of others, and thereby develop a superior sensibility."

"Neither communion with other students nor extracurricular activities played any significant part in the process" of Carl Becker's development at Wisconsin, according to Guy Stanton Ford.[30] An extreme statement perhaps, but there is no direct evidence to the contrary. There are, if we may speak schematically, two kinds of challenges that seem to produce notable literary activities. The compulsion to self-expression may be strengthened by severe challenge in the form of trenchant criticism, or it may be built up by group indifference to the individual in question. Probably there are more cheerful reasons why a man chooses to write, and one must always say, with Becker, that a man is what he is because he has "it in him" to be that way, or as Becker once said of Voltaire, Voltaire was Voltaire because he was Voltaire and not because of a beating he received at the hands of a nobleman's lackeys.[31] In Becker's own case, however, it seems plausible that the overall indifference of the student body at Wisconsin to him did serve as a spur to his literary ambitions. Becker's being alone and ignored seems to have helped renew, for a time, a dream of adolescence, namely, that of being a novelist.

It is indeed possible that Becker's growing awareness of the indifference of the universe to man was much sharpened, first by the unexpected death of his cousin, and then by the indifference of the undergraduates at Wisconsin to Carl Becker. It must come as a shock for the gentle and unassuming son of a successful man in a small town to discover that, by university standards, he is awkward and shy. One recovery might be to acquire certain pretenses of one's own, including a condescension towards others. Becker's "Notebook" has its full share of caustic comments on the manners and intellects of his contemporaries. Caustic comments, for example, about students who attended performances at the Madison Opera House and sat with Becker in the gallery. Becker, while observing quite closely the behavior of these

---

[28] See Leo Gershoy's Introduction to *Progress and Power* (New York, 1949 edition), ix-xxxvii.

[29] Undated entry.

[30] *Op. cit.*, 341.

[31] Review of Cleveland B. Chase, *The Young Voltaire, American Historical Review*, XXXII (April, 1927), 608-610.

students — even to the point of eavesdropping on their conversations — insisted that they were too young and demonstrative to exhibit "other than a sort of child like nature which is not particularly interesting."[32] Then there are notations about the demonstrative nature of the young, especially their being in love, that reveal Becker as *thinking* it may be better to play the part of a fool than no part at all.[33] The son of the Waterloo County Recorder had in him the makings of a "Tonio Kroger," after Thomas Mann: the artist who feels that he can live only vicariously, whose "sensibility" throttles his own "demonstrative" urges.

There is a clear, unbroken line of development from the Becker of the "Notebook" to the adult historian as recalled by one of his students, Leo Gershoy:

> The mildest and most endearing of men, he suffered fools less than gladly. He was disposed also to exaggerate the differences between the sophisticated and unsophisticated levels of awareness and appreciation, because he himself moved and had his being on an unusually high level of honesty and abstraction. Cut off, too, by his own choice [?] from the generality of men, and uncompromisingly severe with his own mental processes, he tended to fall into the error of many intellectuals and underestimate the common man's capacity to resist manipulation and not be hoodwinked.[34]

To exaggerate the differences between the enlightened and the unenlightened is, at the age of twenty-two or so, an excellent way of shortcircuiting one's own enlightenment, and only Becker's being "uncompromisingly severe with his own mental processes" saved him from such a fate. He worked at being creative. He read what William Dean Howells and Henry James had to say about the artist's task. And what were the results? From the point of view of literary criticism, nothing. Nor, despite renewed attempts in later life would there ever be any direct results, save some unpublished (and probably destroyed) sonnets, and an allegory, in verse, "The King of the Beasts," done in 1920 and rejected by several publishers. From the point of view of those interested in the graceful production of histories or essays about history, character sketches, political commentaries, and other works of nonfiction, the results of Becker's early literary aspirations must, however, be regarded as highly beneficial. The desire to write well can survive a false start; it can be channeled into more productive undertakings. If it has been sharpened in any way by experiences in them-

---

[32] "Wild Thoughts Notebook," February 5, February 6, 1894.
[33] *Ibid.*
[34] *Op. cit.*, xxiv.

selves fruitless, then the gain and not the loss must be remembered. In the development of Becker's talent, the transfer of certain modes of thought from the literary preoccupations of his youth to the historical activities of his maturity is so apparent that it is well worth the effort to piece together from his "Notebook" exactly what these early modes of thought were.

They were, in brief, the modes of "Realism," or more precisely the "Realism" of William Dean Howells in which realism is softened by a note of sympathy.[35] The first tenet of this realism embraced by the Wisconsin undergraduate stresses the necessity of perpetual observation; the second has to do with the question of what are fit subjects for our observations. Becker answers this question directly in his "Notebook": "indeed to the careful students of human nature the common uninteresting sort of every day people" form "a greater attraction" than do students, for example.[36] Why uninteresting people are so interesting Becker neglects to say; at the same time he reveals why his "Notebook" contains so many observations about commonplace people. What made this "Realism" so attractive to Becker appears to have lain in its methodology. Just as Becker's concern with the problems of testimony in religion ties in with his interest in the same type of problems in historiography, so does his interest in literary methodology anticipate his interest in historical method, which was to become his particular *forte*.

"It is the character that is formed and manners that result from formed character that make the chief interest of any character study that can in any way be reduced to a method," Becker wrote in his "Notebook." There is a positivistic note in this opinion, which Becker qualified by adding the proviso:

> Not that rules can be formed under which all character will fall. So far from that we know that no two minds coincide and character presents endless variety. But in formed character every thing that is natural means something and however strange it may be does not startle or surprise the thorough student to any great degree.[37]

This is dated February 6, 1894. On February 14, Becker returned to

[35] Becker quoted other authors besides Howells in his "Notebook," Chaucer and Goethe, for instance; but his quotations from Howells always had to do with the problems of literary craftsmanship. For expositions of Howells' realism, see William Dean Howells, *Criticism and Fiction* (New York, 1891) and Everett Carter, *Howells and the Age of Realism* (Philadelphia, 1954).

[36] February 6, 1894.

[37] *Ibid.*

this subject, and by then his pluralism had given way to monism, his caution to confidence: "For there are unformable laws of character which apply to all human kind and which once comprehended furnish a key to the life of any character."[38] The comprehension of unformable laws may seem rather an incomprehensible proposition. "I am sorry to confess," Becker added, "that this has been written during history recitation."

In "formed character" all things are "natural" however strange they might appear. Here, in young Becker's mind, there was the danger of a lapse from Realism into Naturalism: the observation of things simply because they are strange. Becker saved himself from this flat reporting of the freakish by concerning himself with the more philosophical problem of how a novelist can study a state of mind: "I have often wondered," he wrote, "whether any novelist has ever been able to place himself in the life and feeling of any person."[39] Twice Becker recommended to himself Howells' dictum that the way to enter the consciousness of others is through one's own consciousness. The young writer "needs expression and observation not so much of others as of himself," Howells had written, "for ultimately his characters will all come out of himself and he will need to know motive and character with such thoroughness and accuracy as he can acquire *only* through his own heart." Once one has seen all of humanity written in one's own heart then the strange will become natural. The actions of a character will follow logically from his nature, or, as Henry James might put it: incident will then serve to illustrate character,[40] which is the principal way Becker would use incident in his adult writings, after the hurdle of the Ph.D. had been passed. "To me," Carl Becker would later confide to his teacher Turner, "nothing can be duller than historical facts, and nothing more interesting than the service they can be made to render in the effort to solve the everlasting riddle of human existence."[41]

"If I were Henry James," Becker would wistfully exclaim to a friend in one of his letters written as late as the 1930's.[42] If Becker had been

[38] *Ibid.*, February 14, 1894.

[39] *Ibid.*, February 6, 1894.

[40] Dr. Smith makes much the same point as this, *op. cit.*, 127.

[41] Draft of a letter from Carl Becker to Frederick Jackson Turner, May 15, 1910.

[42] Carl Becker to Charles Crump, Ithaca, New York, January 5, 1935. This phrase is quoted back to Becker in a letter to Becker, London, dated March [1935]. Becker's letters to Crump, whom he regarded as the best letter writer alive, have been lost, so we do not know the ending of Becker's sentence beginning "If I were Henry James. . . ." We do know that he had an abiding interest in James. See F. O. Matthiessen to Carl Becker, Boston, January 13 [1944]. "I'm delighted to

Henry James, I think he might have written much of what he wrote, especially his character studies, much as he did write them. Like James, he would circle his characters carefully and at first without commitment, and his descriptions would be in a style that has been called an "American Laconic."[43] Like James, Becker had an unusual capacity for an almost impersonal detachment relieved occasionally by irony and humor. Usually the ironic undertone and the comic relief would be presented with a mellowness that would identify Becker more with the Victorian world of Henry James than with the more modern world of Lytton Strachey or Aldous Huxley.

In his "Notebook" the apprentice Becker was careful to record Howells' observations that the main business of the novelist is to present his readers with "a due conception of his characters and the situation in which they find themselves." Howells also said, and Becker records this too, that Henry James's most characteristic quality is the "artistic impartiality" with which he treats his characters.[44] Detachment and artistic impartiality in time became two characteristics for which Becker's own writings were noted, although more recent critics have chosen to emphasize Becker's biases instead.[45] At this point it seems proper to consider whether Becker's youthful self-exposure to the precepts of Howells and James helps to explain a central paradox in his later career as a professional historian, the paradox being that Becker, who did more than any other American historian (aside from Charles A. Beard) to puncture the myth of the historian as a detached, impartial observer of man, was himself often said to be most detached and impartial.

Certainly Becker's interest in Howells and James was an excellent introduction to the problems involved in the production of literature, as well as a way to avoid the cruder forms of provincialism. Howells

---

have satisfied such a life-long reader of James," a reference to Matthiessen's *Henry James, The Major Phase* (New York, 1944).

[43] J. B. Brebner, Review of Carl Becker's, *Freedom and Responsibility, Yale Review*, XXXIV (March, 1946), 556.

[44] William Dean Howells quoted by Carl Becker, "Wild Thoughts Notebook," October 5, 1894.

[45] I shall have more to say later about Becker and his critics. Meanwhile, it is clear that an author is detached if his conclusions coincide with his reader's; biased, if they do not. No one could deny, however, that there is an air of detachment emanating from many of Becker's books and essays. A. M. Schlesinger's comments on Becker's *The Declaration of Independence* are pertinent here: "The book is written with so high a degree of detachment that one sometimes receives an impression of the author in the role of an entomologist studying a quivering specimen impaled with a pin." A. M. Schlesinger, Review of Becker's *The Declaration of Independence, Mississippi Valley Historical Review*, IX (March, 1923), 334.

and James together probably helped answer for Becker questions he had futilely asked of various rhetoric books in his first days at college.[46] Also, there is a third novelist, even more than Howells a son of the Middle Border, whose work Becker much admired. In the Becker Papers there is a letter from Hamlin Garland: "Your letter gave me great pleasure and made me feel that perhaps my work will live after me."[47] In admiring the cosmopolitan James and the Mid-Western Howells and Garland, Becker, one feels, was admiring just the right sort of writer, properly situated between the raw, unschooled contributors to *Saturday Night* and those who, like Walter Pater, polished the life out of their style.[48] The life depicted by Howells and Garland in their novels was not one of distant Italy but one with which Becker was familiar; and their style was casual enough, without being craftless, not to distract the reader from his subject. Howells and Garland avoided, as Becker would, that extreme self-confidence and experimentalism which would mark — and mar — a subsequent generation of authors. No one could have justly said of the efforts of Howells and Garland what Becker would later say about the rebellion of many American authors against Victorianism: "I get the impression that many American writers felt that since it wasn't necessary to copy foreign writers, it wasn't necessary to know what they were doing; and that since the Victorian writers were defective in certain respects it wasn't necessary to bother about them in any respect," the result being that in attempting to avoid the provincialism that is associated with imitation they fell into the provincialism that is associated with ignorance.[49]

Returning to the style of these writers, it met all the requirements that Becker would ever make. If you take care of the thought, the style will take care of itself, is the way Max Lerner summarized Becker's advice to him.[50] Becker did not altogether care to be known in his later years simply as a stylist among historians. Good style, to Becker, was good thought. It was good thought possessed of an "organic structure — logical arrangement and continuity" running through the entire work. "Good form, in short," Becker would say in his "The Art of Writing" (1941), "is a matter of mastering the content, of ex-

[46] "The Art of Writing," *Detachment and the Writing of History*, 124-127.
[47] Hamlin Garland to Carl Becker, New York, undated.
[48] From reading "The Art of Writing" one gets the impression that Pater was the one Victorian author whom Becker could not abide.
[49] "Benét's Sympathetic Understanding," *Mark Twain Quarterly*, VII (1943-1944), 13.
[50] Max Lerner to Carl Becker, New York, December 13, 1932.

ploring with infinite patience every part of the subject, in all its rami-
fications, letting the mind respond, with as much suppleness as may be,
to the form and pressure of the matter in hand. The style if there is
to be any worth mentioning, must wait upon the idea, which is itself
form as well as substance."[51] Style then is not just a matter of felicity or
decoration, but a matter of thought. The farm boy from Iowa and the
distinguished historian of later years were one in their suspicion of
highly polished, smooth surfaces — the "Notebook" brings the two
together and lets us see the continuity between them.

So much then for Becker's most important "Wild Thoughts." A few
feeble epigrams, "A Christian conscience is a curious thing; a little
conscience is a dangerous thing," a few ambiguous phrases, "Politicians understand variables but constants are beyond them"[52] — from
these modest beginnings would come an epigrammatist and historian
noted for the unusual clarity and subtlety of his thought. By the time
of his graduation in 1897, however, the *Badger* yearbook placed under
his picture, perhaps because of his senior honors thesis and his known
literary aspirations, possibly from want of anything else to say: "Rare
is the worthiness of Authorship."[53]

Certainly the "Wild Thoughts" and the self-examination were worth
that much. What is more, they helped prepare Becker for a long and
faithful association with the historian, Frederick Jackson Turner, himself
no mean writer and one who could move from the most minute inquiry about particulars to the most breathtaking generality. If a man's
style doesn't run away with him, then it is good that he has a style,
Turner had written in his essay "The Significance of History" in 1891.
For "in itself an interesting style, even a picturesque manner of presentation is not to be condemned, provided that truthfulness of substance rather than vivacity of style be the end sought."[54] Becker's
indirect apprenticeship to the works of novelists was about to lose first
place to a direct apprenticeship to Frederick Jackson Turner; if the
new apprenticeship proved successful, the result would be a harmony
of form and substance.

[51] "The Art of Writing," *Detachment and the Writing of History*, 132.
[52] "Wild Thoughts Notebook," undated entries.
[53] *The Badger, Student Yearbook for 1897* (Madison, Wisconsin).
[54] *The Early Writings of Frederick Jackson Turner*, with an Introduction by
Fulmer Mood (Madison, Wisconsin, 1938), 44.

Chapter III

How Becker Decided to Become a Professor of History: The Example of Frederick Jackson Turner

CARL BECKER in his "Wild Thoughts Notebook" had been searching for, among other things, an explanation of character and for the "unformable laws" that shape our natures. His search was, by and large, still in the highly individualistic tradition of evangelical Protestantism; even Howells' literary counsel of introspection, which Becker had accepted, was in essence not far removed from Methodist soul searching. At the University of Wisconsin, however, character was beginning to be studied environmentally or sociologically; and a method comparable to another of Howells' suggestions was being applied — that is, the study of individuals in relation to their social circumstance. Wisconsin was pioneering in the social sciences just as surely as any of the Eastern universities such as Harvard, Columbia, and Johns Hopkins.[1] In the Mid-West Wisconsin stood out, a strong state university relatively untroubled by the problems of denominationalism that were adversely affecting the finances and curriculum expansion of some other Mid-Western institutions of higher learning.

Each of the three most distinguished scholars under whom Becker studied at Wisconsin, Frederick Jackson Turner, Charles Homer Haskins, and Richard T. Ely, had recently been exposed in one way or another to the enlightening ways of European scholarship in the social sciences, as these ways were understood at Johns Hopkins University. Ely indeed had had the advantages of study at Heidelberg, and of the three he was the oldest and — in the 1890's — the most important. Only he had a national reputation, and his acquisition by the University had been one of its biggest coups, one for which Turner, formerly a student of Ely's at Johns Hopkins, had been in large measure responsible.[2] A man of broad learning and voluminous scholarly output, Ely prob-

[1] Merle Curti and Vernon Carstensen, *The University of Wisconsin*, (Madison, Wisconsin, 1949), I, 630-633.
[2] For Turner's rôle in bringing Ely to Wisconsin, see *ibid.*, 618-619.

ably played a larger part than any other American economist of his day in turning economics back into what it had been in the days of David Hume and Adam Smith, a branch of moral science. It was, however, a moral science fully equipped with charts and statistics. Its speculative philosophy was set forth by a highly efficient organization, the American Economic Association, whose founding in the 1880's had seen Ely associated with young Woodrow Wilson, also of Johns Hopkins. Its orientation was directed against the laissez-faire ethics of Adam Smith; and its method was Roscher's not Ricardo's, or historical rather than deductive.

Probably Richard T. Ely's autobiography, *Ground under Our Feet*, is one of the best case histories of how the evangelical tradition became the sociological, reformist tradition, with which the name of the University of Wisconsin is forever linked.[3] Since Becker, as a graduate student, was to do a "minor" in economics under Ely, it might be assumed — despite the absence of direct proof — that Ely helped, however indirectly, to show Becker that the evangelical spirit could be directed toward ends more satisfying than the search for evidences of Original Sin. Ely had tried, as Becker had, to be an orthodox Protestant until he discovered, apparently to his amazement, that "Good works had nothing to do with it."[4] Ely's subsequent approach to good works in the guise of an economist was always moderate and thoroughly respectable.[5] While this did not save him from charges of radicalism and socialism, his advanced thinking was far removed from the demagogic strains apparent in Bryan's presidential campaign in 1896.

Becker in his adult years would be somewhat embarrassed at having cast his first vote in a national election for McKinley and for having been overcome by his fears of Bryan's alleged radicalism; but his own devotion to reform (while sometimes concealed or corroded away in his moments of skepticism) would always be more in the moderate tradition of his teacher Ely than, for instance, in the maverick tradition of his future friend, Charles A. Beard. Exactly what the sources

[3] John Rutherford Everett's *Religion in Economics* (New York, 1946) contains a good account of Ely's fusion of evangelicalism with economics.

[4] Richard T. Ely, *Ground under Our Feet* (New York, 1938), 16.

[5] In his moderation Ely followed the precepts of Wilhelm Roscher, whose work he assigned at the University of Wisconsin: "A people should, if they would have it go well with them, in the changes in the form of things which they make, take as their model time, whose reforms are the surest and most irresistible, but at the same time, as Bacon says, so gradual that they cannot be seen or observed at any one moment." Wilhelm Roscher, *Principles of Political Economy* (Chicago, 1878), I, 109.

were from which Becker eventually learned, *contra* his father, that the voice of the reformer and the voice of the devil need not be the same cannot be documented. Nowhere in his writings did Becker mention Ely, and he may have been unaware of any connection between his literary problems of character study and Ely's none-too-inspiring lectures on the character of economic and social institutions. It seems likely, however, that the tentative, empirical method of Ely symbolized by the very title of his autobiography, *Ground under Our Feet,* was not uncongenial to a young man who had just about had his fill of the Absolute. Ely claimed to have learned at Heidelberg a "contempt for the dogmatic English economics" from Karl Knies, who taught him instead "a fundamentally scientific approach in which relativity and evolution played a large rôle."[6] And who could name a historian in the twentieth century more aware of relativity and evolution than Ely's student, Carl Becker?

With the exception of the young medievalist, Charles Homer Haskins, who had a mind too fine for theories,[7] Wisconsin seems to have provided Becker with a large number of teachers possessed of theories about character. In view of this the comparative absence of dogmatism from the campus was surprising — as was the absence of the usual warfare between science and theology; and it was the absence of dogmatism in one man, Frederick Jackson Turner, that helped make that man the most important teacher in Carl Becker's life. An example of the humility and enthusiasm of Turner lies in the fact that he was instrumental in persuading President Chamberlain to bring Ely to the University in 1892 to head the new School of Economics, Political Science, and History, although this had the effect of placing Ely above Turner, who was at that time Chairman of the History Department. "The reason for grouping the social sciences was to justify the unusually large appropriation which was granted to organize graduate and research work in this field," explained Ely.[8] Still the practical reason does not discount the theoretical one, which places Turner as a

---

[6] Ely, *op. cit.*, 58.

[7] If this statement seems too extreme, one might compare Haskins' *The Renaissance of the Twelfth Century* (Cambridge, Massachusetts, 1927), his best known work in intellectual history, with his student Becker's *The Heavenly City,* or Haskins' *The Rise of Universities* (New York, 1923) with Becker's *Cornell University: Founders and the Founding* (Ithaca, New York, 1943). The comparative absence of the speculative element, or of attempts to enter into the consciousness of others, in Haskins' otherwise excellent works is striking.

[8] Ely, *op. cit.*, 179.

pioneer in the social sciences and as a believer in their essential unity.

Turner's explanation of character, like Ely's, was social, and it had to do with the influence of westward expansion, of the moving frontier, upon national character. But behind this single thesis or "beyond" it, as Turner would later write to Becker, was "the conception of history as a complex of all the social sciences, the conception of the Oneness of the thing."[9] Turner then was a historian who had an interdisciplinary method as well as a vision in the form of the frontier thesis. It is no reflection upon Turner's subsequent eminence in historical inquiry that a host of thinkers, from Jefferson and De Tocqueville to Godkin and Bryce, had anticipated his basic thesis;[10] for he remains the first man to have had both the thesis and a method strong enough for him to proceed a long way towards its verification.

Turner had written his famous essay on "The Significance of the Frontier in American History" in 1893 when he was just past thirty. The thesis presented in this essay is a simple one: "What the Mediterranean Sea was to the Greeks, breaking the bond of custom, offering new experiences, calling out new institutions and activities, that and more, the ever retreating frontier has been to the United States directly, and to the nations of Europe more remotely."[11] There had been, according to Turner, a number of physical frontiers as the political frontiers of the United States had moved westward, and these frontiers had all gone through certain uniform stages of social evolution — the farmers' frontier had always followed, for instance, the ranchers' frontier. The overall tendency of these frontiers had been to strengthen two currents in American life: the nationalist and the democratic modes of thought and activity.

Young Carl Becker, brought up in a region of strong Unionist sentiments, could surely understand the significance of the following clue to the understanding of national character: "The economic and social characteristics of the frontier worked against sectionalism."[12] The frontier, Turner believed, was usually more receptive to the ideas and customs of the middle section of the country, which in turn served to mediate the differences between North and South. "The Middle region, entered by New York harbor, was an open door to all Europe,"[13] and here Carl Becker could have paused, as he did in his *The United*

9 Frederick Jackson Turner to Carl Becker, Madison, Wisconsin, 1925.

10 See Herman Clarence Nixon, "Precursors of Turner in the Interpretation of the American Frontier," *South Atlantic Quarterly*, XXVIII (January, 1929), 83-89.

11 *The Early Writings of Frederick Jackson Turner*, 229.

12 *Ibid.*, 216.

13 *Ibid.*, 217.

States: An Experiment in Democracy, to recall the arrival and settlement of his Irish and German ancestors in New York. The mixture of
peoples, not all of them of English origin, seems to have made for
more democratic ways. Then, too, and this was essential to the Turner
frontier thesis, there had been "the cheap lands of the frontier. . . .
So long as free land exists, the opportunity for a competency exists,
and economic power secures political power."[14] Here was a large
generality that did justice to at least one particular: the career of
Charles Dewitt Becker in his evolution from dirt farmer to County
Recorder.

Democracy, or Republican democracy, had been practiced in Waterloo, Iowa, certainly; and apart from his unfortunate contact with social
fraternities Becker could see that it was accepted, enthusiastically, at
the University of Wisconsin. Turner shared this enthusiasm for democracy and believed, almost messianically, in the mission of the United
States at the same time as he gloried in the uniqueness of her democratic attainments. "Pure history," observed Lord Acton, echoing Dove,
"cannot satisfy the needs of a struggling and travailing nation."[15] One
reason why Turner was to become the most significant figure in modern American historiography, at least in terms of his influence upon
other scholars, lay in the fact that he was so perfectly devoted to the
ideas of nationalism and democracy that he found emanating from the
various frontiers in American history. The past of his beloved Mid-
West was a mirror which, properly handled, reflected the virtues of
Turner himself.

Turner was, however, a conservative democrat, quite distrustful,
for example, of what the wave of East European immigration at the
end of the nineteenth century might do to American institutions;[16]
and he was totally uncommitted to the radical agrarianism that was
making headway in the West and Mid-West in the 1890's. Altogether
he was a man whom Charles Dewitt Becker could, without fear, en-
trust with the instruction of his son. For he stood, with his mixture of
intellectual curiosity and political conservatism, as proof of his own
thesis — that the Mid-Westerner loved not only innovation but that,
with the closing of the frontier, he was coming to love some measure
of conservatism as well. As a boy in Portage, Wisconsin, Turner had

14 *Ibid.,* 210, 221.
15 John Dalberg Lord Acton, "German Schools of History," *Historical Essays
and Studies* (London, 1907), 358.
16 See Edward Norman Saveth, *American Historians and European Immigrants*
(New York, 1948), 122-137.

seen more of the Old West than Carl Becker saw in Waterloo, Iowa; Turner despite his aristocratic bearing was more of a mixer than Becker and naturally saw more of his fellow men. What he saw in the past, however, sometimes pleased Turner more than what he saw in the present of the Mid-West. He was only thirty-three when Becker first met him, and he lived long enough to be profoundly disturbed by ugly manifestations of the growing Mid-Western zeal for uniformity of thought: manifestations that had been painfully in evidence in the charges of socialism made against Ely before the Regents of the University in 1894.[17] "There is a growing insistence on conformity to community public opinion," Turner would write in 1926, "compared with the days of the frontiersman and the 'self-made man.' " The perennially hopeful Turner could, however, still believe that the Mid-West "may yet make new contributions to America, by its union of democratic faith and innovation with a conservative subconscious."[18]

These reflections appeared in the same year as his essay "The Children of the Pioneers," an act of regional piety, in which Turner sought to outline the contributions of the children of the pioneers to national culture and literature, and thus to prove that neither the "goers" to the frontier nor their children could have been "mere materialists." He gave a kind of who's who among the children of the pioneers as proof of this contention; being statistically inclined, Turner was pleased to note that the Mid-West had cut down the disproportionate representation of New England in *Who's Who in America*. The composite picture that Turner drew conveys somehow the impression that he believed all talents to be equal, but he did single out William Dean Howells for mention. Among notable historians whose careers had begun in the Mid-West, he was able by 1926 modestly to include himself and his student of the 1890's, Carl Becker. "A country town in Iowa gave birth to Becker of Cornell. . . ."[19] The Becker in question was no longer the somewhat awkward and retiring farm boy and son of Waterloo; and the Cornell in question was not the Methodist college in Mount Vernon, Iowa, but Cornell University in Ithaca, New York. Probably more than any single man, outside of Becker himself, Turner was responsible for this change. He had helped bring it about in

---

[17] For an account of these charges of socialism and Ely's exoneration, see Curti and Carstensen, *The University of Wisconsin*, I, 508-9, 514-17, 524. Becker in his "Notebook" makes no mention of this famous incident.

[18] "The West — 1876 and 1926," *The Significance of Sections in American History*, 254, 255.

[19] "The Children of the Pioneers," *The Significance of Sections in American History*, 277.

Becker's case, as in so many others, by an act of faith, which began in 1894 and did not end until Turner's death in 1932.

Becker of course had heard of Turner before Turner had seen his future disciple. Already by the time Becker began to consider attending the University of Wisconsin, Turner's influence had spread as far as Waterloo, Iowa. There was, Becker later recalled, a young lawyer in the town who sang the praises of Frederick Jackson Turner. The lawyer in question, a recent graduate of the University of Wisconsin, confessed that he didn't remember much American history after studying it under Turner, but he recalled vividly the man's personality: "It is something he gives you, inspiration, new ideas, a fresh light on things in general. It's something he makes you want to do or be."[20] Becker didn't want to have anything to *do* with history, and certainly he didn't want to *be* a historian, not after studying high school history. The young lawyer's case for Turner had been so strong, however, that Becker did know that he would take a course with Turner if he got to Wisconsin.

Becker arrived in Wisconsin in 1893 and caught his first glimpse of Turner shortly thereafter. His first impression of Turner, who was hurrying up Bascom Hill carrying an "immense leather portfolio bulging with books and notes," was that Turner — for a man of thirty-three — seemed essentially youthful and adventuresome, as if he hadn't yet settled all the disturbing questions of life.[21] In 1894 when Becker enrolled in Turner's general history course, he came forward after the first lecture to ask a question, "a totally unnecessary question, invented for the precise purpose of standing there and being spoken to," as Becker remembered it. Turner answered. "The answer was nothing, the words were nothing, but the voice — the voice was everything. . . ." It was warm, intimate, and magical. "An upward lift of the eyes, a few friendly words, and I, like I know not how many other lads of nineteen, was straightway a devoted disciple and a questionless admirer,"[22] Becker wrote with a warm glow, many years afterward, which doubtless helped obscure the fact that he was twenty-one when he took his first course with Turner.

Becker was, by some standards, something of a late starter in the study of history. By the time he took his second course with Turner he still had not overcome completely the fact that historical facts

20 Quoted by Becker, "Frederick Jackson Turner," *Everyman His Own Historian,* 191-192.
21 *Ibid.,* 193.
22 *Ibid.,* 194.

seemed dull — that Reuben Thwaites' history of the colonies, which Turner assigned, resembled in this essential his high school text, from which Becker could remember only one sentence: "Egypt has been called the gift of the Nile." Becker found, however, that Turner's university method of teaching was not the high school method of recitation. True, Turner would sometimes ask questions about the usually neglected text, which Becker, "being an obedient boy" (self-styled and rightly so), had read; and Becker, during the second term of his second year, was able to give the answer "1811" to a question he was never able to remember afterwards. " 'Precisely,' said Turner, in a tone implying that he now recognized me as of that select company of scholars who would see at once the peculiar significance of 1811," Becker proudly recalled.[23]

Still there were embarrassing moments when Becker couldn't remember "dull, . . . uninteresting facts." And the desire to remember such facts never became an acquired characteristic of Becker's, and never did he solemnly exalt history above all else. There is an undated entry in the "Wild Thoughts Notebook" in which, with apparent approval, he repeated the jibe that history is only gossip for kings and queens. Becker could never, under the supervision of Turner or even Osgood, take seriously *all* the known historical facts. "For Becker," as one of his more prominent students, Louis Gottschalk, would later recall, "was not the kind of historian that is 'overwhelmed by everything that once existed.' "[24]

Why then did Becker become a historian? The answer, he said, lay partly in Turner and partly in Haskins.[25] Turner playfully and Haskins seriously wondered what there was in their teaching that had so affected Becker. Turner felt it must have been Haskins' "ideal of critical scholarship" that had done the trick.[26] Haskins felt modestly that Becker gave him more than his due; Haskins gave credit mainly to Becker himself and to Turner.[27] The story of how Turner affected Becker is given in full in Becker's essay "Frederick Jackson Turner," which is one of the best pieces Becker would ever write. It is especially

[23] *Ibid.*, 195.
[24] "Carl Becker: Skeptic or Humanist," *Journal of Modern History*, XVIII (June, 1946), 161.
[25] "Frederick Jackson Turner," *Everyman His Own Historian*, 195.
[26] Frederick Jackson Turner to Carl Becker, Cambridge, Massachusetts, October 26, 1920.
[27] Charles Homer Haskins to Carl Becker, Cambridge, Massachusetts, May 23, 1927.

valuable to Becker's biographer because, as Turner wrote to Becker in 1927 after reading this essay,

> If, at times, I feel you are writing your youthful enthusiasms *over finding history*, rather than painting the man [Turner] as he really is (or was), I . . . seem to see the young and ardent adventurer 'beyond the edge of cultivation,' and I get a real thrill from the evidence that, at least, I had a part — a too generously recognized part — in shaping such careers as yours, and by companionship, not by schoolmaster's drills.[28]

By companionship, and by a contagious enthusiasm that Turner never lost. Turner in the 1890's was just maturing into the Turner known to the historiographer, and it still looked as if he might continue to be overshadowed by the older Ely or even surpassed by the younger Haskins, whom Turner had also helped bring to Wisconsin from Johns Hopkins as an instructor when Haskins was only twenty. Turner's Ph.D. thesis on the fur trade in Wisconsin had been published in the Johns Hopkins *Studies in Historical and Political Science* in 1891, and during the same year his essay on "The Significance of History" had appeared. He was, however, a long way from having a national reputation when Becker first met him. His "The Significance of the Frontier in American History," written in 1893, had largely gone unnoticed by contemporaries; his challenge to H. B. Adams, his former teacher at Johns Hopkins, for his overemphasis upon the European origins of American institutions was met with silence on the part of Adams' friends and followers. No one, not even Fulmer Mood,[29] has yet explained how between the years 1891 and 1893, between the two essays on "Significance," Turner had changed from believing that "our history is only to be understood as a growth from European history under the new conditions of the New World"[30] to believing in the primary importance of these "new conditions," especially the frontier, in shaping American history. The change in emphasis certainly indicated a quickness of mind, an enthusiasm for hypotheses.

In the mid-1890's Turner's most evident assets were little more than

[28] Frederick Jackson Turner to Carl Becker, Madison, Wisconsin, May 14, 1927. This point was also made by Felix Frankfurter: "You thought you were 'doing' Turner; you also did Becker!" (Felix Frankfurter to Carl Becker, Cambridge, Massachusetts, 1927.)

[29] For Mood's attempts to explain the evolution of Turner's thought, see his "Turner's Formative Period," *The Early Writings of Frederick Jackson Turner*, 3-39; and his "The Development of Frederick Jackson Turner as an Historical Thinker," *Publications* of the Colonial Society of Massachusetts (December, 1939).

[30] "The Significance of History," *The Early Writings of Frederick Jackson Turner*, 64.

this irrepressible enthusiasm and the capacity for communicating it to others. Probably in the 1890's he needed students more than at any time in his life, and he always needed them a great deal, to write the books that he himself wrote so slowly or only hinted at in his essays, to carry forward the "frontier thesis" with all the enthusiasm of a soldier delivering "A Message to Garcia."[31]

Turner himself, Ulrich B. Phillips would recall, really had two messages: the first was the frontier thesis; the second was "the importance of being eager." Most people do not remember Becker as being "eager" — the word *skeptical* comes to mind more easily, but there is in some of Becker's early works a spirited quality that approaches eagerness. "Kansas," written in 1910, has this ebullience, and in the least ebullient decade of Becker's life, the 1920's, it reappeared just once — in the essay on Turner. Turner, Phillips also wrote, was a "glutton for data" who early in his career became "overwhelmed by his accumulation."[32] He would even take notes on students' reports, and he treated his students as if their passion for knowledge equaled his own. Becker responded eagerly. Only a "glutton for data" could have written the early articles and the Ph.D. thesis that Becker would do, after Turner had captured him completely. "The implication [of Turner's method as a teacher] was that we were searching for something, ferreting out hidden secrets."[33] There was the Draper Collection of manuscripts in the Wisconsin State Historical Society where Turner had mastered "Kanuck" French and the fur trade; there one might find something that even Reuben Thwaites, who had a local reputation for omniscience, might have missed.

Turner would impart to Becker an enthusiasm for history by encouraging him to do research in it, by discouraging him from thinking that Turner or Thwaites or anyone could give him final answers about history or anything else. "Turner might have said, with Mr. Justice Holmes, that one important article of his creed as a scholar was that he was *not* God."[34] Above all else Turner gave Becker "freedom," and with this freedom came self-confidence. Before Turner, there had been "parents and uncles and aunts and teachers and pastors" who had sufficiently trained and advised Becker and told him what to do and not to do "with such an implication of futility in the telling," Becker re-

[31] For an account of how Turner's Wisconsin students became scattered throughout American universities, see Curti and Carstensen, *The University of Wisconsin*, I, 642-643.
[32] Ulrich B. Phillips to Carl Becker, Ann Arbor, Michigan, October 13, 1925.
[33] Becker, "Frederick Jackson Turner," *Everyman His Own Historian*, 195.
[34] *Ibid.*, 204.

membered, "to leave me clutching the miserable little suspicion that I would probably never, all things considered, be much good at doing anything. Never having talked with my pastor, Turner didn't know this. He blandly assumed that I might amount to something, and at last one day told me that he thought I 'had it in me' to become a scholar and a writer — seemed really to believe it. To be told by this admired master that I could probably do the very thing I most wanted to do" — which was now to be a historian as well as a writer — "released what little ability I had to do it."[35]

Small wonder that when Becker graduated from the "Civic Historical" undergraduate program in 1896 he had honors in history for his senior thesis, in which he had studied national nominating conventions. Between the second and third years there must have been a notable increase in Becker's historical interests; and in the third and final undergraduate year at Wisconsin, a synthesis was attained: Becker could now write because he had something to write about. There were "original sources" that would never be exhausted, as the stories about Madison "local color" had been. Becker is reported to have said, half-seriously perhaps, that he chose to be a historian so that he would not run out of something to write about,[36] which in turn calls to mind Bagehot's jest about how Gibbon chose to write history.

Small wonder also that, as Becker said, "When the novitiate ended, one took the full vows."[37] Following his senior honors work with Turner, Becker remained in Madison to do two years of graduate study under Turner and Haskins. As a minor subject for his graduate work Becker was advised by Turner to do economics or political science instead of literature, which Becker had preferred. In the first letter, or the first letter preserved, from Turner to Becker, written just after Becker's graduation, Turner cautioned Becker that economics or political science was necessary to historical inquiry, "if your work is not to become dilettante. . . ."[38] Turner was a shrewd judge of his students and their weaknesses, and Becker had enough confidence in Turner to follow his advice and pursue economics instead of literature.

On Mondays, Wednesdays, and Fridays, Becker met with Professor Turner's seminar at the old State Historical Rooms in the State Capitol, or in the Law Building. Reports were given by the students, from whom Turner expected a thorough mastery of their subjects of inves-

[35] *Ibid.*, 206.
[36] Professor Walter French of Cornell University quoted in Smith, *op. cit.*, 45.
[37] "Frederick Jackson Turner," *Everyman His Own Historian*, 200.
[38] Frederick Jackson Turner to Carl Becker, Madison, Wisconsin, July 3, 1896.

tigation. Each man, and occasionally a woman such as Louise Kellogg, was expected "to be ready like a cabinet minister to answer such questions, bearing upon it, as might be asked by the opposition."[39] In this seminar Becker is remembered as having been "a studious fellow and rather shy and unobtrusive. He was certainly not aggressive."[40]

Becker's work, however, was promising enough to encourage Turner and Haskins to recommend him for a fellowship to Harvard University for his second year of graduate study. Turner was no longer afraid of Becker's becoming a literary dilettante, and he took pride in praising Becker's "powers of literary expression" in a letter to A. B. Hart of the Harvard History Department.[41] In a letter to President Eliot of Harvard, Charles Homer Haskins spoke of Becker's "considerable power of literary expression."[42] But all to no avail. First Haskins and then Turner would later be called to teach history at Harvard, but in 1897 their advice could still be ignored; their student Becker would never be called to Harvard. Instead he was given a fellowship at Wisconsin, and during the year 1897-1898 he taught a freshman history course. Probably it was just as well, for no one in his right mind would, at least in retrospect, have left the Wisconsin of Turner and Haskins for a Harvard which hadn't yet had the foresight to acquire these two teachers. In the following year, however, Becker did succeed in winning a fellowship to Columbia University. In writing to President Seth Low, Haskins, who had taught Becker not only ancient and medieval history but historical method as well, commented that Becker now had, in addition to his "exceptional proficiency in English . . . a good grasp of historical method and exceptional aptitude for investigation."[43]

At Columbia, Becker would enjoy the same good fortune he had experienced at Wisconsin: he would come into contact with three more seminal minds — those of John W. Burgess, James Harvey Robinson, and H. L. Osgood. It is, however, no reflection upon these teachers, not even upon Osgood and Robinson with whom Becker had most contact, to say that they would only help add lines to a character already sketched, would only strengthen a professional choice already made. Under the stimulus principally of Turner, Becker had chosen to be a historian and a professor. The only man whom Becker had known as a

[39] "Frederick Jackson Turner," *Everyman His Own Historian*, 201.

[40] O. A. Oestereich to Phil Snyder, Janesville, Wisconsin, January 5, 1956.

[41] Frederick Jackson Turner to A. B. Hart, Madison, Wisconsin, March 5, 1897.

[42] Charles Homer Haskins to President Charles William Eliot, Madison, Wisconsin, March 12, 1897.

[43] Charles Homer Haskins to President Seth Low, Madison, Wisconsin, February 23, 1898.

"professor" before leaving Waterloo had been a local eccentric, so named because he was of no practical value. At Madison, if not at Mount Vernon, Becker came to encounter a much wider variety of individuals bearing that name, some of them as impractical as the town eccentric, but some of them actively concerned with being good citizens. The wonderful thing about them all, Becker would recall in his essay "On Being a Professor," was that they could live as they chose, in the world of the mind. Thanks to them, college had seemed to him "a wonderful adventure in the wide world of the human spirit, an adventure which at the time seemed well worth while, quite apart from any question of its practical application."[44]

[44] *Unpopular Review,* VII (April-June, 1917). Reprinted in *Detachment and the Writing of History,* 93.

Chapter IV

*Becker as a Graduate Student at Columbia: The "Lessons"
of History and the Social Sciences*

CARL BECKER arrived in New York State thirty years after his father
had left it. He enrolled in the Graduate Faculty of Political Science at
Columbia University on October 1, 1898, as a candidate for the degree
of Doctor of Philosophy.[1] Whether or not he was seriously committed
to the idea of taking his Ph.D. at Columbia instead of at Wisconsin
(where he did eventually take it, in 1907), Becker could look forward
with some confidence to his year at Columbia. At the very least Columbia might serve as a kind of finishing school, to round off some of the
rough edges of the Mid-West. By 1898 Becker had largely given up the
religious speculations of his youth; one path that might have led him to
a "tragic view of life" had been closed. With it had been closed the
road of literary hazards; Becker would never be a Tonio Kroger, nor
would he ever know the less sublime agony of having to live by his
pen alone.

For his year of graduate study Becker registered for courses in constitutional law, European history, international law and American history. Constitutional law was his major subject, and European history
his minor.[2] Becker's fellowship was in constitutional law, and it would
be quite misleading to say, as Guy Stanton Ford has, that "the title of
the fellowship in no way represented his interests."[3] Constitutional law
is not so far removed from a study of political conventions, which
Becker intended to undertake for his Ph.D. thesis. Turner had long
been of the opinion that "we need a political history of the United
States which shall penetrate beneath the surface of the proceedings of
national conventions to the study of the evolution of the organs of
party action and of those underlying social and economic influences in

[1] The Registrar, Columbia University, to the author, New York, December 6,
1957.
[2] *Ibid.*
[3] Ford, *op. cit.*, 341.

49

the states and sections which explain party action."[4] Becker was planning to meet part of this need as outlined by Turner, and Columbia was an ideal place in which to prepare further for this undertaking.

At Columbia the divisions separating law, politics, and history from one another had lost much of their importance in the hands of John W. Burgess, who had had more to do with making Columbia into a graduate university than any other single man. Burgess's two-volume *Political Science and Comparative Constitutional Law* had already appeared,[5] and in it Burgess had attempted an Hegelian synthesis of the State and the individual, of law and freedom. Freedom defined as the freedom of the State to do what is historically necessary is a notion now in disrepute, and even at that time E. L. Godkin of *The Nation* and Woodrow Wilson were pointing out to Burgess the limitations of his synthesis, in a way which Burgess found highly offensive. In the 1890's, however, Burgess's position as an architect of higher education was more secure than it had been in the 1880's, or than it would be after critics such as Charles A. Beard got hold of it. In the 1890's Burgess still had hopes of making Columbia's Faculty of Political Science into a great school of public administration, after the Hegelian notion that the civil servant stands closest to God. In this he hoped to make Columbia the equal of certain German universities, or at the least to make Columbia do directly and scientifically what Oxford and Cambridge in Britain had done, apparently despite themselves: to send her sons into careers of public service.[6] Burgess would himself teach two future Presidents of the United States, the two Roosevelts; unfortunately neither of them followed the canons of the master, and Burgess had eventually to call the first Roosevelt a dishonest man for his jingoism and imperialism.[7]

As head of the Faculty of Political Science and Professor of Political Science and Constitutional Law, Burgess had long been practicing what Turner had preached in his Essays of 1891 and 1893, namely, the value of the interdisciplinary approach to the social sciences. And Columbia had the financial resources to support Burgess, far more than the Wisconsin legislature was willing to grant Turner and Ely. Like

[4] "Problems in American History," *The Significance of Sections in American History*, 16.

[5] Boston, 1893.

[6] John W. Burgess, *Reminiscences of an American Scholar* (New York, 1934), *passim*. Charles Merriam, "John W. Burgess," *Dictionary of American Biography*, XXI, 132-134.

[7] Burgess, *Reminiscences of an American Scholar*, 312-321. Burgess, *Recent Changes in American Constitutional Theory* (New York, 1923), 41.

Ely, Burgess had learned the value of the interdisciplinary method in Germany; his approach to his own discipline of political science was in method identical with Ely's approach to economics — it was evolutionary and comparative. What Ely had learned at Heidelberg from Knies, Burgess had learned at Leipzig from the master of the German historical school, Wilhelm Roscher.[8]

Identical methods do not, alas, produce identical results, and Burgess's conclusions about politics and economics often ran counter to the Progressive ideas that Becker had encountered at Wisconsin; in fact they often were contrary to the ideas of the bright young men such as Frank J. Goodnow and E. R. A. Seligman whom Burgess brought to Columbia. Opinion at Columbia was not so undivided as opinion had been at Wisconsin, and for the first time Carl Becker could observe at first hand a very real competition of ideas in the open market. However conservative Burgess may have been personally, in his views on the sanctity of property and the private corporation, the characterization of his Faculty of Political Science as an "institutional stereotype" of the tendency of laissez-faire believers of the 1890's to separate political science from economics (a charge made later by Charles A. Beard,[9] who came to Columbia the year after Becker did) is grossly unfair.[10] Burgess had only followed the example of Roscher, who had pointed out the interdependence of the social sciences. More of a statesman or organizer of higher education than an original thinker, Burgess had nevertheless pioneered in America in doing exactly what Beard would accuse him of not doing; perhaps Beard never forgave the legalist Burgess for having anticipated Beard's "revolutionary" hypothesis that the adoption of the American Constitution had been more of a coup d'état than an orderly step in legal development.[11]

There is no evidence that Burgess's political science returned Becker, even momentarily, to the Republicanism of his father; nor is it even certain that Becker had given up the Republican ghost by the time of his arrival at Columbia. It is, however, evident that Burgess's deification of the Teutons and the Germanic reconciliation of authority and liberty had no effect upon Becker, who, despite his German ancestry,

---

[8] Burgess, *Reminiscences of an American Scholar,* 109.

[9] *Public Policy and the General Welfare* (New York, 1941), 134.

[10] See Ralph Gordon Hoxie (and others), *A History of the Faculty of Political Science, Columbia University* (New York, 1955), which shows the importance attached by Columbia to interdisciplinary approaches and Burgess's tolerance of heterodoxy.

[11] Burgess does this in *Political Science and Comparative Constitutional Law,* I, 105.

never cared enough for things German to acquire more than a graduate student's knowledge of the language. A racial interpretation of history, for such Burgess's was despite his protests to the contrary, must seem remarkably naive, at least in comparison with the "frontier thesis." Doubtless Burgess's exaltation of the Teutonic genius for government was, in 1898, harmless; but to judge from Becker's subsequent reactions to the cruder kinds of racial theories current in the First World War and during the days of Adolph Hitler, Becker never saw anything in racial "explanations" except pseudo-science.[12]

Burgess did, however, strike certain notes that must have raised a response in the mind of Frederick Jackson Turner's student. There was a concern on the part of both Turner and Burgess for the preservation of traditional American liberties. These liberties, Turner felt, were threatened by the complex social conditions that came with the closing of the frontier and the disappearance of free land; Burgess felt, even more strongly, that liberty was endangered by a decline in public morality, a decline particularly in evidence in our foreign policy. Both Turner and Burgess, especially the latter, feared the Slavic immigrant and doubted whether he could be easily assimilated by the Republic.[13] Both men loved the Republic and feared the conflict of democracy and individualism — a fear that would provide the basic theme for Carl Becker's later political speculations, the reconciliation of liberty and equality, of freedom and responsibility.[14]

Finally Turner and Burgess had in common a belief that if any reconciliation is ever to take place between the community and the citizen, it will be because we have learned to think historically. Unless a State knows itself and its traditions, it is likely either to advance too far in the direction of liberty, resulting in anarchy, or to move too far in the direction of authority, thus bringing about the destruction of personal liberty — and property. It simply isn't enough, Turner and Burgess argued, to have general ideas about our past; we must have exact knowledge. Hence comes in part their reasoning by analogy from the natural sciences to the social — the ideal is precision in facts so that we might choose wisely in the realm of values.

[12] For the earliest example of Becker's distrust of "Teutonism," see his review of Houston Stewart Chamberlain, *The Foundations of the Nineteenth Century, The Dial,* L, (May 16, 1911), 387-391.

[13] See Frederick Jackson Turner, *Chicago-Record Tribune,* October 16, 1901. See also John W. Burgess, "Uncle Sam," an address given in Cologne, Germany, March 3, 1907, and reprinted in his *Reminiscences,* 300-401.

[14] Becker's last book, *Freedom and Responsibility in the American Way of Life,* is a fitting symbolic end to his lifetime preoccupation with this problem.

The most "brilliant" lectures Burgess had heard in Germany were those given by the physicist Helmholtz on the principles of logic; Helmholtz had been chiefly concerned with their application to the "domain of natural science, but they were equally applicable to metaphysics, law, and social relations," Burgess thought.[15] Turner was not quite so innocent; he was personally too much of an artist to be quite so literal in his scientific faith. But notice the italics in the following passage by Turner (notice also the national self-consciousness that immediately follows it): "*As successive terminal moraines result from successive glaciations, so each frontier leaves its traces behind it, and when it becomes a settled area the region still partakes of the frontier characteristics.* Thus the advance of the frontier has meant a steady movement away from the influence of Europe, a steady growth of independence on American lines. And to study this advance, the men who grew up under these conditions, and the political, economic, and social results of it, is to study the really American part of our history."[16]

No one could fail to discern the mixture of descriptive and normative in the above, or overlook the value judgment which lies in the phrase "really American"; and if one missed it here, one could find it on almost any page by Turner. Turner may have gone one step beyond the generation of his teacher, H. B. Adams, and that of Burgess, too, far enough to see that liberty, as we know it, didn't come from German forests; but he apparently had not gone far enough to see that liberty wasn't just as dependent upon another kind of national history, the history of the American frontier. Turner's essay on "The Significance of History" (1891) is freer from the idea that history is an exact science than is Burgess's more philosophical lecture "Political Science and History" (1896), but Turner was equally bound to the thesis that history has certain lessons to teach, the lessons of civic responsibility and national self-consciousness. This kind of thinking is sometimes known as historicism, and it calls to mind George Sabine's summary of Hegel's philosophy of history: "Properly studied, history provides the principles for an objective criticism, immanent in the course of development itself, which distinguishes the true from the false, the significant from the trivial. . . ."[17] Turner had not studied at several German universities, as Burgess had, but Turner's way of looking at history was saturated with the same kind of historicism. Becker especially remem-

[15] Burgess, *Reminiscences*, 126.
[16] "The Significance of the Frontier," *The Early Writings of Frederick Jackson Turner*, 189.
[17] *A History of Political Theory* (New York, 1950), 626.

bered Turner's saying that history is "the self-consciousness of humanity";[18] the phrase is central to an understanding of Turner's "The Significance of History" where he acknowledged that he had taken these words from Burgess's beloved teacher at the University of Berlin, Johann G. Droysen (to whom Burgess had dedicated his *Political Science and Comparative Constitutional Law*).[19]

"As well try to understand the egg without a knowledge of its developed form, the chick, as to try to understand the past without bringing to it the explanation of the present," Turner had written in "The Significance of History," "and equally well try to understand an animal without study of its embryology as to try to understand one time without study of the events that went before." History, said Turner, is "ever *becoming*, never completed."[20] In the light of this, doesn't Turner's use of the word *significance* take on a special importance of the kind Sabine spoke of in connection with Hegel? I am not interested in linking Turner with Hegel, or in showing the "influence" of the Hegelian Droysen upon him, but certainly the affinity at this point is striking. The question "Significant for whom?" did not interest Turner in the way that it would come to interest Becker and Beard. For Turner, no less than for Burgess, the essential question was "Significant for what?", and the answer seemed to be "Significant for objective History and the ethic immanent therein." Small wonder that Allyn A. Young later commented judiciously that Turner's history was "not only 'past politics,' but also present politics, present economics, and present sociology."[21]

Burgess, too, seemed at times to be reading history backwards. "History in the making," was to his mind always an uncompleted story in need of interpretation "as the progressive realization of the ideal of the human spirit in all the objective forms of their manifestation, in language, tradition, and literature, in customs, manners, laws, and institutions, and in opinion and belief. And history, in the writing, is the true and faithful record of these progressive revelations of the human reason, as they mark the lines and stages of advance made by the human race toward its ultimate perfection."[22] Where the meaning and the use of history were concerned, Burgess thought rather like the

---

18 Draft of a letter from Carl Becker to Frederick Jackson Turner, May 15, 1910.

19 "The Significance of History," *The Early Writings of Frederick Jackson Turner*, 53.

20 *Ibid.*, 53, 52.

21 Allyn A. Young to Carl Becker, Cambridge, Massachusetts, October 9, 1925.

22 "Political Science and History," *Annual Report of the American Historical Association for the Year 1896*, I (Washington, 1897), 205.

younger Turner. History is not simply the past; it is development and progress. It is the total story of man's achievement, and it is a story that must be utilized by any political scientist who wishes to think — or to act — effectively in the present.

Burgess, from his experiences as a Unionist soldier in the Civil War, saw history as being on the side of nationalism, a lesson confirmed by Hegel and Droysen. Like Turner, Burgess thought of history as an "organic whole" and, again like Turner, he saw that it still consists of competing organic wholes in the form of sovereign political states. If Turner wrote history to convince Americans of the uniqueness of their heritage, Burgess had written history and political science to heal the wounds caused by the Civil War, to "clear up the confusion in the common consciousness." Even more than Turner, Burgess believed that useful history would be objective history and the opposite of partisan history; before the First World War involved the United States in a war with his beloved Teutons, Burgess happily believed that his ethical convictions and the course of historical development coincided. He could, therefore, be generous to lost causes; his efforts at sympathy are apparent in his writings about the American Civil War: "Keenly conscious of my own [Yankee] prejudices, I have exerted my imagination to the utmost to create a picture in my own mind of the environment of those who held the opposite opinion . . . and to appreciate the processes of their reasoning under the influence of their own particular institution."[23]

The "historicism" and the "presentism" apparent in both Turner's and Burgess's thinking must have impressed young Carl Becker; his own "presentism" and "relativism" may be said to commence here, with his studies under Turner and Burgess. Becker remembered that Turner had said at Wisconsin: "The question is not whether you have a Philosophy of History, but whether the philosophy you have is good for anything."[24] Both parts of Turner's off-the-cuff remark appear fatal (1) to Burgess's claims to objectivity and (2) to the particular way in which Burgess hoped history might be useful. It was difficult to see the relevance of Burgess's eulogy of nationalism to the pressing social and economic problems of his day, once the Civil War was forgotten. In comparison, Turner's "frontier thesis" at least called attention to the impact of social and economic forces upon national development and predisposed one to give these questions priority over abstract discussions of the State, the Spirit of the People, and the formal as-

[23] Preface to The Middle Period 1817-1858 (New York, 1897), vii.
[24] "Frederick Jackson Turner," Everyman His Own Historian, 207.

pects of constitutional theory. "I had a great advantage over you," Becker wrote to Felix Frankfurter in 1937. "I studied 'sound political science' (under Burgess), and the result is that it was settled once for all, so that I have never had to bother about it since. But you have had to study it all your life, and still you aren't sure."[25]

If, as is obvious, Becker thought, after forty years, that he had learned little of lasting worth from Burgess concerning political science or the historical process, one cannot altogether omit Burgess from a listing of "formative influences." Burgess had an awareness of the philosophical implications of historical writing that would be hard for an observant student to miss; and even today he seems curiously modern, although he is largely ignored even by those historians who are influenced by Croce and Collingwood and thus ultimately by Hegelianism and historicism. It is not a very long way from the position of either Burgess or Turner to the one reached later by Becker in his first essay on historiography, "Detachment and the Writing of History" (1910), or even to his "Everyman His Own Historian" (1931). History conceived of as the "memory of things said and done . . . running hand in hand with the anticipation of things to be said and done," what Croce and Becker after him called *"living* history,"[26] is not so far removed from the living history of Burgess ("history in the making") or of Turner (history as "ever *becoming,* never completed"). It is just more sophisticated. Becker's famous "relativism" is, in a sense, simply "historicism" or "presentism" made aware of its own presuppositions and hence self-conscious; the historian has come, as Droysen advised, really to know himself, and as a result to see the mote in his own eye.

If Becker learned anything about the philosophy of history, and especially about the mote in the historian's eye, while at Columbia, he probably learned most from James Harvey Robinson, for never has there been in the history of American scholarship a historian more critical of historians — even Henry Adams must take second place for once. Robinson had come to Columbia in 1895 from the University of Pennsylvania, and he had been hired not as a controversialist but as a specialist in medieval and modern history. His preparation in these fields had been undertaken at Harvard University and at the University of Freiberg in Germany, where he took his Ph.D. under von Holst. His doctoral thesis was a reworked version of a paper he had done at Harvard on "The Original and Derived Features of the Constitution of the United States," but after this he had worked exclusively in Euro-

[25] Carl Becker to Felix Frankfurter, Ithaca, New York, January 3, 1937.
[26] "Everyman His Own Historian," *Everyman His Ow.. Historian,* 242.

pean history. He continued, however, to write in political history for some time, as one would expect of a student of von Holst's, and his *The German Bundesrath, a Study in Comparative Constitutional Law* was published in 1891. At Pennsylvania he also began to acquire a reputation as an editor and translator of historical documents, an activity he continued at Columbia. During his first years at Columbia he gave courses in the Renaissance and the Reformation, in the history of France and the French Revolution, but he did not begin his famous course in the intellectual history of Western Europe until 1904. His *The Development of Modern Europe,* written in collaboration with Charles A. Beard, did not appear until 1907, and his *The New History* was not published until 1912.[27]

Robinson had, however, already shown certain maverick tendencies. At Harvard he had studied under William James, and the effects of James proved ultimately more durable than those of von Holst. James imparted to Robinson an interest in psychology, as well as a pluralistic, pragmatic philosophy; he was, according to Robinson, the only teacher who had left a permanent mark on his thinking.[28] At the University of Pennsylvania Robinson had had as colleagues Edward P. Cheyney, who is now remembered for having discovered six laws of history where most historians find none,[29] and John Bach McMaster, who was still working on his *History of the People of the United States,* probably the most influential piece of social history written in the English language apart from John Richard Greene's earlier *Short History of England.* Before coming to Columbia, Robinson had already begun to lay into orthodoxy. He had insisted, for instance, that the infant science of sociology was of value to the historian, and he had tried to show that the conventional historian was too interested in dramatic events at the expense of historical continuity or evolution. Later, in *The Mind in the Making,* published in 1921, and in his presidential address before the American Historical Association, "The Newer Ways of Historians," the emphasis would again be upon what the historian could learn from the social scientist, but here the psychologist would definitely rank higher in importance than the sociologist.[30] Robinson would remain

[27] See Luther V. Hendricks, *James Harvey Robinson, Teacher of History* (New York, 1946), 1-19.

[28] Harry Elmer Barnes, "James Harvey Robinson," *American Masters of Social Science,* 326-327.

[29] "Law in History," *American Historical Review,* XXIX (January, 1924), 191-202.

[30] *The Mind in the Making* (New York, 1921), *passim.* "The Newer Ways of Historians," *American Historical Review,* XXXV (January, 1930), 245-255.

more impressed by James than by all the other social scientists put together; and by some thinkers he himself would come to be regarded as the William James of American historiography. "For me," H. G. Wells would write in his Preface to the English edition of *The Mind in the Making*, "I think James Harvey Robinson is going to be as important as Huxley in my adolescence and William James in later years. . . . The spirit of the school he has organized liberates something of my private dreams into the world of reality."[31]

It is hard to imagine Wells as having private dreams, just as it is hard to recapture the spirit of the school, the school of "New Historians" allegedly organized by Robinson — the "New Historians" who were really quite old by the time Robinson began to publicize their virtues and who were aptly referred to by Becker, in his essay on Turner, as "an ancient and honorable company."[32] Robinson's "New History" was very old history indeed, as old as Voltaire and John Richard Greene. It was also old in the sense that Turner and even Burgess had made it old before Robinson; both Fulmer Mood and Merle Curti have pointed out that Turner's "The Significance of History" anticipates the more important precepts of *The New History*,[33] and to a lesser degree the same can be said for the theories outlined in Burgess's "Political Science and History." The idea of the present's depending upon the past, the belief that we need in the study of history all the help we can get from *all* the social sciences, even the continuing faith in the genetic method — a carry-over from the days of H. B. Adams[34] — are in evidence in *The New History* and in Robinson's and Beard's textbook, *The Development of Modern Europe*. And they are present without much evidence that the present has improved upon the recent past of Turner or Burgess. "One may look to history to explain almost everything," Robinson and Beard would confidently exclaim, "great and small, from the constitution of a state to the form of a written character or the presence of useless buttons upon a man's coat sleeve."[35]

The last illustration given by Robinson and Beard in this quotation

[31] H. G. Wells, Introduction to the English edition of *The Mind in the Making* (London, 1923), 7.

[32] "Frederick Jackson Turner," *Everyman His Own Historian*, 229.

[33] Mood, Introduction to *The Early Writings of Frederick Jackson Turner*, 31. Curti, "Frederick Jackson Turner, 1861-1932," *Probing Our Past* (New York, 1955), 40.

[34] See H. B. Adams, "Special Methods of Historical Study," *Johns Hopkins University Studies in Historical and Political Science*, II (Baltimore, 1884), 5-23.

[35] James Harvey Robinson and Charles A. Beard, *The Development of Modern Europe*, I (New York, 1907), 2.

is an unintentional piece of symbolism: what separates the "New Historians" from Turner and even Burgess is not so much history as it is politics, not the question of whether history is something more than "past politics" but the question of what the historian ought to do about "useless buttons" left behind by the past. Turner and Burgess, in their "presentism," were more interested in explaining the present in terms of past evolution; Robinson and Beard would be more interested in explaining the past from the vantage point of the present, in terms of new hypotheses or points of view — or as Becker would express it — not only is the present the product of all the past, but the past is even more the product of the present.[36] Turner, it is true, had called attention to present economic problems, and the conservative Burgess had sometimes taken time off from his metaphysical speculations about the State to express his fears concerning a possible warfare in the United States between plutocracy and proletariat; but Turner, as Beard would complain, did not write about labor union versus employer in the way in which he wrote of frontiersman versus Eastern capitalist;[37] and Burgess's doctrines of constitutional limitations and laissez-faire made his fear of the social consequences of unrestrained wealth remain only a fear.

Robinson and Beard, on the other hand, had read too much of Marx to believe that either the virtues of a primitive, frontier society or the sanctification of liberty under law (Teutonic law, of course) could long keep an industrial society in a state of "organic wholeness."[38] Robinson could not believe, as Burgess did, that the State is "the human organ least likely to do wrong" and that we must therefore "hold to the principle that the state can do no wrong."[39] He did, however, believe enough in the State, more apparently than Burgess, to accept the desirability of state planning and the collective use of intelligence, which he felt was being wasted individually. Later, along with Beard,

[36] "Detachment and the Writing of History," *Detachment and the Writing of History*, 3-28.

[37] Beard, "The Frontier in American History," *New Republic*, XCIX (June 14, 1939), 148.

[38] However much they learned from Marx, both Robinson and Beard preferred to believe in ameliorative intelligence rather than in intelligence used as an instrument for furthering the class struggle. For Robinson's debt as a historian to Marx, see James Harvey Robinson, "History," *Columbia University Lectures on Science, Philosophy and Art, 1907-1908*, 5-29. For Beard's debt to Marx, see William Appleman Williams, "A Note on Charles Austin Beard's Search for a General Theory of Causation," *American Historical Review*, LXII (October, 1956), 59-80.

[39] *Political Science and Comparative Constitutional Law*, I, 52-54. Some scholars suggest that when Burgess said *State* he really meant *Society*, but that does not seem satisfactory in this context.

Thorstein Veblen, Alvin Johnson, and John Dewey, Robinson would help organize the New School for Social Research; and it was Robinson who wanted to make it into a kind of Ruskin Hall for America, a truly "labor college."[40]

Robinson, like Turner, had enthusiasm. More than Turner he was certain of what buttons to keep and what buttons to remove from the historical fabric; and he was a thousand times more certain than Burgess, despite Burgess's talk of the "ultimate perfectibility of man," of man's ability to progress. "When we read the descriptions of our nature as given by William James, McDougall, and even Thorndike . . . we get a rather impressive idea of our possibilities. . . ."[41] Enthusiasm about the future and skepticism about the present alternated in Robinson's mind, much as the ideas of good and evil do in the Christian mind. Enthusiasm over the possibilities of social science was Robinson's specialty, so that he is a central figure in what Cushing Strout has called "the twentieth century enlightenment" in American social thought.[42]

Equally strong, however, was Robinson's skepticism over the ability of the unenlightened, especially unenlightened historians, to perceive this potential; nor did his skepticism spare those who fell into the opposite error of claiming too much for reason. Robinson the pragmatist never allowed his audience to forget that the human mind is, as H. G. Wells following Lord Balfour succinctly put it, "essentially a food-seeking system and no more necessarily a truth-finding apparatus than the snout of a pig."[43] Robinson's high-low estimate of human reason was accompanied by a disillusioned and ironic attitude toward mankind for having accomplished so little thus far. A dark past, a bright future, this was Robinson's estimate of man's nature and destiny. All these sentiments combined to turn von Holst's student into one of America's outstanding polemicists: a polemicist of much wit and erudition. What is so-called objective history, he asked later, but history without an object? And what, if the historian ever does learn his lessons from all the social sciences, will it profit him to gain the whole world if he loses his soul?[44]

[40] Robinson quoted by Hendricks, *James Harvey Robinson, Teacher of History*, 25. In 1937 Robinson's student Becker would be invited to join the Faculty Council of the New School, and he would accept. (Alvin Johnson to Carl Becker, New York, March 19, March 29, 1937.)

[41] Robinson, *The Mind in the Making*, English edition, 92.

[42] *The American Political Science Review*, XLIX (June, 1955), 321-339.

[43] H. G. Wells, Introduction to the English edition of *The Mind in the Making*, 9.

[44] James Harvey Robinson, *The New History* (New York, 1912), *passim*.

In the 1890's, however, Robinson was still mainly a historian and classroom teacher. The scholar who, along with Cheyney and Munro had edited *Translations and Reprints from the Original Sources of European History,* was still predominant in Robinson, and his graduate students probably learned as much "sound" history as Burgess's did "sound" political science. The methods of the two differed, however; Robinson had, like Turner, some of the humility that had managed for the most part to escape Burgess, the man of the world and the friend of the Kaiser's. Himself the most certain of men in his judgments of value, Robinson the painstaking scholar and teacher was fond of quoting Abelard's "By doubting we learn to inquire; by inquiry we find out truth."[45] As a teacher Robinson had a following as illustrious as Turner's, especially when one bears in mind that he had no single thesis or historical explanation around which the zealous could rally. (Compare Turner's students, Solon J. Buck, Ulrich B. Phillips, Frederick Merk, Avery Craven, and Guy Stanton Ford, with Robinson's, James T. Shotwell, Carlton J. H. Hayes, Lynn Thorndike, Dixon Ryan Fox, and Irwin Edman.)

Both Turner and Robinson would be able to take pride in the achievements of Carl Becker, and Robinson is only slightly less important to Becker's biographer than Turner. Turner (and Haskins, too) had had the advantages of being first, but what Turner had given Becker in the field of American history and in the way of enthusiasm about history, Robinson would give him in the field of French history and in the way of a polite skepticism about historians mixed with an enthusiasm for examining their presuppositions. In a way more scholarly than the Reverend Van Ness's, Robinson introduced Becker to French culture, a fact of some significance since Becker's future classic, *The Heavenly City of the Eighteenth Century Philosophers,* reflects not only Robinson's interests but seems to be organized around a distinctly Robinsonian point of view.

"In 1898 I enrolled in James Harvey Robinson's seminar in eighteenth century thought," Becker recalled in 1937, "which met one evening a week in the old Columbia library. The professor talked so charmingly and entertainingly that taking notes seemed out of place. He had wit, a dry, mordant humor, and a fund of striking, unacademic bits of information which I had not found in textbooks or formal histories; and there was a sadness in the countenance, a quality, half plaintiveness, half resignation in the voice that made even simple statements of fact, amusing or illuminating, or both." Becker did a

[45] Henry Johnson, *The Other Side of Main Street* (New York, 1943), 162.

paper for Robinson on the Physiocrats, and in so doing "acquired an abiding interest in why people think as they do."[46]

It was the beginning of a long and cordial relationship between Becker and a man whom he regarded as "one of the ablest and most thought-provoking teachers of history in our time."[47] Of course, Becker's interest in why people think as they do had been much in evidence long before he met Robinson — as the "Wild Thoughts Notebook" amply demonstrates. Robinson's *forte*, however, was intellectual history (which must not be confused with the history of philosophy); and he was keenly interested in the factors, either subconscious or economic, that lie behind formal thinking. Probably nothing is more appealing to a young man determined to penetrate to the essence of things through a maze of cant and humbug than the word *rationalization*, which Robinson used with the greatest effectiveness — and Becker's entire literary output, even his maturest works such as *The Heavenly City*, is shot through with this word or this *attitude* towards the opinions of others. What Becker had to say about the Physiocrats during his seminar under Robinson is lost; but what he had to say later about them and the natural-rights school in general, in his *The Declaration of Independence* (1922), was as penetrating, and at times as mordant, as Robinson could have wished. In 1899 Robinson wrote the first of his cordial letters to Becker: "I am happy to say that the work which you pursued under my direction was entirely satisfactory. Your reports in the seminar showed industry and insight and made it clear that you had a good grasp of historical methods."[48]

It is important at this point to note that all of Becker's principal teachers chose to comment on his grasp of historical method. Just as Robinson had qualified, in Becker's later opinion, to be a critic of historians by first becoming a good specialist himself, so Becker was qualifying as a future critic of historical method. Robinson's importance in this qualifying process was probably profound; if we are correct, he is the connecting link — hitherto ignored or underestimated by Becker scholars — between the "historicism" or "presentism" of Turner (and Burgess) and the "relativism" of the later Becker. Insofar as Becker criticized the idea of "objective history" as defended, for example, by C. M. Andrews[49] and by those who considered Reason as

[46] Review of James Harvey Robinson, *The Human Comedy*, *The Nation*, CXLIV (January 9, 1937), 48-50.

[47] *Ibid.*, 50.

[48] James Harvey Robinson to Carl Becker, New York, September 3, 1899.

[49] See C. M. Andrews, "These Forty Years," *American Historical Review*, XXX (January, 1925), 225-250.

a Logic detached from passion or special interest, Robinson could claim much of the credit. Insofar as Becker came to share the opinions of the "New Historians" and their reformist sentiments, here, too, much of the credit would be Robinson's. When Becker would weary somewhat during his own middle age of "twenty-five years" of talk by Robinson on the "New History" — which Robinson never really wrote but only hinted at in his textbook written with Beard — and when Becker at times despaired of incessant talk about reform, his skepticism was tempered, in part by love, the love of an "admiring and grateful" student for a man who, if he sometimes tilted at windmills, "exerted a profound and beneficial influence upon the thought of his generation."[50]

Robinson was the first rationalist of any caliber, outside of Ingersoll, whom Becker had observed — a fact which suggests that Robinson helped complete or at least to solidify Becker's philosophic detachment from religion. Robinson had, as Becker was to have, many of the strengths and weaknesses of the eighteenth century *philosophes*. He had also certain characteristics as a teacher that would later become Becker hallmarks: there was his dry manner, his Midwestern accent, combined with an impassivity, an absence of affectation, and a determination to convince by rational means alone. Becker became more aware than Robinson of the limits of reason, but central to the lives of both men is the paradox of trying to convince by a reason that is known beforehand to be a frail, thin reed. Small wonder that in such a hopeless task both men placed so much emphasis upon clarity and the well-chosen word. Even to undertake such a task is the mark of the honest man, but integrity of this kind must be relieved by wit and even irreverence. Robinson found pleasure, as Becker sometimes would, in exposing human stupidity,[51] this being the rationalist's equivalent of the Christian's search for evidences of Original Sin. Another paradox in Robinson, as in Becker, is that a man who found so little of value in religion was of some consequence in directing the attention of students and readers to the importance of religion and of the medieval Church as a key to the understanding of modern history. Robinson knew his medieval history too well to fall into clichés about the Dark Ages and the anti-science of the Church; Robinson's attitude suggests Becker's later attempts to explain the eighteenth century *philosophes* as Christians-not-Christian.

[50] Review of James Harvey Robinson, *The Human Comedy*, *The Nation*, CXLIV (January 9, 1937), 50.
[51] Irwin Edman, *Philosopher's Holiday* (New York, 1938), 134-156.

If Robinson and Becker were men of paradox, the third most important of Becker's teachers at Columbia was a man almost totally devoid of this quality. He was Herbert Levi Osgood, whom Burgess considered "the most profound and original scholar in English and American history our country has ever produced."[52] From Osgood's famous seminar at Columbia came Charles A. Beard's doctoral dissertation on the English Justice of the Peace and A. M. Schlesinger's study of the colonial merchants of New York. Between these two works appeared Becker's history of political parties in the province of New York,[53] which Becker finally completed for the University of Wisconsin but which may be regarded as having come, at least in part, from Becker's studies with Osgood. Of all Becker's teachers he was the most orthodox in his conception of what history ought to be, probably because he spent so much time with documents that he had no time left for the philosophy of history. Although critical at times of von Ranke, Osgood was a firm believer in "political history." He thought, "The political and constitutional side of the subject should be given first place, because it is only through law and political institutions that social forces become in a large sense operative. The directions which these forces take are also largely determined by the political framework within which they act. They are ever modifying institutions, but it is by acting on and through them."[54] The only paradox of this man's career is his influence upon and sympathy with men such as Beard, Schlesinger, and Becker, and the fact that he managed to keep their earlier researches within the limits outlined above. Osgood was a model of industry not of style; he was the bread to the wine of Robinson, as Robinson became more of a polemicist and less of a research historian. After Becker began to study under Osgood, he turned from a study of national nominating conventions, suggested by Turner, to the more modest, Osgood-like plan for a history of political parties in New York on the eve of the Revolution. Whether Osgood was responsible for this change is unknown; for want of documentary evidence Osgood's influence upon Becker, like Haskins's and Ely's, must remain a matter for conjecture. Even the conjecture will have to wait its proper chronological place, for Becker waited nearly a decade from the time of his leaving Madi-

[52] Burgess, *Reminiscences of an American Scholar*, 159.

[53] Charles A. Beard, *The Office of Justice of the Peace in England in Its Origin and Development* (New York, 1904). A. M. Schlesinger, *The Colonial Merchants and the American Revolution* (New York, 1918). Carl L. Becker, *The History of Political Parties in the Province of New York: 1760-1776* (Madison, 1909).

[54] Quoted by Dixon Ryan Fox, *Herbert Levi Osgood, An American Scholar* (New York, 1924), 86.

son, Wisconsin, before returning there to submit his Ph.D. dissertation, and without the urging of Turner and Haskins he might never have done so.[55]

If Becker did not get very far in his studies toward the Ph.D. during his year at Columbia, he got far enough to win the Tappan Prize for the best work done in constitutional law that year, and far enough for J. W. Burgess to write that his career at Columbia had been an "eminent success." No grades were given, which was the custom at that time,[56] but "The uniform testimony of his instructors," according to Burgess, "is that he is an able, conscientious and industrious scholar, and an entirely trustworthy and upright man."[57] On the basis of his work at Wisconsin and Columbia, Becker was offered the Harrison Fellowship in American History at the University of Pennsylvania to commence in September, 1899. Haskins had written John Bach Mc-Master a letter stressing Becker's capacity for hard work and his "power of happy, lucid statement":[58] two virtues possessed in abundance by McMaster himself. Had Becker accepted the Fellowship, his biographer would be able to state almost without qualification that Becker, by working next with McMaster and Cheyney, had studied under every major American history teacher responsible for pushing historical inquiry beyond the famous dictum of E. A. Freeman, which H. B. Adams had placed above the doorway to his seminar room at Johns Hopkins in the 1870's: "History is past Politics and Politics present History." Becker, however, denied us the artistic completeness of such a statement. Instead of accepting the fellowship he chose to go to Pennsylvania State College as an instructor — his days as a graduate student were over.

It might be well at this point to summarize the promises and the limitations that Becker would carry with him into the teaching world. Just as the provincial had brought with him respectable intellectual equipment for his year's study at an Eastern university, so he carried with him to Pennsylvania State College an even better potential as both a research scholar and a thinker on historical questions. At Columbia he had, for the first time, lived among equals or near equals. Ulrich Phillips, Charles Merriam, and James Shotwell were all fellow

[55] See, for example, Charles Homer Haskins to Carl Becker, Madison, Wisconsin, October 27, 1902.

[56] The Registrar, Columbia University, to the author, New York, December 6, 1957.

[57] John W. Burgess to Carl Becker, Montpelier, Vermont, August 30, 1899.

[58] Charles Homer Haskins to John Bach McMaster, Madison, Wisconsin, March 7, 1899.

students of Becker's. The classes had been small enough for Becker to measure himself against Columbia's best, and he had not been found wanting.[59] Also, by attending Columbia Becker acquired an advantage, however intangible, over other Turner students, some of whom never escaped the master's charm. Becker's own interpretations of American history would be essentially Turnerian, and most of his writings would actually be in the fields of American history and government. As a teacher, however, he would come to specialize in European history and his most provocative book, *The Heavenly City of the Eighteenth Century Philosophers*, would be in that field. Not only did Columbia help prepare Becker for work in European history, Robinson having carried on the work begun by Haskins, but Columbia also probably helped save Becker from the intellectual provincialism that sometimes affected Turner's followers.

At both Wisconsin and Columbia Becker had acquired the tools essential for an informed understanding: what R. G. Collingwood rightly describes as the Question-and-Answer procedure of historical inquiry.[60] Since history and politics were so interwoven at Wisconsin and Columbia, history having nearly become in some instances *present* politics, Becker's teachers had asked questions that no technical historian, however refined his methods, could answer, questions as large as life itself, which Becker said is how history is when seen through the eyes of someone like Turner.[61] No student of Turner's and Burgess's could be unaware of the conflict between individualism and democracy; no student of Turner's and Robinson's could be unaware of questions concerning the influence of ideas or environment, European or American, upon character. Nor could a man who had studied under Turner, Haskins, Burgess, Robinson, and Osgood fail to know something about historical method in both its philosophical and practical aspects.

Only one thing was lacking in Becker's preparation, and that was the quality which the social fraternities at Wisconsin had missed. He had studied under men of considerable charm. He had, while at Columbia, begun to court the woman he would later marry, but he was still too reserved or shy for the teaching profession. After two years at Pennsylvania State College Becker accepted a position at Dartmouth College, where he encountered problems of discipline. Letters from Turner and Haskins reveal considerable worry on this

---

[59] James T. Shotwell to the author, New York, August, 1957.
[60] R. G. Collingwood, *The Idea of History* (Oxford, 1946), 269-274, 278-282.
[61] "Frederick Jackson Turner," *Everyman His Own Historian*, 191-232.

score; their student who wrote so well talked so poorly and without enthusiasm. Turner had hoped in vain that Becker would *"find"* himself as a teacher at Pennsylvania State College;[62] Haskins worried about Becker and the "lively" Dartmouth boys and was almost as relieved as Becker when the latter returned in 1902 to the Mid-West to teach at the less lively University of Kansas. Even at Kansas all would not go well. It must have been embarrassing to Becker to receive after a year at Kansas — he was by then thirty years old — a letter from Haskins urging him to overcome a defect that Haskins had noticed years before when Becker was in Madison. "Look them fiercely in the eye!", the distinguished medievalist advised him, as a means either to win or subdue his students.[63] Becker would have been even more embarrassed, and somewhat worried, to know that his superior at Kansas, Wilbur C. Abbott, had written Turner complaining about Becker's stand-offishness. "The only doubt I ever had about Becker," Turner admitted to Abbott, "was just on the point which you mentioned. I have a feeling that Becker's training under Osgood emphasized traits that were somewhat too pronounced already."[64]

If there seemed to be a Gresham's Law working against Becker in favor of what Haskins called the "hustler," there were by now brighter elements in the story. In the first place, the Kansas appointment would prove to be, despite Abbott's initial misgivings, a long one. Becker went there in 1902 as an assistant professor of history and did not leave until 1916, when he had a full professorship and a growing reputation as a historian. With the preparation of lectures demanding less of his time, and with a more tranquil student body, Becker had leisure in which to write. He had begun to publish before going to Kansas, but the distinctive qualities that mark his mature writings date from his Kansas years.

Also, Becker had married in 1901 Maude Hepworth Ranney, the New York widow and physician's daughter whom he had met during his Columbia days. Mrs. Ranney was several years his senior, with a seven-year-old daughter by her first marriage, but Becker's assumption of his new responsibilities seems to have been without unusual effort. Becker's family had been "greatly shocked" by the marriage, his sister has recalled; he had been rather expected to marry a "gracious and

[62] Frederick Jackson Turner to Carl Becker, Madison, Wisconsin, November 17, 1899.
[63] Charles Homer Haskins to Carl Becker, Madison, Wisconsin, January 4, 1903.
[64] Frederick Jackson Turner to Wilbur C. Abbott, Madison, Wisconsin, March 9, 1903.

talented girl" in Waterloo.[65] The family soon recovered, however, enough for Mrs. Becker to write a gracious letter to Becker's bride and another one to her son, telling them both that Mrs. Ranney was getting "the best husband in the world."[66] Afterwards, Becker, owing to the affliction of his step-daughter, an affliction of an obscure but serious nature that dated from an overdose of medicine during the Beckers' stay in Kansas, would need to be the best husband in the world. No one familiar with the story of his solicitude for his wife and her daughter can doubt his capacity for understanding. Some would say that he had to give more understanding than he got, especially in the later years of his life; his wife, alas, was not intellectual enough to please all of Becker's acquaintances, who never stopped to reflect that understanding is not a purely cerebral affair. She was, however, a motherly woman who gave Becker a home, enough to provide many an introvert with a feeling of security. In 1910 she gave him a son, Frederick; and she continued to be a faithful and loyal wife to Carl Becker until his death in 1945.[67] No one who has read any of Becker's letters to his wife, from whom he was seldom separated, or her letters to him during his one trip to Europe in 1924, when he was recovering from one of a series of painful illnesses, could fail to understand the dedication of one of his books "To Maude Hepworth Ranney who possesses and has needed forbearance and understanding."[68] By the time of Becker's arrival in Lawrence, Kansas, in 1902, the process of "settling in" — into a marriage and into a career — had got well under way, or so it seems in retrospect.

[65] Jessie Becker to Phil Snyder, Waterloo, Iowa, December 12, 1955.

[66] Mrs. Charles Becker to Carl Becker, Waterloo, Iowa, June 6, 1901.

[67] This sympathetic assessment of Mrs. Becker is confirmed by a letter from "one of Becker's closest friends" reprinted in David Hawke's "Carl L. Becker," Master's thesis, University of Wisconsin, 1950, 208-210.

[68] There are about twenty-five letters from Maude Becker to Carl Becker in The Becker Papers of the sincere "take care of yourself for I love you" type. The book dedicated to Maude Hepworth Ranney is *Progress and Power* (Stanford, California, 1936).

Chapter V

Becker and Kansas: The Development of a Career and of a Pragmatic Point of View

"SOME YEARS AGO, in a New England college town, when I informed one of my New England friends that I was preparing to go to Kansas, he replied rather blankly, 'Kansas? Oh!' "[1] This recollection was made by Becker in 1910 in his essay "Kansas" when he was still in Kansas and when it looked as if the names of both Kansas and Becker might never arouse a more spirited response in Eastern centers of learning. By 1910 Kansas had become the object of a perverse kind of pride on Becker's part. He shared the native's belief that Kansas, having passed through a "superior heat" and worse calamities ranging from a civil war to drought and depression, deserved to be known affectionately as "Dear Old Kansas." The spirit of Kansas, Becker wrote, was the "American spirit double distilled . . . a new grafted product of American individualism, American idealism, American intolerance," the very qualities that Becker's teacher Turner had singled out as part of the frontier heritage. Moreover, Kansas, according to Becker, was "America in microcosm."[2]

Becker stayed in the microcosm, or on the educational frontier, for fourteen years, long enough to be remembered. A student of Becker's at Kansas, later to become vice-president of the publishing house of Appleton-Century-Crofts, remembers Becker "pushing a baby carriage slowly along the sidewalk, slightly stooped, pipe in mouth," so abstracted that passersby went unnoticed. The same student recalls Becker's introductory course in European history: "his quiet approach to the teacher's chair, his detached air as he peered at the ceiling before opening the class with almost hesitant remarks, and then perhaps one of his Socratic questions delivered in an unemotional voice and an

[1] "Kansas," *Everyman His Own Historian*, 1.
[2] *Ibid.*, 5, 25, 27.

69

absentminded manner which for the first few days left me wondering whether he was of this world or not."[3]

From Becker's days at Kansas there also dates a revealing anecdote — revealing even if it were untrue — about this most detached and otherworldly of men. Another student of Becker's tells how one day an undergraduate committed suicide by throwing himself from the top floor of a building directly behind the one in which Becker lectured. Becker lectured facing the windows and the students sat with their backs to the window facing Becker. Becker saw the body hurtling downward, according to this legend; but he said nothing about the incident and continued his lecture. The students in Becker's class knew nothing about the suicide until after the class was dismissed.[4]

If Becker kept the students in ignorance of the spectacular — and his students also recall that he tended to underplay the drama in history — he also kept them in ignorance about his home life. "We were never invited to his house but we went in and out of the homes of Abbott and [Frank H.] Hodder," one of his students recalls.[5] Mrs. Becker, although remembered as a gracious hostess by some of Becker's students after he had gone to teach at Cornell University, is not remembered at all at Kansas. This is not surprising as she was of a retiring disposition; she was quite different from those hellions who later appeared (and not only in the novels of Sinclair Lewis) determined to transform a place of heat and dust into one of light and beauty. If Becker succeeded in having some measure of privacy at the University, which was still little more than a college, he did not isolate himself entirely. Although he began to be plagued at Kansas with the ulcer trouble that would not leave him until a few years prior to his death, he still found time and strength for an occasional game of tennis and a few close friendships.

Becker at Kansas is remembered as a man "small in stature, slender, with dark hair and eyes and a rather dark tone in his skin," who to the casual observer showed "no warmth" and "apparently did not enjoy company."[6] Becker, by his own admission, found teaching especially painful at this stage in his career, presumably because of his shyness.[7] "I have a feeling that Mr. Becker suffered from a kind of intellectual

[3] Allen S. Wilbur to Phil Snyder, New York, December 14, 1955.

[4] Alicia M. Siefrit to Phil Snyder, Tonganoxie, Kansas, February 27, 1956.

[5] Frank Klingberg, Professor of History at the University of California at Los Angeles, to Phil Snyder, Los Angeles, November 10, 1955.

[6] Richard R. Smith to Phil Snyder, West Rindge, New Hampshire, November 14, 1955.

[7] Leo Gershoy, Introduction to *Progress and Power*, xxv.

loneliness," one of his more distinguished students from Cornell University has remarked; and from this loneliness there came about a certain uniformity in his ideas "not from assertion in arguments, but from not having argued with people of different opinions. . . . Of course I only knew him in the last thirteen years of his life. But perhaps even earlier, probably from the Kansas days, he had too few intellectual friends. . . ."[8] Such is the familiar, Eastern opinion, more often spoken than written, but one that is often repeated to the student of Becker's life. Becker had ulcers; he was alone and probably miserable, with no friends of any consequence. In order to test parts of this opinion it is necessary to ask who were Becker's friends at Kansas. Were they so few as to justify the opinion that Becker didn't enjoy company, and so unintellectual as to confirm the suspicion that Becker's Kansas days were really marked by "intellectual loneliness"?

Becker's principal friends at Kansas were Wallace Notestein, Frank H. Hodder, Olin Templin, and Frank Egbert Bryant. Of these, only the two historians, Notestein and Hodder — especially Notestein — ever acquired reputations going much beyond Lawrence, Kansas. Notestein came to Kansas after Becker did and left sooner, first for the University of Minnesota, to which Becker was later called, and finally for Yale University, to which Becker was nearly called. Behind Becker's call to Minnesota and his near-call to Yale lay the hand of his friend Notestein, who greatly admired Becker's literary style and philosophical acumen. Notestein, the student of British institutions, was more nearly the detached scholar than Frank H. Hodder, more polished in his style, and more productive in his historical writings. Hodder is now remembered principally for his efforts to show that the Kansas-Nebraska Act was passed more for railroad purposes than for political reasons.[9] In his interpretation of this period in American history, his most important disciple has been, by an odd twist of fate, one of Becker's severest critics where historiography is concerned, James C. Malin.[10]

Hodder was considerably less detached from his environment than either Notestein or Becker; he was to teach for forty-four years at

[8] Robert Palmer to George Sabine, Princeton, New Jersey, November 17, 1945.
[9] "The Genesis of the Kansas-Nebraska Act," State Historical Society of Wisconsin, *Proceedings,* 1912 (Madison, Wisconsin), 69-86. "The Railroad Background of the Kansas-Nebraska Act," *Mississippi Valley Historical Review,* XII (June, 1925), 3-22.
[10] See James C. Malin, *The Nebraska Question, 1852-1854* (Lawrence, Kansas), 1953. Also "Frank Heywood Hodder, 1860-1935," *Kansas Historical Quarterly,* V (May, 1936), 115-121.

Kansas, where he was known as a painstaking scholar and teacher deeply interested in the administration of the University and in the protection of academic freedom. Hodder was a man "Deeply, Richly Human," and his speeches at faculty meetings were devoid of "reserves" or "concealment."[11] He was personally the very opposite of Becker, bluff and genial, with no feeling for nuance and distrustful of irony. Yet he passed from Becker's severest critic at Kansas to one of his closest friends — they seemed to complement one another. "If Frank were one of your best friends, you were one of his," his widow wrote Becker in 1936, "it would seem there was mutual admiration."[12] There was; and long after Becker left Kansas he received many blunt but affectionate letters from Hodder, some of them complaining that the University had been in a perpetual state of decline ever since Becker's departure. "I envy Cornell in the acquisition of Professor Becker, whom we first lost to Minnesota. He was the best man we had," Hodder would wistfully exclaim in 1917.[13]

One other man at Kansas knew Becker's strength; that was Olin Templin, Dean of the University. Templin, too, was devoid of pretense and pettiness; and he knew Becker's worth as a teacher sooner than most men at the University. "A lot of us are still wishing," he wrote to Becker in 1941 after his own retirement, "you had staid with us, but what would you have been if you had?"[14] Finally there was Frank Egbert Bryant, an associate professor of English at the University, a man who had the run of the Becker household and whose untimely death in 1910 at the age of thirty-three cut short a promising career of research and teaching. He had literary interests in common with Becker, and Becker loved him for his "unshakable conviction that truth is different from falsehood, that right is different from wrong."[15]

The evidence is strong enough to warrant the conclusion that, appearances notwithstanding, Becker at Kansas had need of company and enough warmth to find and keep friends. As for the question of "intellectual loneliness" that is largely a subjective question — a man is lonely if he feels lonely. The evidence, however, suggests that there

[11] E. H. Holland, Tribute to Frank Heywood Hodder, *The Graduate Magazine* of the University of Kansas, XXXIV (January, 1936), 3.

[12] Mrs. Florence M. Hodder to Carl Becker, Lawrence, Kansas, January 18, 1936.

[13] Frank H. Hodder quoted by A. A. Young to George Lincoln Burr, [Cambridge, Massachusetts], July 28, 1917. The George Lincoln Burr Papers.

[14] Olin Templin to Carl Becker, Evergreen, Colorado, June 30, 1941.

[15] Becker, Tribute to Frank Egbert Bryant, *Frank Egbert Bryant 1877-1910* (Lawrence, Kansas, March, 1911), 20-24. Delivered at the Kansas University Chapel memorial service, January 24, 1911.

is no objective reason to regard Becker's years at Kansas as years wasted among philistines and mediocrities. Notestein was no Robinson, Hodder was no Turner, but at that time Becker was not yet fully Becker. It is even possible for us to imagine that some feeling of dissatisfaction with one's present state, call it loneliness if you will, is ultimately advantageous. Arnold Toynbee's phrase "Withdrawal and Return" fits Becker's story rather nicely. In two ways, actually. One can look upon Becker's few years in the East as a withdrawal, and upon his going to Kansas as a return to his own kind of Mid-West, or one can regard his stay at Kansas as a period of withdrawal and testing with his departure to Cornell via Minnesota as a return to "Culture." In either event, Becker might be adduced as additional proof that Toynbee is in a sense correct, that it is better to go away and then to return than to remain forever, if in going away one does not destroy one's promise through loneliness.

At Kansas Becker was what he had been as a student at Wisconsin, a slow starter; but, as at Wisconsin, Becker slowly proved his worth, emerging from his apprentice days as a teacher and author in his own right. Becker's success as a teacher dates, insofar as University recognition is concerned, from the year 1907 when he finally took his Ph.D. at Wisconsin and was promoted to associate professor of history at Kansas. In 1908 Abbott left for Yale, and Becker was made full professor of history. With Abbott's departure the two history departments, European and American, were consolidated into one, with Becker responsible for the work in European history. If Becker's enrollment continued to be less than Abbott's had been — a matter of grave concern sometimes irreverently referred to as "the numbers game" — both Hodder and Templin were by now unqualified champions of Becker. Becker's salary was raised, from $1,400 to $2,000, and it is said that in the year 1908 he appeared on campus with a "brand new look."[16]

If Becker, as a teacher, could never feign interest in student activities or athletics, he managed to capture the interests of the students in his small classes by taking the course along with them. In the course that he now gave in historiography he would, for example, end the semester by reading an essay on his own. In classes where the enrollment was larger, in sophomore history, for example, where the enrollment was as high as forty, Becker is remembered mainly for his soporific powers — at ten in the morning.[17] During Becker's last year at

[16] Frank Klingberg to Phil Snyder, Los Angeles, November 10, 1955.
[17] *Ibid.*

Kansas, he had in his course on the French Revolution James C. Malin as a graduate student; Malin was definitely not impressed except by the fact that Becker's successor Frank Melville did a great deal more, in language preparation, for example, for his graduates than Becker ever bothered to do.[18]

If Becker did not go out of the way for his students at Kansas — he may secretly have doubted that it was worthwhile — he took his responsibilities seriously enough to earn the respect of Hodder and Templin, and he went so far as to speculate seriously on the mission of a state university. Perhaps he shared with his teacher Burgess a preference for a university built along the lines of a private corporation, but he defended the state university on the grounds that while it educated only a few it would ultimately benefit the many, if certain dangers could be avoided. One danger was that of over-specialization, of too great an emphasis on the professional school. The purpose of a state university, he maintained in a brief essay, "Value of the University to the State," was not to produce professional people capable of earning larger fees, but leaders who, scattered throughout the state, could resist the appeal of demagogues. Studies designed to produce such an elite within a democracy would in the long run prove more "practical than any professional school with its emphasis upon short-run practicality."[19] The other danger, already hinted at in "Value of the University," Becker developed more fully in two letters to William E. Dodd of the University of Chicago. It was that the University in trying to train an elite would yield to quack nostrums, to the notion that the organizer of playgrounds, or the YMCA director, was "the sort of man who performs the most effective social service." Under the influence of such thinking, students might come to regard the "learned historian as a parasite on the body politic."[20]

"It goes without saying," Becker wrote to Dodd, "that universities should be concerned, however indirectly, with the vital problems of society."[21] Becker's own preference was for the "however indirectly" method. It was against this background at Kansas that Becker began writing in 1915 his essay "On Being a Professor," which appeared in 1917 in Henry Holt's *Unpopular Review*. This essay was a well-written

[18] James C. Malin to the author, Lawrence, Kansas, August 25, 1956. For Malin's formal criticism of Becker, see his *Essays in Historiography* (Lawrence, Kansas, 1946).

[19] "Value of the University to the State," *The University Press Bulletin*, Lawrence, Kansas, I (December 3, 1910), No. 36, no page numbers.

[20] Carl Becker to William E. Dodd, Lawrence, Kansas [1915].

[21] Carl Becker to William E. Dodd, Lawrence, Kansas, undated.

plea for an education that enlightens but leads nowhere directly, and it had a full quota of irony and sarcasm directed against those who felt otherwise. Irony at the expense of young women who considered the university "so excellent a place in which to be initiated into literature and the fine arts, into history and the social sciences, and into a sorority."[22] Sarcasm directed mainly, however, at "the more serious youths who deeply pondered the problems of existence." Writing in a vein that would later win for him the respect of H. L. Mencken, Becker showed his ability at debunking. "Very modern in their ideas of Social Service, wishing not to be thought irreligious although not subscribing to any formal creed, they appeared to enjoy a high sense of having reconciled all the antinomies, inasmuch as they willingly accepted, with certain reservations, the doctrine of evolution, and yet found it not inconsistent to be present at meetings designed to promote the cause of true Christianity through the discussion of 'Jesus Christ as Head Coach,' or other up to date and opportune topics."[23] Becker was having it back at the Methodists and the self-assured, high-minded students of his own youth, but it is important to remember that the debunking was aimed not at the idea of utility but at some of its more puerile expressions. After leaving Kansas, Becker had the opportunity to read Thorstein Veblen's *Higher Learning in America,* which Charles A. Beard called "the Hire Learning" in America. Happy at last at Cornell University, Becker mused, "It is understood that Veblen got much of his thunder from Chicago. But if Chicago gives him so much thunder I wonder what some other institutions would do?"[24]

A certain note of bitterness creeps into Becker's reflections on the state university. As an antidote to this feeling of disaffection, and perhaps of intellectual loneliness among students who would be YMCA directors, Becker found refuge in writing. The boy who had dreamed of writing for *Saturday Night* became a man who, while at Kansas, managed to write successfully for the *American Historical Review,* as well as for *The Nation* and *The Dial.* In addition to doing reviews and articles for these and other magazines, Becker had two books published during his stay at Kansas: his doctoral thesis, published in 1909 by the University of Wisconsin as *The History of Political Parties in the Province of New York, 1760-1776,* and a textbook, *The Begin-*

---

[22] *Detachment and the Writing of History,* 99.
[23] *Ibid.*
[24] Carl Becker to William E. Dodd, Ithaca, New York [1919].

nings of the American People, published in 1915 and aimed at a wider audience (which it didn't succeed in reaching).

Becker had published several articles before coming to Kansas. The first dealt with "The Unit Rule in National Nominating Conventions," and was published in the *American Historical Review.* It was a competent piece of research, written with lucidity but without distinction, although it did show that its author had an eye for the larger generalities involved. The Democrats, he noticed, had tended to use the unit rule as a gesture towards states' rights; the Republicans, on the other hand, didn't use it because the Republican Party had come into being at a time "not when powers were to be estimated, but when rights were to be asserted."[25] This was followed by a second article, "Law and Practice of the United States in the Acquisition and Government of Dependent Territory," written in 1900, probably in response to the issues raised by the Spanish-American War.[26] After this he published in 1901 two articles, "Nominations in Colonial New York" and "Growth of Revolutionary Parties and Methods in New York Province 1765-1774."[27] Taken together these articles indicate that Becker's interest was shifting away from the national nominating convention to the revolutionary parties in New York on the eve of the Revolution; they also indicate that he was learning how to write, if only in the academic vein.

From this modest beginning Becker went on until by the time he left Kansas he had acquired the relaxed, laconic style that became so apparent, for example, in "On Being a Professor." And by the time he left Kansas he had to his credit two of the best essays he would ever write, "Kansas," which attracted considerable attention from historians, and the less well-noticed "Detachment and the Writing of History" — the latter being outstanding, however, according to the editors of the *Atlantic Monthly,* for its "brilliant common sense."[28] Becker at Kansas went through the evolution common to all historians who would write about history for an audience wider than their own guild: the final mastery of writing with footnotes for thesis purposes, and the far more difficult mastery, never a "final" one, of writing without footnotes — the going beyond "two independent witnesses not self-deceived."

[25] *American Historical Review,* V (October, 1899), 82.
[26] *Annals of the American Academy of Political and Social Sciences,* XVI (November, 1900), 404-420.
[27] *American Historical Review,* VI (January, 1901), 260-275; VII (October, 1901), 56-76.
[28] Editors of *Atlantic Monthly* to Carl Becker, Boston, November 10, 1909.

When Becker's first writings are compared with his more mature ones, we are reminded of how necessary a thing practice is in the transformation of a research historian into one distinguished for his style. Becker got much of the necessary practice by reviewing books for *The Nation,* which he commenced to do in 1903; in fact he did eighteen reviews that first year. From Haskins, who was now at Harvard, came the promise that he would be on the lookout for them. "No doubt," Haskins prophetically added, "you will strike their high and mighty tone the first time, if you try — it's rather the easiest tone to hit at first."[29] So it was, at first; one finds Becker commenting intelligently but tersely and in an "objective" tone on the first not very important books he was asked to review, commenting on bibliographies, sources and the like, being still very much the graduate student. But gradually humor and life made their appearance — the books reviewed, and the reviewer, became more important. The success was largely anonymous, for the reviews were unsigned. Dr. Smith has rightly discounted the myth that in Becker the wish to write was so weak that it depended mainly upon external stimuli, such as attractive financial offers made during Becker's later life by various foundations for a few public lectures;[30] there is no stronger proof of Becker's early determination to write than in his willingness to write anonymously for *The Nation.*

The reviews first for *The Nation* and then also for *The Dial* reveal more than the emergence of a style; they reveal an intellectual growth, of such proportions as to justify almost entirely Henry Holt's subsequent praise of Becker's "On Being a Professor," which Holt described as being noted for its "wisdom, temper, and temperance" as well as for its "wonderful expression of what it does not say, and its indication of the undefinable; and thank God! its humor."[31] Taken in conjunction with Becker's longer articles and books, his reviews allow the reader to make a composite picture of Becker's intellectual achievements during the years before World War One and before he became the Carl Becker of Cornell University. The reviews and articles contain reflections on history and historical method; they also tell us something, although not enough, about Becker's politics. First, however, it is desirable to consider Becker's earliest contributions to his-

[29] Charles Homer Haskins to Carl Becker, Cambridge, Massachusetts, January 4, 1903.
[30] See Footnote 56, Chapter I.
[31] Henry Holt to Carl Becker, New York [1916].

torical knowledge, mainly in his Ph.D. thesis, as these contributions form the base from which all other operations developed.

During the course of his life, Becker's literary production far exceeded that of either Frederick Jackson Turner or James Harvey Robinson, but where the writing of many-volumed histories was concerned he shared their reluctance — or inability — to rush into print. To write on the scale of Francis Parkman or of the Henry Adams who wrote a *History of the United States,* one has to believe that it is worth doing, Becker once confided to one of his later students — the implication being that he, Becker, had his doubts.[32] He always had his doubts, from the very beginning; he had begun to scatter away the results of his thesis research in the pages of the *American Historical Review* before he succeeded in bringing his materials together. However useful his first reviews and articles may have been personally, some would regard them as no more than exercises for learned histories that were not for the most part forthcoming. Of the three reasonably orthodox, i.e., footnoted, histories Becker brought himself to write, only one, his thesis, was in the field of political history. Of the other two, one would be a study in intellectual history, *The Declaration of Independence,* and the other in the history of higher education, *Cornell University: The Founders and the Founding.*

The thesis, *The History of Political Parties in the Province of New York, 1760-1776,* began with the usual acknowledgements of indebtedness, to Wilbur Abbott and Frank Hodder, but mainly to the example of "certain inspiring teachers": Turner, Haskins, and Victor Coffin of Wisconsin, Osgood, Burgess, and Robinson of Columbia. Of these teachers only Osgood and Robinson were specialists in the eighteenth century, "one of those important periods about which every one talks and few write," as Becker described it in 1908.[33] Only Osgood was a specialist in eighteenth-century America, and by 1907 he had completed only three volumes of his history of the colonies in the *seventeenth* century; his *The American Colonies in the Eighteenth Century* did not appear until after his death in 1918. Moreover, it is important to bear in mind that A. M. Schlesinger's *The Colonial Merchants and the American Revolution* and J. F. Jameson's *The American Revolution Considered as a Social Movement,* which have an interpretation of the Revolutionary period similar to Becker's, did not appear until 1918 and 1926 respectively. The question then becomes

[32] A conversation between Harold T. Parker and the author, Durham, North Carolina, December 17, 1956.

[33] Review of Edward Channing, *A History of the United States, II, The Nation,* XXCI (November 5, 1908), 440.

one, not of how Becker was influenced by contemporaries writing in the same vein, but of whether Becker's thesis is to be regarded more as a product of Turner's or Osgood's seminar.

Although Osgood was aware of the importance of the frontier as a factor in the American Revolution, and Turner conscious of Osgood's awareness,[34] Osgood preferred to look upon the Revolution as "but an episode in the development of the English colonial system" while Turner would have objected strenuously to Osgood's condescending use of the word *but*. However much Osgood's patient craftsmanship impressed itself upon Becker, Becker's thesis itself was, at least in its hypotheses, a Turner triumph. "The American Revolution," Becker wrote, "was the result of two general movements; the contest for home rule and independence, and the democratization of American politics and society. Of these movements, the latter was fundamental; it began before the contest for home rule, and was not completed until after the achievement of independence."[35] And the thesis in its attempts to show the democratization of New York is proof of another, later thesis of Becker's: that "in giving direction to the methods of investigating American history and in furnishing new light for its interpretation, the share of Mr. Turner has been the most profound and abiding of this generation."[36]

Becker's thesis is especially Turnerian in its emphasis upon the importance of property in the democratization of New York: "If political conditions determined the nature of party alignment, party methods were equally determined by social and economic factors."[37] According to Becker there were "three distinct classes" in colonial New York: an "aristocracy" of "closely related families of wealth," the freeholders, and the unfranchised.[38] Becker's thesis is quite simple, namely that the agitation within the colony against Parliamentary legislation such as the Stamp Act opened the way for direct popular activity, often of an extra-legal sort, which served to break the exclusive hold which men of means had hitherto had over the politics of that most conservative of colonies. Becker tried to show how the question of who shall rule at home was one in which "merchants" became pitted against the

---

[34] Osgood's "England and the Colonies," *Political Science Quarterly*, II (September, 1887) was cited by Turner as evidence of the importance of frontier conditions in the shaping of the American Revolution. ("The Significance of the Frontier in American History," *The Early Writings of Frederick Jackson Turner*, 220.)

[35] *The History of Political Parties in the Province of New York*, 5.

[36] "The American Frontier," Review of Frederick Jackson Turner, *The Frontier in American History*, *The Nation*, CXI (November 10, 1920), 536.

[37] *The History of Political Parties in the Province of New York*, 8.

[38] *Ibid.*, 8-11.

"mob," "conservatives" against the "radicals," with the result that the merchants and the conservatives were propelled, partly against their wishes, into advocating more radical measures for the securing of independence, out of fear of losing control completely of affairs *within* the colony.[39] Hence the Revolution was, in Becker's eyes, what is now called a "conservative revolution," but one which nevertheless democratized the politics of New York.

Becker's thesis was well received. Max Farrand wrote from Yale University that he was holding it up to his students as an illustration of what might be done with a Ph.D. thesis.[40] William E. Dodd of Chicago[41] and Allen Johnson of Yale were favorably impressed, so much so that each would shortly ask Becker to contribute a volume to the series of histories they were editing. Johnson expressed the hope, which proved to be futile, that Becker would carry his study on "through the Revolution and beyond."[42] Had Becker done this, his reputation would have been assured; as it is, few would venture to quarrel with a thesis so heavily documented, so obviously the product of intimate association with the rich archival materials of New York State. Yet Edmund S. Morgan has recently ventured to do just that. As for Becker's celebrated aphorism that the Revolution arose less from questions about home rule than from problems as to who should rule at home, Morgan comments:

> It cannot be denied that both disputes existed, but to magnify the internal contest to the same proportions as the revolt against England is to distort it beyond recognition. Both before and after the struggle Americans of every state were divided socially, sectionally, and politically; but these divisions did not with any consistency coincide with the division between patriot and loyalist, nor did they run so deep as to arouse the same intensity of feeling. The Revolution cut across the old lines and plucked loyalists and patriots alike from every class and section.[43]

My own criticisms of Becker's thesis would be mainly derivative; I should be inclined to apply some of the criticisms that Robert E. Brown has made of Charles A. Beard's *An Economic Interpretation of the Constitution*[44] to Becker's interpretation of New York politics, insofar as Becker's interpretation is an economic one. In the first place

---

[39] *Ibid.*, 192.
[40] Max Farrand to Carl Becker, New Haven, Connecticut, December 22, 1909.
[41] William E. Dodd to Carl Becker, Chicago, March 19, 1911.
[42] Allen Johnson to Carl Becker, Brunswick, Maine, January 4, 1909.
[43] *The Birth of the Republic* (Chicago, 1956), 100.
[44] *Charles A. Beard and the Constitution* (Princeton, New Jersey, 1956).

Becker took for granted the existence of distinct cleavages within the society of colonial New York, which no one would deny; he further assumed that these cleavages were economic in origin, which may be true, and that one could speak of "classes," of a "coterie" of the wealthy, of the "mass" of freemen. This is to speak of eighteenth-century New York in the language of the twentieth century. It could be argued that Becker exaggerated the importance of class differences and even of the democratic ferment, perhaps because of his own democratic bias. Witness, for example, the value judgment contained in the following: "the prestige of landed wealth and social position was everywhere sufficient to confer an *excessive* influence upon a few men."[45] When Becker characterized the assembly of New York as representing a "privileged class" but not "the people," the same democratic bias was apparent. When he wrote, "It is *perhaps* safe to say that over half of the male population above the age of twenty-one years was without political privilege of any sort,"[46] he revealed the flimsy structure upon which his democratic-anti-democratic thesis partially rests. Also, Becker wrote of the "mob" in the city of New York in a language that seems more appropriate to the Paris of the French Revolution than to a small colonial seaport. At stake here are the still unanswered questions of how democratic or undemocratic colonial society was, what difference internal class differences made in shaping the Revolution, and how important the city was as a force in bringing about independence. According to present-day scholarship Becker is safest in his emphasis upon the importance of the city as a place for the conception and propagation of revolutionary sentiments.[47]

I think colonial historiographers might do well to take up the possible contradiction within Becker's thesis of the Turner frontier hypothesis and what is now known as the "Beard-Becker bias," or the emphasis upon divisions between social and economic classes. The difference is not clear-cut. Turner knew the importance of class differences; but there is, as Beard knew,[48] a latent hostility between the

---

[45] *The History of Political Parties in the Province of New York*, 14. Italics added.

[46] *Ibid.*, 11. Italics added.

[47] See Carl Bridenbaugh, *Cities in Revolt: Urban Life in America, 1743-1776* (New York, 1955), which would seem to confirm Becker's position.

[48] Beard acknowledged his own indebtedness to Turner for calling attention to the economic factor, and he wrote that Turner "is in fact thinking of American history mainly in terms of economic group conflicts." He could not resist adding, however, that Turner talked mainly of capitalist versus pioneer, not of capitalist versus organized labor. (Review of Frederick Jackson Turner, *The Frontier in American History, New Republic*, XXV (February 16, 1921), 349-350.) See also Footnote 37, Chapter IV.

two conceptions. If classes in colonial New York were as "distinct" as Becker insisted, how is this to be reconciled with the following Turnerian observation by Becker? "In the first place, the colony was a part of the English frontier and the conditions inseparable from a frontier community were levelling here as elsewhere. . . . In any case, a certain democratic flavor always characterized the aristocracy inasmuch as it was based on wealth and not on birth."[49] Also, if the second of these propositions is correct, it may be that the class conflict within New York wasn't as important as the conflict between colony and Parliament. Certainly Becker *succeeded* more in the Osgood-like task of showing the economic differences between New York and England, although this was secondary to his thesis, than in establishing the Turnerian position as to the importance of dissentions within the colony over the question of land ownership and the political privileges that went with it.[50] Finally, if this is so, it may have been that, in taking the steps that led directly or indirectly to the Revolution, the "conservatives" joined the "radicals" not, as Becker thought, to make the radicals more moderate (and thus to insure conservative supremacy), but because they had become more radical themselves, not domestically, but in reaction to British colonial policy. Neither Becker nor Turner seems to have considered these problems; Becker, although he later played down the class-conflict hypothesis in his *The Eve of the Revolution,* never ceased to believe that this conflict was fundamental.

If Becker's thesis proved that history is not only past politics but to some extent present politics as well, it might be of interest to note in passing his impressions of the first two volumes in *A History of the United States,* written by Edward Channing. Channing was a man who thought himself "scientific" and objective, and who at the same time appeared to be the last American historian capable of writing monumental narrative history. "Half insensibly," Becker remarked, "we have been led to suppose that such works were to be replaced by manuals, dictionaries, and cooperative histories. . . ."[51] Channing's method was that of straightforward narration; Lord Acton's dictum that the historian should study problems not periods had not impressed him as it had Turner, nor was he impressed by any Turner-like contempt for "merely narrative" histories.[52] Channing's method, Becker wrote innocently in reviewing Volume One in 1905, is such that it "permits

[49] *The History of Political Parties in the Province of New York,* 16.
[50] *Ibid.,* 23-53.
[51] *The Nation,* XXCI (July 13, 1905), 40.
[52] Turner, "The Significance of History," *The Early Writings of Frederick Jackson Turner,* 45.

one to tell the exact truth."[53] In his more critical review of Volume
Two, written in 1908, Becker imagined Channing as saying that, if
history is the orderly unfolding of a definite plan, historians have had
no luck in discovering that plan. Professor Channing eschewed theories
and abstractions. "The even narrative flows on without storm or stress,
following the subject. . . . Professor Channing has the air of 'This is
what happened in this place, and at this time, to these people; interpret as you please.' "[54] Becker pointed out, however, the limits of
Channing's objectivity. First, he chided him for having *no* interpretation of the colonies as part of the British empire, for exalting the personal over the legal or constitutional; in short, for not doing as Osgood did. If Channing had no philosophy of history, he had his likes
and dislikes, caring for neither Stuarts nor Whigs — which is a kind
of interpretation. Becker concluded: "Well, it is difficult to write
history without having any theory about it. We believe that Professor
Channing has some very good theories about it, and only regret that
he has concealed the best part of them."[55] The second review marked
a considerable advance over the first and is more consistent with
Becker's subsequent reflections on historical method, since it makes no
mention of "exact truth" and recognizes the importance of theory in
the composition of even the most objective narratives. From New
York, Paul Elmer More of *The Nation* wrote, telling of a dinner at
which one of the deans of American historians, James Ford Rhodes,
had expressed his pleasure at the review and inquired as to its author.[56]

The applause by the discriminating few was on in earnest, and
Becker carefully kept every letter of praise that he received. The reception awarded his Ph.D. thesis and his reviews proved to be no
short-lived enthusiasm. The appearance of his essay "Kansas" in a
volume of essays presented to Turner, who had by now joined Haskins at Harvard, brought forth favorable responses from James Bryce
at the British Embassy in Washington, as well as from Henry Adams.[57]

[53] See Footnote 51.

[54] *The Nation*, XXCVII (November 5, 1908), 441.

[55] *Ibid.*

[56] Paul Elmer More to Carl Becker, New York, December 2, 1912. Becker reviewed Volume Three of Channing's *History* in *The Nation*, XCV (November 21,
1912), 482-483.

[57] James Bryce to James Franklin Jameson, British Embassy, Washington, D.C.,
March 22, 1911. A copy of Adams' letter to Jameson about Becker was later published by Becker in the *American Historical Review*, L (April, 1945), 675-676, and
has appeared in Harold Dean Carter, *Henry Adams and His Friends* (New York,
1947), 709-710. Jameson was editor of the *American Historical Review* and had

Adams, mindful of his own reputation for eccentricity among historians, felt it necessary, however, to warn against the dangers of being a wit among historians, and W. A. Dunning of Columbia cautioned Becker that he might make a reputation as an epigrammist. In "Kansas" Becker displayed to the utmost that "whimsy," "light-hearted gaiety," and "exuberance," which, as Leo Gershoy has observed, was to disappear little by little from his later works when he would be overburdened by ill-health and doubts.[58] "Kansas," Dunning wrote, "has evidently been a very stimulating region to you,"[59] and Dunning's irony notwithstanding, this is what Kansas, despite itself, was proving to be.

Never was Becker more of a Turner disciple in interpretation and even in style than in his essay on "Kansas," and this devotion to Turner proved to be a connecting link between Becker and William E. Dodd. Dodd was the man most responsible for introducing American historians to Karl Lamprecht,[60] his master at Leipzig, whose social psychology promised to illumine all of history and to make history at last into an exact science. Despite Dodd's introduction Lamprecht never really caught on, and Dodd's own enthusiasm for Lamprecht soon waned. "I used to think history as a science was possible," he would confide to Becker, "led to that idea by Lamprecht; but I have long since got over that."[61] Dodd could not live without a hero; his favorite personage in the past was Thomas Jefferson, whom he considered a complete egalitarian — being quick to criticize Charles A. Beard for saying this wasn't so. Dodd's love of democracy may have predisposed him to love Turner, and for his short-lived enthusiasm for Lamprecht he substituted a lifelong admiration of Turner.[62] Following Turner's lead, Dodd would go along with Beard in emphasizing the importance of economics in human conduct, all the way to Monticello, where he would draw back. His religion was democracy, and he believed, not in salvation by faith, but by good works; of all the historians who could be considered "New Historians," Dodd held to

---

sent Becker's "Kansas" to Bryce and Adams as a sample of recent writings in American history.

[58] Gershoy, Introduction to *Progress and Power,* xxxi.

[59] W. A. Dunning to Carl Becker, New York, March 7, 1911.

[60] See William E. Dodd, "Karl Lamprecht and Kulturgeschichte," *Popular Science Monthly,* LXIII (September, 1903), 418-424. William Holmes Stephenson, *The South Lives in History, Southern Historians and Their Legacy* (Baton Rouge, Louisiana, 1955), 28-57.

[61] William E. Dodd to Carl Becker, Chicago, April 8, 1917.

[62] Stephenson, *The South Lives in History,* 31-32.

the notion that "history teaches" with unswerving devotion. It is good to have simple men who aren't simple-minded, and knowing the warm-hearted and loyal Dodd was one of the most attractive features of Becker's life; against the unyielding Jeffersonian bias of Dodd, Becker would hammer out some of his own best thoughts, which were often Jeffersonian. If Becker came to doubt more than Dodd that "history teaches," no one could doubt that Dodd "taught" Becker; for all his later-day fame among historians for a Henry Adams-like irony and subtlety, Becker always got along best with the unsophisticated. Nowhere could he find a man more deliberately unsophisticated than Dodd, or a man who had more passion for liberty *and* equality than was common even among Kansans, except perhaps for John Brown.

Dodd's specialty was Southern history — he is now remembered mainly for his *The Cotton Kingdom* — and the first evidence of any contact between Becker and Dodd is in a review Becker did of Dodd's *The Life of Nathaniel Macon* in 1904. Becker approved of it as a biography and as proof of a growing interest in Southern history on the part of Southerners — Dodd had not yet been called from Randolph Macon College to Chicago — but he feared that Dodd had "as little realization as Macon had of the vital forces at work from 1816 to 1828."[63] The review was unsigned; Becker at least thought enough of Dodd at this time to send him copies of his thesis and of his essay "Kansas." Dodd, in turn, asked Becker in 1912 to write a book in the series, Riverside History of the United States, which he was editing. Becker replied diffidently that he had got "very rusty" in American history and that he still wrote "very slowly and with difficulty."[64] A luncheon with Dodd that June helped Becker overcome his fears, and by March, 1913, he sent Dodd the first chapter of his *The Beginnings of the American People*. The years 1913-1914 mark an extensive correspondence between the two men. Becker depended a great deal upon Dodd for comments and encouragement, and in return he read parts of Dodd's *Expansion and Conflict*, which would appear in the same series. Turner and Notestein also read parts of Becker's manuscript; Notestein praised it for its "philosophical insight" and mastery of the sources, although he found parts of Becker's generalizations about Puritanism in England "more suggestive than true."[65] Finally on December 12, 1914, came word from Dodd that he regarded the finished manuscript as a huge success, that no one, not even the colonial historian C. M.

[63] *The Nation*, LXXVIII (May 12, 1904), 878.
[64] Carl Becker to William E. Dodd, Lawrence, Kansas [1912].
[65] Wallace Notestein to Carl Becker, Minneapolis, Minnesota [1914].

Andrews, could outshine Becker — in fact, "There is no one now writing history in this country who has written so well. . . ."[66] He wondered only about how the lowly history instructors would use it as a text, and so did the publishers.[67]

Although history was, according to Becker, "one of the most difficult subjects in the world to make literature out of,"[68] that is exactly what he had done in *The Beginnings of the American People*. Haskins found it the "most notable piece of historical writing" he had seen in the United States for some time.[69] The reviewer for the *American Historical Review* commented on the "rare charm" of its literary form,[70] and the reviewer for the *Mississippi Valley Historical Review* noted its "beauty of diction."[71] Although the book seems remarkably lucid and uncomplicated today, the reviewers doubted that it would succeed as a textbook. It was more a "brilliant piece of interpretation" than a "sufficiently solid narrative." The reviewers were correct, for *The Beginnings* sold only 24,000 copies,[72] which made it a commercial failure.

Aside from its literary appeal, *The Beginnings* provided a good summary of the works of Osgood, Turner, and Channing. Becker followed Osgood's example in keeping his social and economic happenings within a political framework; he followed Turner in calling attention to the rivalries between seacoast and frontier, although he did not neglect the European background; like Turner, he emphasized the importance of land; and the reviewers notwithstanding he wrote, I think, an adequate narrative, which was, like Channing's, not altogether free from reflections on the personalities of the illustrious dead. His bias was unmistakable; he was on the side of men such as Franklin, "the first American,"[73] and he prized in the colonial mind what he had loved in the Kansas mind — its passion for liberty and its practical flair. And the book shows that while, in Becker's opinion, America was free before it won its independence, Becker was in his way as much a patriot as Henry Cabot Lodge, whose patriotic history Becker criticized.[74]

[66] William E. Dodd to Carl Becker, Middlebrook Farm, Round Hill, Virginia, December 12, 1914.

[67] Houghton Mifflin Company to Carl Becker, Boston, January 31, 1915.

[68] Carl Becker to William B. Munro, Lawrence, Kansas, July 19, 1915.

[69] Charles Homer Haskins to Carl Becker, Cambridge, Massachusetts, July 1, 1915.

[70] XXI (January, 1916), 352.

[71] II (September, 1915), 276-277.

[72] Houghton Mifflin Company to David Hawke, Boston, January 31, 1950.

[73] *The Beginnings of the American People* (New York, 1915), 199.

[74] Review of Henry Cabot Lodge, *The Story of the Revolution*, *The Nation*, LXXVII (November 9, 1903), 366-367.

Like Turner and Burgess, Becker showed himself a revolutionary only in the sense that Edmund Burke was, the champion of a revolution long past. If he saw in the Revolution sordid motives, he also saw a conflict between different ideals of justice and welfare, this being "one of those issues which touching the emotional springs of conduct are never composed by an appeal to reason."[75] The least passionate of men, Becker saw the passion in others, but above passion he saw the Declaration of Independence whose "sweeping generalities formulated those basic truths which no criticism can seriously impair, and to which the minds of men must always turn, so long as faith in democracy shall endure."[76]

The Beginnings is a seminal book. It was Becker's first attempt at textbook writing, during which he proved only that he was caviar for the general; the irony is that his failure to write a text intelligible to college students would later be obscured in the 1930's by his enormous success as the author of two textbooks for high-school students. The book is seminal in a more serious sense, also. Those subjects which he had handled with obvious relish in *The Beginnings* he would treat at length in subsequent works, in his brief biography of Benjamin Franklin, his study of America on the eve of revolution, and his analysis of the Declaration of Independence.

Finally, *The Beginnings* points up the paradox, so central to Becker, of how "basic truths" can emerge from emotional conflicts which in themselves cannot be resolved by appeals to reason or truth; how, in other words, a reign of truth and order can emerge from a history of conflicting passions and disorder, such as we have in the American Revolution. This problem recurs again in Becker's *The Eve of the Revolution.* In both works, Becker's proclamation of loyalty to the principles contained in the Declaration of Independence, those principles to which the "minds of men must always turn," provides us with a convenient yardstick with which to measure Becker's subsequent moods of optimism and pessimism, and thus to determine how far Becker would be carried in either direction from the faith of the Fathers, and of Turner.

"To say of any historian, ancient or modern, that he is scientific, or literary, or patriotic tells me little that I care to know," Becker once wrote, "and particularly, to regard the term 'scientific' as an adequate characterization of any group of historians is but to dispense with dis-

[75] *The Beginnings of the American People,* 203.
[76] *Ibid.,* 253.

tinctions, and with that discrimination which is essential to genuine criticism."[77] But one thing the historian is bound to do, according to Becker, is not to judge a man "by standards that were foreign to the age in which he lived."[78] This means, again according to Becker, that the truth or falsity of ideas which a given man entertains about himself is not so important to the historian as the understanding of these ideas and why they were entertained. A generation of historians, such as that of H. B. Adams and J. W. Burgess, which regards a seminar room as a laboratory and *thinks* itself "scientific," is scientific enough in its orientation if not in its achievement to warrant its being called by that label — regardless of whether we think history is a science. A historian who loves his country, and this would include practically every American historian, *is* by definition patriotic. And a historian who takes great pains with the writing of history and whose literary gifts are much admired and commented upon *is* a literary historian, — and this is Carl Becker, at least from the time of his essay on "Kansas" until his death.

Becker is, however, correct in saying that labels never tell enough. Becker himself was thinking about the "meaning" of history, at the same time as he was writing about historical happenings. More specifically, he was thinking about the philosophy of history, a subject which can be divided into two categories: (1) epistemology, or the question of how historical knowledge is possible, and (2) the nature of the forces at work in history, or the question of the direction in which history moves. Becker is most remembered for his reflections on the first of these topics, although certainly his criticisms of "objectivity" and "detachment" were not so detached that they can be altogether isolated from the second topic. What should be established here is that every principal idea to be found in his presidential speech before the American Historical Association in 1931, "Everyman His Own Historian," occurs remarkably early in his writings, so that the major ingredients in his "relativism" were already present before the First World War, although Becker did not speak of "relativism" at this time or see fully the skeptical implications of his position. As Becker emphasized in his essay "What Is Historiography?",[79] the historian must be seen as a creature of his own age not ours, which means that here Becker must be seen not in relation to the logical positivism of A. J. Ayer or the

[77] "Labelling the Historians," Review of John Spencer Bassett, *The Middle Group of American Historians, Everyman His Own Historian,* 135.

[78] Review of Norwood Young, *The Life of Frederick the Great, New Republic,* XX (November 12, 1919), 329-331.

[79] *American Historical Review,* XLIV (October, 1938). Reprinted in *Detachment and the Writing of History,* 65-78.

Neo-Orthodoxy of Reinhold Niebuhr, but in relation to the pragmatism of John Dewey and Warner Fite, not in relation to the politics of Eisenhower, but in relation to the "New Freedom" of Wilson.

The first point to establish is that Becker fully accepted the changes in the dimensions of historical study for which Turner had been in part responsible, changes which stretched the historian's province to include the study of social and economic problems. Becker wrote that "for the last quarter-century social problems have been in the ascendant. History is therefore conceived more in terms of social conditions; and historians concern themselves less with the mechanism of government than with the general welfare — less, one might say, with the freedom of the free than with the happiness of the unfortunate."[80] Those historians who clung to the ideal of ethical neutrality and scientific objectivity were mistaken, Becker explained in his gentle burlesque of G. P. Gooch's *History and Historians in the Nineteenth Century*, where he derided Gooch's "naive and altogether pleasant conception of history," a conception which holds that the past can be known scientifically and in some "ultimately true and final manner."[81]

Our histories change, Becker thought, as the context in which they are written changes; in periods when political problems predominate, history will be past politics, but when social and economic problems become central, then history will be past sociology and economics. It was not that Becker rejected the authenticity so much as the immortality of the histories that may emerge from any given age or period. Man is mortal, he seemed to say, and so are his truths. Against the absolutist view of truth which holds that a statement once true is always true of the circumstances its purports to describe, however much these circumstances themselves may subsequently change,[82] Becker would insist that, while this may be true, the relevance of such "true" statements *certainly* may be expected to diminish over the years. It is not so much that Becker started out to question the "scientific" nature of historical knowledge as that he began with a philosophy which was largely functional, one in which relevance and truth are strictly related;[83] ultimately, by the early 1930's relevance became "relativism"

---

[80] *The Nation*, XCVI (April 24, 1913), 642.

[81] *The Nation*, XCVII (September 4, 1913), 208-210.

[82] For a realist's defense of the "once true, then always true" position in questions concerning factual propositions, see G. E. Moore's "William James' Pragmatism," *Philosophical Studies* (New York, 1922).

[83] Becker has been much misunderstood on this point. See Perez Zagorin, "Carl Becker on History, Professor Becker's Two Histories: A Skeptical Fallacy," *American Historical Review*, LXII (October, 1956), 1-12.

and truth in effect became indistinguishable from myth in Becker's reflections.

So many truths, Becker thought in 1912, lose their value because they lose their relevance; and like William James, Becker strongly implied that the loss of relevance ultimately becomes a loss of truth itself, along the line of reasoning which claims that the truths of yesterday become the falsehoods of tomorrow. We can never know the whole truth; "the definitive history" seldom stays that way, he said in a review of Robinson's *The New History*, and he confessed, with exaggeration, to "an entire lack of interest in all such works — if they really *are* definitive."[84] One might reply that it is not necessary to know all the truth to know some truth, but this criticism could then be used to strengthen Becker's general thesis. What truths shall we *select* to record for our public, assuming we write well enough to have a public? Selection can be distortion: if we say that a man is free (to use an illustration not out of keeping with the concerns of Becker, Robinson, and Beard) but neglect to say that he starves in his freedom, isn't this a rather arbitrary procedure? What criteria then shall we use? If we were nationalists like Burgess, we should minimize the importance of sectionalism; if we were Marxists, we should write of the past with an eye to the future triumph of socialism. In short, we should, if Becker is correct, be guided inevitably in our judgments of fact by our judgments of value.

The "should" in the last sentence is both descriptive and normative. This is both the way it is and ought to be. Historical knowledge, however, cannot be practically applied, Becker wrote in 1915, in that the historian cannot make predictions in the manner that the natural scientists can. This separates Becker from the Marxist, but Becker insisted that history does have value: "Knowledge of history cannot be . . . practically applied, and is therefore worthless except to those who have made it . . . a personal possession. The value of history is indeed, not scientific but moral." History, Becker continued, liberalizes the mind, fortifies the will, above all else it deepens the "sympathies" — and no one except the misanthrope Schopenhauer commended sympathy more highly than Becker. History, Becker concluded, "enables us to control, not society, but ourselves, — a much more important thing; it prepares us to live more humanely in the present and to meet rather than to foretell the future."[85]

[84] *The Dial*, LIII (July 1, 1912), 19.
[85] Review of L. Cecil Jones, *The Interpretation of History*, *The Dial*, LIX (September 2, 1915), 148.

On the basis of sentiments such as these, Dr. Smith has concluded: "Becker neither fought the reforming New Historians nor joined them. . . ."[86] This appears to be one of the principal conclusions of her *Carl Becker: On History and the Climate of Opinion,* and it is, I submit, hopelessly wrong. Becker both fought the New Historians *and* joined them. He fought them with the heresy, to which he did not always subscribe, certainly not in time of war or depression, that it is better to reform ourselves than society — which is, however, a mild heresy since we *are* society. He joined them, insofar as a man as detached as Becker could actively join anyone, by pointing out the limits of detachment and by encouraging Robinson and anyone else who believed that history — regardless of its scientific status — could aid the social sciences and ultimately mankind.[87] And when Charles A. Beard somewhat belatedly proclaimed in the 1930's with more heat than understanding that he had been cheated, that history was no objective science after all,[88] Becker could have modestly claimed to have known that practically all his life.

Where Dr. Smith errs is in underestimating Becker's emphasis upon "the sympathies." Becker's own sympathies, it is clear, did not lie with "literary" historians, which points to another paradox in Becker's career: his Osgood-like refusal to acknowledge the supreme importance of style at the same time he was developing into the foremost stylist of his generation. As for literary historians of the past, Becker shrewdly suggested that the appeal of someone like Macaulay came less from his "style" than from the fact that he was writing after the French Revolution, when men were seeking to rediscover in the past historic rights in place of those natural rights which had failed so disastrously. "But in our own day," Becker wrote in 1914, "when we are again, *somewhat as men were in the eighteenth century, seeking a 'new freedom'* when we are less intent upon stability and more insistent upon 'social justice,' the past seems unable to furnish what we want. The past seems to be on the side of vested interests."[89]

If the past seemed to be on the side of vested interests, Becker himself was on the side of those who, like James Harvey Robinson, were

[86] Smith, *Carl Becker: On History and the Climate of Opinion,* 117.

[87] See Carl Becker, "Some Aspects of the Influence of Social Problems and Ideas Upon the Study and Writing of History," American Sociological Society, *Publications,* VII (June, 1913), 73-107.

[88] "That Noble Dream," *American Historical Review,* XLI (October, 1935), 74-87.

[89] "An Interview with the Muse of History," Review of G. M. Trevelyan, *Clio, a Muse and Other Essays, The Dial,* LVI (April 16, 1914), 337. Italics added.

seeking to turn upon the past and use it in the interest of social advance. Becker's "sympathies" lay with his friends, and his friends had politics rather different from his father's. They were reformers, and no one who has read Becker's writings in the pre-World War One period can doubt his sympathy for those who seek to reform society, even before they have reformed themselves. He had at times, moreover, the Robinson-reformer tendency to see history in terms of conspiracy: social justice has eluded us, not because justice is indefinable, but because of "vested interests." This is the historical teleology of men like Robinson, and only the coming of the war taught Becker the limits of looking at history in this way. Before the war he shared the "Progressive faith." "Accept my congratulations," he wrote to Wendell Phillips Garrison in 1906 when Garrison retired as editor of *The Nation*, "on having fought, for so many years, and no less uncompromisingly than your illustrious father, the enemies of the Republic — with what results, who shall say?"[90] The cryptic ending is typical of Becker, but the important thing is that Becker believed the Republic had enemies.

Who were these enemies? Some of them, according to Becker, had shown their hand in the American occupation of the Philippines, and on this question it is useful to contrast the positions of Burgess the conservative and Becker, who by now had lost faith in McKinley. Burgess regarded the Spanish-American War as immoral, as a failure of republican political institutions to function responsibly and honestly.[91] Becker, too, was critical of the government. "From first to last, the Philippine business has been managed for the people by the Government. The public has been allowed to know, not what happened but what if it had happened, would have been to the credit of the party in power," Becker wrote in reviewing Judge James Blount's *The American Occupation of the Philippines*. Have we developed the resources of the islands, or are they of military value? Becker asked. "Can it be, then, that we have raised an army of 120,000 troops and spent $300,-000,000 in order to increase the profits of the Tobacco Trust, the Sugar Trust, and the International Harvester Trust? Judge Blount's account of it would lead one to think so."[92] Here, in the trusts, were some of the enemies of the Republic; and here, in Becker's review, was an economic interpretation of governmental misconduct and of imperialism along the lines of J. A. Hobson.

Clearly the trusts weren't contributing to progress, except perhaps to

[90] Carl Becker to Wendell Phillips Garrison, Lawrence, Kansas, July 1, 1906.
[91] Burgess, *Reminiscences*, 312-321.
[92] *The Nation*, XCV (October 3, 1912), 310.

the progress of the trusts, but "What after all is progress?," Becker asked of Robinson in reviewing Robinson's *The New History* in 1912. Becker hastened to add that "one may venture to feed the starving before formulating a definition of progress. But if one wishes to remove the causes of poverty, a definition of progress might prove useful."[93] Certainly if the historian is to help better the lot of man, he needs a more definite idea of progress than Robinson's "the most bewildering opportunities for betterment summon us on every side." One is apt to stay bewildered, Becker seems to have thought, unless this moral desire for social justice is accompanied by "*a genuinely scientific definition of progress.*"[94] Here is the scientific complement to Becker's emphasis upon history as a moral force, which Dr. Smith has ignored.

"It need hardly be said," Becker continued, "that present-day ideas of progress are most intangible. A profound faith in progress, we have; a world of light talk about it. . . ." But can we yet tell what is progress until it is past? "If conscious efforts towards social regeneration are to issue in anything more than temporary expedients, the distinction between what is natural and permanent in human society and what is artificial and temporary must be drawn again in some manner or other. But to be in any way effective the distinction must be based upon genuine scientific knowledge as well as upon an emotional faith."[95] These were helpful criticisms and one can only regret that there was no Diderot or Jefferson on hand to assist the New Historians, or to give a definition of progress that would be more than a summary of historic achievement.

Becker thought that perhaps the "newer sciences of mankind," sociology, anthropology, and psychology, might assist in the solution of these problems. Meanwhile, he believed that the historian should, as Robinson had advised, study anything in the past that he finds interesting or important, the implication being that he might by chance stumble upon keys to unlock doors hitherto closed. Robinson's franchise, Becker felt, is one "which surely includes us all. Meanwhile, by all means let the historian learn all he possibly can about the newer sciences of mankind, and about the older sciences too, and about philosophy, about literature, about art, about everything that is under the sun."[96] A sympathetic if not a very dogmatic conclusion, one quite in harmony with the "New History."

[93] *The Dial*, LIII (July 1, 1912), 21.
[94] *Ibid*. Italics added.
[95] *Ibid*.
[96] *Ibid*.

Actually Becker had in 1910 already kicked the props out from any distinction that he or anyone else, in 1912 or afterwards, might try to make between scientific knowledge and emotional faith, just as in his study of the Declaration of Independence in 1922 he denied the distinction between what is "natural and permanent" and what is "artificial and temporary." The occasion for Becker's attempt to break down the antithesis between science and faith, although he did not express it as strongly as that, lay in his "Detachment and the Writing of History." Here in 1910 he went further than Charles A. Beard would ever go, in denying explicitly the traditional distinction between historical analysis (the "scientific" research) and historical synthesis (the written history presented to the public). "Strictly speaking, analysis and synthesis cannot be rigidly distinguished," he wrote.[97] Subjective elements are present in the analysis as much as in the conclusion; the historian is part of the very process he would analyze and interpret. "Instead of 'sticking to the facts,' the facts stick to him, if he has any ideas to attract them. . . ."[98] Truth, he insisted, is not a fixed quality, facts are not objective realities, they are only inferences that the historian makes from his sources.[99]

Becker was pleased to notice that "the Pragmatists are asking whether, if everything is subject to the law of change, truth be not subject to the law of change, and reality as well — the very facts themselves." And what is a historical truth, what distinguishes a sound historical synthesis from a bad one? "If useful and necessary, then true — true in the only way that historical synthesis is ever likely to be true, true relatively to the needs of the age which fashioned it."[100] Small wonder that Becker, when asked in 1938 what books had influenced his thinking most, would list William Graham Sumner's *Folkways* as having impressed upon him "the relativity of custom and ideas" and the ideas of John Dewey as having "confirmed a native tendency to pragmatic theory."[101]

Sound science and truth, according to the pragmatist Becker, would

[97] "Detachment and the Writing of History," *Detachment and the Writing of History*, 15.

[98] *Ibid.*

[99] Becker never changed his mind on this point and was unaffected by criticism of his "Detachment and the Writing of History" or of his later "Everyman His Own Historian." (See Carl Becker to Carl Horwich, Ithaca, New York, June 11, 1940.)

[100] "Detachment and the Writing of History," *Detachment and the Writing of History*, 28.

[101] Becker, "Books that Changed Our Minds," *New Republic*, XCVII (December 7, 1938), 135.

then be useful and necessary, which on the surface sounds highly commendable and quite innocent. But perhaps useful and necessary are, like the idea of progress, best validated *a posteriori*. Becker had run into the classic problem of pragmatism: when the useful has proved useless and the necessary has proved expendable, where do we look for truth? This is the kind of criticism Randolph Bourne would make of John Dewey during the First World War with telling effect;[102] perhaps it could also be made of Becker and many of his contemporaries. In 1912, however, it looked different; then the question was not whether it is pragmatic to be a pragmatist, but how to insure a fuller commitment to the idea of progress. There was no time for a careful distinction between faith and science, only time for destroying the detachment of the scientist so that his faith might be strengthened.

The idea was intoxicating, and Becker drank deeply. "The state of mind best calculated to find out exactly what happened is perhaps incompatible with a disposition to care greatly what it is that happened," Becker proclaimed; "and whatever value the notion of detachment may have just now," he warned, "the time may come — there have been such times in the past — when it is most important that everyone should care greatly what happens. In that case, one can hardly think of the 'objective man' as possessing qualities exceptionally well adapted for survival."[103] The paradox of the detached man deriding detachment was firmly established; nor could anyone doubt his *intellectual* attachment to the ideas of progress and betterment, at the same time he wondered what these things were. Such are the mysteries of faith.

[102] Bourne, "Twilight of Idols," *Untimely Papers* (New York, 1919).

[103] "Detachment and the Writing of History," *Detachment and the Writing of History*, 28. Studied closely, this article shows an even closer correspondence between Becker's thought and pragmatic *doctrines* than Cushing Strout has assumed in his *The Pragmatic Revolt in American History* (New Haven, 1958).

Chapter VI

Becker's Call to Cornell: The Contributions of a Professor of European History to American Studies

POSSIBLY THERE WAS a certain vagueness in Robinson's definition of progress, enough to disturb Becker, but there is no evidence that Becker himself hungered or thirsted unduly for a more precise definition. During the first Presidential administration of Woodrow Wilson, before the Palmer raids of the second, it was easy for believers in the "New Freedom" to equate progress with social and economic improvement, without inquiring too closely into the meaning of either. The doctrinaire side of Wilson was less apparent then than it would be after America's entry into World War One. The word *pragmatic* comes easily to the lips as the historian speaks of Wilson before Versailles.[1] When one has the "New Freedom," surely the enemies of the Republic are on the run. And when one's own career is advancing at last, surely betterment is universal. There were, it is true, the problems of socialism and militarism,[2] but these were largely confined to Europe, and who in Kansas thought of Europe, outside the classroom?[3]

Already in Becker's mind there was a growing awareness that liberalism in Europe might be "seen to have been the halfway house on the road from absolutism to democracy" and that it might be regarded as a rationalization of class interest, having found "its chief support in the well-to-do middle class."[4] All these things could, however, be seen without undue alarm. Turner, to be sure, had, in his presidential address before the American Historical Association in 1910, commented on the growing conflict between liberty and equality *within* the United

[1] Henry Steele Commager, *The American Mind* (New Haven, 1954), 349.

[2] "Thus in England, as on the Continent, the pressing problems of the new century are militarism and socialism." Becker, "Modern England," *The Nation*, XCVI (April 24, 1913), 643.

[3] Becker, "Europe through the Eyes of the Middle West," *New Europe*, XV (May 13, 1920). Reprinted in *Detachment and the Writing of History*, 177-187.

[4] Becker, "Cavour and the Map of Italy," Review of William Roscoe Thayer, *The Life and Times of Cavour*, *The Dial*, LI (November 16, 1911), 390.

States.[5] Becker reported to the readers of *The Nation* Turner's new thesis: that with the disappearance of free land the nation is "entering on a period of conflict between classes which is bringing to light the fundamental opposition between the notion of liberty and the notion of equality. . . ."[6] Becker, however, was not especially worried. Had not both notions existed side by side in Kansas without grave injury to each other? The possibility that absolutism and democracy might share certain despotic tendencies did not yet bother Becker when he wondered about the future of liberalism. However limited that future might be in Europe, in America the middle class was doing very well, its liberal philosophy had never been more popular; and no one, least of all Becker, was especially disturbed by Turner's prophecy.

Becker had little reason to be disturbed when, at last, it seemed that for him professionally some of Turner's better prophecies were coming true. At the age of forty-three, when even hopeful men might begin to despair of "careers open to talent," Becker was invited to teach at the University of Minnesota, where Notestein had gone before him, and where another Turner student, Guy Stanton Ford, who like Becker had gone over to teaching European history, eagerly awaited him.[7] Becker accepted the offer; and Turner was delighted.[8] "I wish to thank you very sincerely," wrote the Chancellor of the University of Kansas to the departing Becker, "for the important work you have done for the University of Kansas. You have achieved distinction in our midst to the gratification of all of us."[9]

Before Becker could complete even his first semester at Minnesota, he was asked to come to Cornell University at the beginning of the next academic year. There had been a distinct possibility that Cornell would hire Becker before Minnesota did,[10] but no offer was made until December, 1916, at the American Historical Association meeting in Cincinnati. There, in the hotel room where such things traditionally

[5] "Social Forces in American History," *American Historical Review*, XVI (January, 1911), 217-233.

[6] XCII (January 19, 1911), 57. Turner denied the newness of this thesis and insisted that it did not in any way diminish the importance of his frontier thesis. (Frederick Jackson Turner to Carl Becker, Cambridge, Massachusetts, January 21, 1911.)

[7] Guy Stanton Ford to Carl Becker, Minneapolis, Minnesota, January 13, 1916.

[8] Frederick Jackson Turner to Carl Becker, Cambridge, Massachusetts, March 10, 1916.

[9] The Chancellor of the University of Kansas to Carl Becker, Lawrence, Kansas, February, 1916.

[10] See Frank H. Hodder to George Lincoln Burr, Lawrence, Kansas, April 26, 1915, asking if Burr was "still going after Becker for next year." The George Lincoln Burr Papers.

take place, Professor Charles Hull, after introducing Becker to the Cornell history group and pointing out the *limitations* of Cornell, invited Becker to join the faculty. Hitherto Becker had been only offered jobs, an important distinction, as he later remembered it. Despite its sins of omission, including an inadequate salary, Cornell would, as represented by Hull, be highly honored if Becker could "so far condescend to its needs" as to associate himself with it. When Becker asked Hull what courses he would have to give, Hull seemed surprised. "Why, I don't know that anything is *required* exactly," Hull replied — before proceeding to give the requirements. "It has been customary for the Professor of Modern History to give a general survey course in modern history," as well as to offer a more advanced course in some part of it, and to supervise "to whatever extent may seem to him desirable the work of such graduate students as may come to him."[11] Actually, the only appreciable difference between Cornell and other institutions, so far as the work was concerned, lay in the graduate training where the amount of course work, formal preparation, and the like expected of the student was considerably less.[12] If objectively the work expected of Becker was similar to that done at other universities, the attitude toward the work was noticeably different, so much so that Becker pretended always to believe that nothing was ever required of him at Cornell.

"Such a magnification of the professor, such a depreciation of the university," Becker had never seen before. Hull, at least in Becker's presence, did not take either too solemnly. Soon Becker would learn that Hull presided over the history department only because it met in his office, which it did only because of the size and convenience of Hull's location. The president, Hull would later advise Becker, had as one of his principal duties the obviating of the difficulties created by his being president, and the dean was little more than a bookkeeper. No one inquired too closely into the nature of authority — only trouble could come from looking up the statutes.[13] While being certain to point out the limitations of Cornell, Hull shrewdly suggested that it offered a man of Becker's disposition opportunities not present in Lawrence or

[11] The story of how Becker was called to Cornell is told in Carl Becker, "The Cornell Tradition: Freedom and Responsibility," an address delivered on April 27, 1940, and reprinted in *Cornell University: Founders and the Founding* (Ithaca, New York, 1943), 193-204. The "quotations" from Hull appear on page 197.

[12] See Marshall Knappen, a former student of Becker's, to Phil Snyder, Ann Arbor, Michigan, February 18, 1956.

[13] "The Cornell Tradition: Freedom and Responsibility," *Cornell University: Founders and the Founding,* 196, 199-200.

Minneapolis.[14] It offered him, among other things, $4,000[15] and, as it turned out, a lifelong friendship with Hull whom Becker would come to regard as "one of the best of friends and the wisest of counselors. I have never known a man who so happily united great learning with an analytical intelligence of the highest order."[16] A man of independent income, Hull had no reason to be unduly pontifical or to worry himself in the evangelical manner fashionable on the frontier. An excellent teacher, a scholar trained in Germany and especially adept in languages, Hull was not a man given to "bossing," to publishing — he had not published anything of consequence since 1889[17] — or to hurrying — he had first conceived of bringing Becker to Cornell as far back as 1910, after reading Becker's essay on Kansas.[18]

Among the Cornell historians there was another man even more interested than Hull in securing Becker's services. This was George Lincoln Burr, who had admired Becker ever since the publication of his doctoral thesis on political parties in the province of New York, which Burr regarded as a work of "permanent importance."[19] Burr was serving with Becker on the Board of Editors of the *American Historical Review*, and a mutual respect had developed between them. Becker had befriended Burr when Burr, along with the entire administration of the American Historical Association, was under fire from the historian Frederick D. Bancroft. Bancroft had wished to democratize the Association, which he saw as ruled by a self-perpetuating clique. After all, what right had Burr to be elected president, and hadn't Morse Stephens invited those responsible for Stephens's election to the presidency to lecture in sunny California? A slander, of course, although Burr had helped Stephens and had been invited to California. In this tempest in a teapot, Becker, the historian of democracy, was loyal to the "oligarchy," and to Burr.[20]

---

[14] Charles Hull to Carl Becker, Ithaca, New York, January 12, 1917.

[15] Carl Becker to Charles Hull, Minneapolis, Minnesota, January 8, 1917. The Charles Hull Papers, Regional History Archives, Cornell University, Ithaca, New York.

[16] Carl Becker quoted by the *Ithaca Journal*, July 17, 1936, upon Hull's death.

[17] *The Economic Writings of Sir William Petty*, Charles Hull, ed., Cambridge, England, 1889.

[18] Charles Hull to Carl Becker, Ithaca, New York, January 22, 1917.

[19] George Lincoln Burr to Carl Becker, Ithaca, New York, July 22, 1909.

[20] Carl Becker to George Lincoln Burr, Lawrence, Kansas, June 5, 1915. Becker thought Bancroft "had a perfect genius for putting himself in the wrong." Becker advised Burr not to reply to the accusations made by Bancroft in his pamphlet "Why the American Historical Association Needs Thorough Reorganization." (Becker to Burr, Hubert, Minnesota, September 9, 1915. The George Lincoln Burr

There were other reasons why Burr, who shared some of Hull's indifference to publication, would want Becker. In comparison with Hull and Burr, Becker published prodigiously; and unlike the popular Wilhelm Van Loon, whom he was called to succeed, Becker did not practice style at the expense of critical scholarship. His voice would be heard outside Ithaca; and inside Ithaca, he and Burr could talk of historiography, of the relationships between history and politics, and between history and the social sciences. "History must be brought to bear upon life. This had always been Burr's thesis," according to his student and biographer Roland H. Bainton.[21] Had Burr not assisted in solving a boundary dispute between Venezuela and British Guiana?

Both Burr and Becker had sympathy with Robinson and the newer sciences of man, especially psychology; but both differentiated between psychology which deals with the type and history which deals with the individual.[22] Both had a sense of proportion, amounting at times to irreverence for the lessons of the "newer sciences." Shall we forget the theory of evolution on the authority of Henry Adams, Burr playfully asked, only "to accept it again on the authority of Mr. Robinson? Can we test it for ourselves? Has Mr. Robinson tested it?"[23] Whether tested or not, the theory of evolution was in fact accepted by both Burr and Becker, as was the idea that history ought to help rather than hinder the "newer sciences" which had captivated Robinson. Burr, like Hull, became a lifetime friend of Becker's, later applauding Becker's *The Heavenly City*[24] and his presidential address before the American Historical Association. "I am your convert," he would exclaim with enthusiasm at the latter, "though I see still plenty of use for sound research and honest records."[25]

Burr was a man to whom Becker could speak freely, and Becker's first thoughts upon leaving Cincinnati in 1916, he confided to Burr, were that Hull and Burr had "over rated" his attainments. After all he

---

Papers.) For Burr's gratitude to Becker for his support, see Burr to Becker, Ithaca, New York, July 5, September 23, 1915.

[21] *George Lincoln Burr: His Life and Work* (Ithaca, New York, 1943), 70.

[22] See Burr, "History and Its Neighbors." Reprinted in Bainton, *op. cit.*, 316-333. See also Carl Becker to George Lincoln Burr, Minneapolis, Minnesota, January 18, 1917. The George Lincoln Burr Papers. "Let the psychologist explain how the sense of duty, abstractly considered, is a product of psychic responses to external stimuli. That is his business, and a good business it is, but it is not the historian's business." Actually Becker made it his business without recourse to psychological jargon.

[23] Burr, "The Background of History," Commentary on James Harvey Robinson's "The Relation of History to the Newer Sciences of Man," Bainton, *op. cit.*, 335.

[24] George Lincoln Burr to Carl Becker, Ithaca, New York, October 23, 1932.

[25] George Lincoln Burr to Carl Becker, Ithaca, New York, January 27, 1932.

did not have Burr's knowledge of paleography and diplomatic history, or his mastery of languages.[26] In listing his own limitations, Becker didn't say that his publications had been mainly in the field of American history, and it wasn't until later correspondence with Burr that he admitted to not counting himself "much pumpkins as a popular lecturer."[27] Soon, however, Burr and Hull convinced Becker that he was worthy. Becker offered to give a year course in modern history from 1648 to the present, with the emphasis on the years after 1870, a year course in the French Revolution and Napoleon, and a seminar in either the Revolution or eighteenth-century intellectual history. He asked and was given permission to hold his classes in the afternoon so that he might have "undisturbed mornings for study and writing." He confessed to having "thought a good deal about the meaning of history," and he hoped to do work that would please Burr.[28] But he wondered about the dampness of Ithaca's climate, and was it true that Cornell neglected the humanities in favor of the sciences? Burr reassured him on both counts, and helped arrange for Becker to correspond with a real estate agent concerning living quarters,[29] which led ultimately to the Beckers' purchasing a spacious and attractive home at 109 Uplands Road in Ithaca.

By January 27, 1917, the president of Cornell, obviating the difficulties of his office as Hull would have put it, made the offer by Hull and Burr official,[30] and Becker accepted. That fall Burr took Becker, freshly arrived in Ithaca, to see Andrew Dixon White, now retired from the presidency of the university that he and Ezra Cornell had made. At eighty-five, White was still very much alive; and Becker would remember their conversation for his brilliant vignette on White in *Cornell University: Founders and the Founding*, which he would write in his own retirement. Or was it a conversation? White received Becker and Burr "with an unstudied courtesy and an air of pleased anticipation, as

[26] Carl Becker to George Lincoln Burr, Minneapolis, Minnesota, January 4, 1917. The George Lincoln Burr Papers.

[27] Carl Becker to George Lincoln Burr, Minneapolis, Minnesota, January 18, 1917. The George Lincoln Burr Papers.

[28] Carl Becker to George Lincoln Burr, Minneapolis, Minnesota, January 4, 1917. The George Lincoln Burr Papers.

[29] Burr sent Becker the Treasurer's and Librarian's Reports, which satisfied Becker about the humanities if not the climate. For Becker and his family's appreciation of Burr's activities on their behalf, see Carl Becker to George Lincoln Burr, Minneapolis, Minnesota, May 5, 1917. Burr continued to befriend the Beckers after their arrival and once loaned Becker $500 to pay his hospital bills following an illness. (See Carl Becker to George Lincoln Burr, Ithaca, New York, September 17, 1923. The George Lincoln Burr Papers.)

[30] J. S. Schurman to Carl Becker, Ithaca, New York, January 27, 1917.

if we were both old and valued friends," and he began talking and talked for an hour and a half "not so much to us or with us," Becker recalled, "as for us and for himself, and for the pure joy of practicing the art, as if cultivated conversation were God's best gift to man. He spoke of the good fortune of Cornell in inducing me to join its faculty, and of my good fortune in being associated with his friend George Burr whose learning and wisdom he had himself found of unfailing assistance; spoke of the new book he was then reading, and of other new books he had recently read by authors unknown to him, and asked us what we thought of them, and then, before we could start anything, told us what *he* thought of them; spoke of the war and the Fourteen Points and of Bismarck whom he had known and liked, but now thought in some sense responsible, with his blood and iron for the war; spoke of early Cornell days and difficulties, and of Ezra Cornell, a remarkable and lovable man. . . ."[31] And so on; such were the recollections of an urbane, experienced "gentleman and a scholar" by a shy gentleman and a scholar — small wonder that Becker in discussing the curious cooperation between the reticent Cornell and the voluble White would observe that Cornell, after meeting White, probably had felt even less need for words.[32]

This was the Cornell University that Becker loved, the Cornell of President White, whose *Warfare of Religion and Science* had been the first major American contribution to the history of ideas, the Cornell of men of the world such as Ambassador White (who had interrupted his duties at Cornell to serve in Berlin and St. Petersburg), and Arbitrator Burr, and the man of affairs Hull. To the Cornell of these men, with their emphasis upon freedom from "religious or political or social obligation," there was nothing Becker could wish to add or take away, not even after two decades of teaching there. At Cornell his learning would be admired, his solitude would be respected and his eccentricities loved. Among these men of the world, Becker, who knew the world chiefly from books, would be at home. He was finally, as he said, free to be responsible.[33]

Becker would never leave Cornell for another university, except to teach at Chicago or Columbia during their summer sessions, or to give a series of public lectures at Yale, Stanford, or Johns Hopkins; the longest he would ever stay away would be for a full term at Smith College,

---

[31] Becker, *Cornell University: Founders and the Founding*, 66-67.

[32] *Ibid.*, 84.

[33] "The Cornell Tradition: Freedom and Responsibility," *Cornell University: Founders and the Founding*, 193-204.

and this would not be until after his retirement from active teaching. Becker's determination to remain at Cornell became evident soon after his arrival there, for almost at once he began to receive — and reject — attractive offers from other institutions. The most attractive, from a financial point of view, came from the new president of Amherst College and would-be reformer of American higher education, Alexander Meiklejohn. While at Kansas, Becker had in 1907 considered accepting a position at Amherst,[34] but it was nothing so grand as what Meiklejohn now offered, $5500 as against the $4500 that Cornell was paying him. Becker declined. In 1920 Meiklejohn raised his offer to $7000. Becker, who had no independent income, felt independent enough to decline again. Besides, Becker by 1920 would be temporarily sick of reform. "Theoretically I think your scheme an excellent one," Becker wrote to Meiklejohn, "but I am temperamentally inclined to be too much aware of practical difficulties to be a good reformer. As an observer of courageous experimenters," he added, "my interest in your projects is as great as it ever was. . . ."[35] He only hoped Meiklejohn would find someone more suitable, and he gave the same answer to William E. Dodd when Dodd tentatively inquired whether Becker would come to stay at Chicago.[36] Only once would Becker appear to weaken in his resolve to remain at Cornell, and that would be in the 1930's when his friend Notestein tried to secure an appointment for him at Yale, an attempt that failed, according to Notestein, because of the effects of the Depression upon Yale finances,[37] but also probably because of Becker's age.

Becker was never called to the older Ivy League universities — the closest he ever got was the Columbia Summer Session — but he bore this failure to follow the example of his teachers Turner and Haskins and his friend Notestein with good humor. In fact, he behaved as Turner had behaved at Wisconsin before his call to Harvard, unaware that he had failed at all.[38] Cornell, Becker confided to Dodd, was so well suited to the exercise of his "particular talents" that he couldn't have done better had he made it to order himself. The library, famous for its White Collection of materials in French history, was excellent for his researches. The schedule of five hours a week plus a seminar

[34] Smith, *Carl Becker: On History and the Climate of Opinion*, 19.

[35] Carl Becker to Alexander Meiklejohn, Ithaca, New York, June 6, 1920. Meiklejohn's offer of $7,000 was made on May 17, 1920.

[36] William E. Dodd to Carl Becker, Chicago, November 23, 1919. Carl Becker to William E. Dodd, Ithaca, New York, December 2, 1919.

[37] Wallace Notestein to Carl Becker, New Haven, Connecticut, March 2, 1933.

[38] Becker, "Frederick Jackson Turner," *Everyman His Own Historian*, 210.

was agreeable. There was at Cornell "a tradition of liberty for the individual professor." Finally he was "in love" with the place[39] — of all the institutions he attended as a student or served as a teacher, Cornell was the first and the last to provoke such enthusiasm. To his friend J. F. Jameson, he wrote that, in comparison with Cornell, Amherst had only money to offer. At Cornell there were good graduate students — a polite silence about the undergraduates was part of Becker's policy wherever he taught — and there were Burr and Hull, who were all that he had expected them to be — "the finest of the wheat."[40]

Becker proceeded to behave at Cornell in a way that could scarcely have surprised either Hull or Burr. He gave a disappointing first lecture, and he continued to write what were essentially essays about American history rather than monographs. Both activities involve paradoxes. The first paradox centers upon the question of how a man who wrote so well could be so lacking in grace when called upon to speak in public. His first lecture was delivered, a student recalls, "in a dull monotone, with no dramatic flurries and hardly above a whisper."[41] This was pale stuff, especially in comparison with the artistic performances of Becker's predecessor, Wilhelm Van Loon. By the end of the first term, however, there had begun a "Becker cult" at Cornell, one still in evidence today over a decade after his death. One might suspect Becker of a certain artfulness in his apparent deficiencies in the art of public speaking. Granted the genuineness of his nervousness, he followed nevertheless the honored practice of building slowly, of promising less than he could deliver. In time, as he developed facility — and a national reputation — Becker became one of the most popular of lecturers in undergraduate eyes, although he never equaled Robinson's reputation at Columbia in this respect. Becker's first popularity at Cornell came, however, from his contacts with the graduate students. He had brought George Hedger with him from Minnesota, and he had Louis Gottschalk and Leo Gershoy as students during his first graduate seminar: an unusual bit of luck to find two of his most productive students at the very beginning.

For the first time in his life Becker was truly happy to teach. He would come into seminar "his face glowing." Naturally, graduate students could better appreciate his irony, his moments of "savage" judgments at the expense of the "stupid and pompous" — provided the

---

[39] Carl Becker to William E. Dodd, Ithaca, New York, December 2, 1919.

[40] Carl Becker to J. F. Jameson, Ithaca, New York, June 8, 1920.

[41] Barnet Nover of the *Denver Post* to David Hawke, Denver, Colorado, February 10, 1950.

stupid and pompous were adults and not students. For students, there was no "pulling of rank," even for the most naive — at worst there was a chilling silence, or on rare occasions Becker would be compelled to leave the seminar room without commenting upon an especially bad report.[42] In seminar Becker's tendency to play down the dramatic element in history, or at least in historical writing, found constructive expression. When a student used the word *compelling* in a paper, Becker wrote on the margin that such language should be left to "cheap reviewers of trashy novels."[43] On the lecture platform Becker relied heavily upon notes, which may be one source of his insistence that history isn't memory but memory analyzed;[44] but in seminar he could be more relaxed, more casual. Discussions would range from eighteenth-century France to the morning newspaper. Sometimes Becker would read his own work to the students for criticism, a criticism that was given more freely during his first years at Cornell, before it was dampened somewhat by feelings of reverence and awe as his reputation grew. To these critical students Becker would dedicate his *Everyman His Own Historian,* thanking them for not following the example of Hway, the student of Confucius, who took delight in everything the master said.[45]

In seminar Becker taught, largely by example, economy in the use of words and painstaking analysis in the use of documents. Marshall Knappen recalls a two-hour analysis by Becker of the career and character of Mirabeau. In the first hour, he set forth all the evidence showing Mirabeau to be a scoundrel; in the second he made a case for Mirabeau's being a high-minded patriot. All along, he insisted that the evidence was sound and showed that it came from "two independent witnesses not self-deceived." After this, Becker concluded, "Well, gentlemen, we have observed all the rules of the game and come out with two contradictory conclusions. How are we to resolve dilemmas of this sort?" The students leaned forward, waiting to learn how. Becker gathered his papers together and said, "I don't know, gentlemen. Do the best you can." And he left the room.[46]

[42] *Ibid.*

[43] Carl Becker quoted by Barnet Nover. *Ibid.*

[44] Zagorin in his "Carl Becker on History," *American Historical Review,* LXII (October, 1956), 8, makes the mistake of assuming that Becker reduced history to memory. Leo Gershoy in his "Zagorin's Interpretation of Becker: Some Observations," *American Historical Review,* LXII (October, 1956), 12-17, exposes this and other errors in Zagorin's reading of Becker.

[45] Dedication of *Everyman His Own Historian.*

[46] Marshall Knappen of the University of Michigan to Phil Snyder, Ann Arbor, Michigan, February 18, 1956.

Despite his ability in the seminar room and the mark of grave se-
renity that came to be the hallmark of Becker's lectures as he grew
older,[47] the problem remains of how a man of Becker's "peculiar felicity" of written expression could often create so mediocre an impression in the lecture room. "Peculiar felicity" was how John Adams had
spoken of Thomas Jefferson's literary gifts. Becker in writing of Jefferson said that Jefferson's felicity wasn't peculiar; rather it was the kind
most admired and cultivated during the Enlightenment, as it possessed
simplicity, clarity, logical order, and common sense. George Sabine has
remarked that "One wonders whether there was not a trace of autobiography" in Becker's characterization of Jefferson and his literary
style. Sabine has also noticed that Becker, like Jefferson, lacked "'a
profoundly emotional apprehension of experience. One might say that
Jefferson [and Becker] felt with the mind, as some people think with
the heart. He had enthusiasm, but it was enthusiasm engendered by an
irrepressible curiosity.'"[48] Becker lacked emotional apprehension, but
like Jefferson, he was saved by his intelligence, his candor, and his
"humane sympathies."

Saved perhaps but lost, too, as far as public speaking went. He did
not mumble as Jefferson sometimes did, but he did whisper. To feel
with the mind is not to admit to much emotional necessity; Becker
indeed shared the rationalist's distrust for passion and enthusiasm, at
the same time that he detected passion and enthusiasm in the eighteenth-century rationalists. Not to feel compelled may reveal a freedom
from baser passions, but it may also mean that one does not feel compelled to foster one's convictions or "humane sympathies" upon others.
D. H. Lawrence *had* to write, and sometimes to rave. Becker had no
use for Lawrence,[49] or for anyone who took himself so seriously. Probably this is why Sabine fell into the error of saying that Becker's own
will to write was weak.

Becker, like Jefferson, was most at ease among friends. With them he
would sometimes relax enough to take a drink and even to compose
doggerel verse.[50] It is, however, a long way from this state of affairs to
Joseph Wood Krutch's judgment that Becker could be more readily
imagined as "most at home, not in the classroom, but, like a true man
of the Enlightenment, in a drawing-room."[51] The Iowan of rural origins,

[47] Gershoy, Introduction to *Progress and Power*, xxvi.
[48] Sabine, Preface to *Freedom and Responsibility in the American Way of Life*,
xi.
[49] Becker, *New Liberties for Old* (New York, 1941), 33.
[50] Gershoy, Introduction to *Progress and Power*, xxv.
[51] Krutch, "The Doctrine of Recurrence," Review of Becker's *The Heavenly City*

who avoided the drawing-room and the intellectual cocktail party like sin, may have chuckled at Krutch's well-intended compliment; but it contains an element of truth — Becker actually was most at home *at home*, preferably in his study writing, or sometimes entertaining, or visiting friends such as the French scholar Othon Guerlac in the evenings. When Guerlac would have a gathering of intellectuals Becker would usually keep silent; but it is remembered, by Guerlac's son, that Becker would dare to venture an occasional profundity.[52]

Finally, one discovers Becker, in his writing on Jefferson, explaining perhaps why he himself did not shine in public:

> It might seem that a man who can write effectively should be able to speak effectively. It sometimes happens. But one whose ear is sensitive to the subtler, elusive harmonies of expression, one who in imagination hears the pitch and cadence and rhythm of the thing he wishes to say before he says it, often makes a sad business of public speaking because, painfully aware of the imperfect felicity of what has been uttered, he forgets what he ought to say next. He instinctively wishes to cross out what he has just said, and say it over again in a different way — and this is what he often does to the confusion of the audience. In writing he can cross out and rewrite at leisure, as often as he likes, until the sound and the sense are perfectly suited — until the thing *composes*.[53]

In case there remains any doubt that Becker was being autobiographical Becker adds another sentence: "Not that Jefferson wrote with difficulty, constructing his sentences with slow and painful effort."[54] Jefferson didn't, but Becker did, as anyone who has seen his manuscripts knows.[55]

Another problem for those interested in Becker has to do with the question of why Becker, a professor of modern European history, did most of his writing in the field of American history. The problem is lessened somewhat by the fact that Becker as a graduate student had been trained primarily for investigation in American history; his teaching in European history can also be seen as having originated more

---

of the Eighteenth Century Philosophers, New York Herald Tribune Books, December 18, 1932.

[52] Henry Guerlac, "Newton's Changing Reputation in the Eighteenth Century," *Carl Becker's Heavenly City Revisited,* ed., Raymond Rockwood (Ithaca, New York, 1958), 4.

[53] *The Declaration of Independence, A Study in the History of Political Ideas* (New York, 1922), 194.

[54] *Ibid.,* 195.

[55] See Smith, *op. cit.,* 176-184, for an analysis of some of Becker's manuscripts and his methods of revising them.

from necessity than from conviction — American history was already in the hands of Hodder when Becker arrived at the University of Kansas, so that he became a professor of European history partly by default. The problem remains, however, although it has been obscured by two additional circumstances: the first, that his most remarkable book, *The Heavenly City of the Eighteenth Century Philosophers*, was a study in European intellectual history; and the second, that most of the publications of his graduate students would be in eighteenth-century French history.

Prior to his appointment at Cornell, Becker's writings in European history had been meager to the point where, outside the bailiwick of Hull and Burr, he might not have been appointed at all. Book reviews, review articles, an essay on "Juliette Drouet and Victor Hugo," and a brilliant essay, "The Dilemma of Diderot," comprised the total of his contribution. More will be said later about Diderot's dilemma, but as Becker observed, "Few men . . . were philosophers enough to be troubled by the difficulty which Diderot never solved. . . ."[56] The difficulty was really nothing more than Diderot's inability to harmonize his scientific theories with his judgments of value. According to one interpreter this was Becker's difficulty, too,[57] but our present problem is less philosophical. Few men, or few historians, were philosophers enough to be troubled by Becker's excursions into European history either before or after his Cornell appointment, at least not until the 1930's. After his appointment, the book reviews continued; there were other brilliant essays, especially those on Horace Walpole and Madame Roland; but they were studies more in the psychology of historical personages than studies in the movement of historical forces — even the highly technical "Letter from Danton to Marie Antoinette"[58] was, for all its footnotes, largely a study in individual psychology.

At this point, the problem takes on a note of irony, which would have pleased Becker, who regarded history as "profoundly ironical."[59] Louis Gottschalk writes that there was something "quite intelligible and yet

[56] "The Dilemma of Diderot," *Everyman His Own Historian*, 283. Reprinted from the *Philosophical Review*, XXIV (January, 1915).

[57] David Noble, "Carl Becker: Science, Relativism, and the Dilemma of Diderot," *Ethics*, LXVII (July, 1957), 233-248.

[58] "Horace Walpole's Memoirs of the Reign of George III," *American Historical Review*, XVI (January, April, 1911), 255-272, 496-507. "Memoirs and Letters of Madame Roland," *Everyman His Own Historian*. Reprinted from the *American Historical Review*, XXXIII (July, 1928). "Letter from Danton to Marie Antoinette," *American Historical Review*, XXVII (October, 1921), 24-46.

[59] Becker, "Napoleon — After One Hundred Years," *The Nation*, CXII (May 4, 1921), 646.

ironic" in the fact that F. J. Turner's "outstanding student" should owe his reputation so largely to his efforts to show that the new American ideas, which Turner had linked with the frontier, were also interwoven with European culture. Gottschalk sees Becker as a synthesis in which the conflict between H. B. Adams and F. J. Turner is resolved to such an extent that Becker was a party to neither camp, having transcended the false cosmopolitanism of Adams and the excessive provincialism of some of Turner's students. As for the warfare between those who emphasized Europe and those who stressed the frontier, Becker wanted "only to understand how much he was indebted to each."[60] Although Gottschalk has overlooked, apparently, Becker's reliance upon the frontier thesis in his writings on American history, his point can be understood if we assume that Robinson (and Haskins, too) helped influence Becker away from an exclusively American orientation, partly by introducing him to "intellectual history," which was certainly not Turner's medium.

To Becker, however, this problem of interpretation might have seemed nonexistent. *His* Turner had asked more questions than he had given dogmas, and *his* Turner had been less "Turnerian" than many of his students. "Some of Turner's students," Becker would write in 1944, "have, I am afraid, missed the point entirely. Turner's use of the term 'West' has led some of them to suppose that if they made an exhaustive statistical inquiry into, for example, the development of the production of corn and hogs in Iowa, or some other Western state, they would be applying Turner's method: Turner was never himself 'provincial' but too many of his students have been."[61]

Actually any interpretation of Becker that attempted to link his name too closely with any "single-factor" interpretation or thesis concerning the processes of history would do an injustice to the intricacy of Becker's mind. Where problems of historical method are concerned, one can say with considerable ease that Becker followed the "relativist" line; but where problems of interpreting the actual course of historical events are concerned, one can only comment that Becker was a superb lay psychologist. "While bold spirits were talking about the necessity of enlisting psychology in the service of historical writing, Carl Becker in

[60] Gottschalk, "Carl Becker: Skeptic or Humanist," *Journal of Modern History,* XVIII (June, 1946), 260-261.

[61] Becker, Review of Fulmer Mood, *Development of Frederick Jackson Turner as a Historical Thinker, American Historical Review,* XLIV (January, 1944), 263-265.

his quiet way was actually doing so without any borrowing of strange new terms," Merle Curti has written;[62] and by psychology Curti meant both the social psychology evident in Becker's essay on Kansas and the individual psychology revealed with such delicacy in his essays on Diderot and Madame Roland. Where Becker got his grasp of psychology is a mystery; his papers and reading lists are free from authors who might have given him any "strange new terms." Freud, he later recalled, had in his *A General Introduction to Psychoanalysis* taught him that the wish is father to the thought,[63] but the *extent* of his learning from Freud is a matter for hopeless conjecture. Probably he learned more about psychology from the novels of Henry James.

Wherever he learned his psychology, it brought praise from his master Turner, who especially admired Becker's study of the *two* Madame Rolands, one a simple woman, the other determined to be a part of heroic history. Turner wrote to Becker that he felt very comfortable while reading Becker's psychological probings, a feeling he did not always have in the presence of some of the more ambitious attempts then being made by historians.[64] Becker's study of characters such as Madame Roland's greatly exceeded anything Turner might have done in that sphere; but, and here is where argument may commence, he was also capable of surpassing Turner, in my opinion, where social psychology is concerned. As proof of this I should like to examine the first book Becker published while at Cornell, *The Eve of the Revolution*. Then, so as not to exaggerate Becker's achievements, I will examine briefly his *The United States: An Experiment in Democracy*, where he followed Turner to the point of aping him. Finally, I will take account of Becker's *The Declaration of Independence, a Study in the History of Political Ideas*, which reveals an area of study where he was second to none, an area in which psychology, political theory, and popular philosophy could be brought together to make an organic whole.

These three books all appeared in the four years between 1918 and 1922. They represent at once the zenith and the climax of Becker's effective contributions to the writing of American history. The middle

[62] Review of Becker's *Everyman His Own Historian*, *American Historical Review*, XLI (October, 1935), 116-118.

[63] Becker, "Books That Changed Our Minds," *New Republic*, XCVII (December 7, 1938), 135.

[64] Frederick Jackson Turner to Carl Becker, Pasadena, California, October 9, 1928. See also Leland Hamilton Jenks, Review of Carl Becker, *Everyman His Own Historian*, *American Sociological Review*, I (February, 1936), 160-161: "The essay on Madame Roland is worth many case histories as an analysis of roles, compensation and identification, public and private attitudes."

book on the democratic experiment is a kind of patriotic potboiler, but the other two volumes are of exceptionally high quality. There is nothing in them to suggest that Becker could not have gone on indefinitely writing books about the democratic or liberal philosophy and its development in the United States. Of course, he continued to write essays and biographical sketches, those of Sam Adams, Benjamin Franklin, and Henry Adams being the most memorable,[65] but after the First World War the book-making process in Becker seems to have broken down, perhaps because Becker wondered if the democratic process itself wasn't on the verge of collapse. With the exception of his history of Cornell University, written in 1943, Becker would never write another book about American history, and only the coming of the Second World War would lead him to discuss again in book form the type of questions that had provoked *The United States: An Experiment in Democracy.*

The first thing to be said about these works is that their author had certain advantages he had not had previously. They were written during Becker's middle age and were begun while he was still more enchanted with Cornell and the idea of progress than disenchanted with the results of American entry into World War One. There was about these books none of the "forced march to learning" quality that had strained some pages of his thesis and *The Beginnings;* he had time to master much of the material beforehand, and although the books were written to order, only *The Eve of the Revolution* was in any way intended as a textbook, and this rather loosely. Becker finally had the advantage, as a professor of modern European history, of seeing the United States in broader perspective; and actually his French and American studies always tended to reinforce one another and to save his writings from conveying a one-dimensional effect. An example of this occurred as early as 1914 in a review of *The Letters of Richard Henry Lee,* which contains this fruitful idea: "The American Revolution was not without its Girondins. . . ." Lee, Becker thought, had "the Girondin air of loving liberty because he had studied the classics. Faithful to the Roman tradition he christens his son Cassius," and so on.[66] Here in the sentence about Lee is reasoning by analogy, in a way that anticipates Becker's method in both *The Eve of the Revolution*

---

[65] "Samuel Adams," *Dictionary of American Biography,* I (New York, 1928). "Samuel Adams," *Encyclopedia of the Social Sciences,* I (New York, 1930). "Henry Adams," *Encyclopedia of the Social Sciences,* I (New York, 1930). "Benjamin Franklin," *Dictionary of American Biography,* VI (New York, 1931). "Benjamin Franklin," *Encyclopedia of the Social Sciences,* VI (New York, 1931).

[66] *The Nation,* XCIX (December 10, 1914), 691.

and *The Declaration of Independence;* also the sentence indicates Becker's grasp of the psychology of the American Revolution and anticipates one of the major themes of both *The Eve of the Revolution* and his later work, *The Heavenly City.* This theme has to do with the "uses" made of history by interested parties.

The Eve of the Revolution, A Chronicle of the Breach with England, is really the first of Becker's writings in which he drove home the proposition that ideas, whether about history or political philosophy, are more rationalizations than abstract or absolute truths. The American patriots, he wrote, found John Locke's defense of the "glorious revolution" of 1688 useful; they bought his book, which was "conveniently placed on their library shelves."[67] As for the patriots' use of history, Becker cited the large number of letters in colonial newspapers written by a Brutus or a Cato, Sam Adams' reading of Roman history in terms of the struggle between liberty and tyranny, and John Adams' observation that Demosthenes did not go forth from Athens to propose a Nonimportation or Nonconsumption Agreement against Philip.[68] Sometimes Becker pushed this idea to a pointless extreme, as when he depicted George Wythe as "the noblest Roman of them all, steeped in classical lore, with the thin sharp face of a Caesar" — what was Caesar doing in the republican camp? — "and for virtuous integrity a very Cato."[69] Ordinarily, however, Becker proved masterfully that "throughout the eighteenth century, little colonial aristocracies played their part, in imagination clothing their governors in the decaying vesture of old-world tyrants and themselves assuming the homespun garb, half Roman and half Puritan, of a virtuous Republicanism."[70]

History was used by the patriots, some would say to the point of abuse; in any case, ideas are rationalizations, according to Becker. Becker did not propound this thesis as explicitly as his friend Charles A. Beard would, and certainly he wasn't yet committed to the idea that ideas are only rationalizations. He did write that the opposition to the three-penny tax on tea supports the reflection that "mankind in general are bound by interest," and he did see fit to inform us of the economic distress of young John Adams and the economic incompetence of his cousin Sam.[71] "I would have come right out and said that Sam Adams was a deadbeat," Becker's friend Hodder wrote, and he

---

[67] *The Eve of the Revolution,* 59.
[68] *Ibid.,* 64, 163-165, 212-213.
[69] *Ibid.,* 66-67.
[70] *Ibid.,* 60.
[71] *Ibid.,* 202-203, 90-91.

complained that there was something "a little illusive" about Becker's method of treating his subjects.[72] What was illusive to Hodder is artful or subtle to more sophisticated readers who are pleased that Becker was not too explicit about the "factors" which "caused" the American Revolution. *The Eve of the Revolution* is a pleasant relief from omniscience in this respect; it is, however, not a retreat from responsibility: Becker was on safe ground when he pointed out that property rights were *among* the natural rights being defended by the patriots against British "tyranny." His irony about the tea tax is instructive: that Britain should have insisted upon the tea tax in "acknowledgment of her right, that America should have refused it in vindication of her liberty, may be taken as a high tribute from two eminently practical peoples to the power of abstract ideas."[73]

Clearly *The Eve of the Revolution* is not "thesis-ridden" or doctrinaire, and what is surprising, as we mentioned earlier, is that Becker's own thesis concerning the origins of the Revolution (that the "Revolution was not merely a question of 'home rule'; it was also a question of who should rule at home"[74]) was not made too explicit, although certainly it was suggested by Becker's presentation of the differences between the incendiary Sam Adams and the loyal Governor Thomas Hutchinson. The theme is there, but *The Eve of the Revolution* will not collapse if future research invalidates the emphasis that Becker had attached to it in his *Political Parties in the Province of New York*. Becker never changed his mind on this point, but *The Eve of the Revolution* is so subtle that he seems to have moved beyond it, to have comprehended better the "logic of events." This phrase isn't Becker's, but clearly it does justice to the following proposition of his: "Ten years of controversy over the question of political rights had forced Americans to abandon, step by step, the restricted ground of the positive and prescriptive rights of Englishmen and to take their stand on the broader ground of the natural and inherent rights of man."[75] And there is the Pennsylvania Farmer, John Dickinson, who sadly symbolizes men caught in the web of changing circumstance: he had "no mind for anything but conciliation, to obtain which he will go to the length of donning a Colonel's uniform, or at least, a Colonel's title, perfecting himself and his neighbors in the manual of arms against

[72] Frank H. Hodder to Carl Becker, Lawrence, Kansas, March 23, 1919.

[73] *The Eve of the Revolution*, 149.

[74] Becker would repeat this aphorism again in 1924 in his review of H. E. Egerton, *The Causes and Character of the American Revolution*, *American Historical Review*, XXIX (January, 1924), 344-345.

[75] *The Eve of the Revolution*, 254-255.

the day when the King would graciously listen to the loyal and humble petition of the Congress."[76]

This is at once the individual *and* the social psychology of the Revolution, because it was part of Becker's genius or gift that he shows us that individual psychology *is* social psychology, and his final demonstration that this is so lay in his presentation of two archetypes, the intriguer Sam Adams and the royal administrator Thomas Hutchinson. The plight of the Pennsylvania Farmer notwithstanding, *The Eve of the Revolution* is not weighed down by any high sense of tragedy, and Becker's treatment of Adams and Hutchinson, and even of Hutchinson's fall from power, is done in a nearly comic vein. There is humor aimed at Hutchinson's impeccable social background and his administrator's logic — for example, "Governor Hutchinson finally reached as a conclusion the prepossession with which he began; namely, that whereas a disturbed state of mind is, *ex hypothesi,* a vital evil, assertions or denials which tend to cause the evil must be unfounded";[77] and there is Samuel Adams with the "soul of a Jacobin," "born to serve on committees," as competent in secret societies as he was incapable of providing for his family. In his chapter on these two individuals, ironically entitled "A Little Discreet Conduct," Becker showed his talent for using individuals as symbols without depriving them of their individuality.[78] He made them into his pawns, or perhaps history's pawns, as illustrating the development of a revolutionary situation. He used them in preference to the usual narrative method, the march of external events, but he remained faithful to their essence by a liberal use of quotations, and by employing an impressionistic prose style of his own. (Such a style, in the words of Herbert Read, is "one that gives the illusion that the reader is participating in the events, scenes or actions described."[79] — to which we might add, "or sharing in the thoughts and feelings of the participants.")

The Eve of the Revolution marks Becker's emancipation from what he regarded as the poverty of what Herbert Butterfield calls "technical history,"[80] and his coming into an inheritance, not of technical history, but of history written as literature, psychology, and even as ethics. He did this consciously and stated that his intention was to enable the

[76] *Ibid.*, 233.
[77] *Ibid.*, 184.
[78] *Ibid.*, 150-199.
[79] *English Prose Style* (New York, 1955), 155.
[80] See Becker's critical review of Butterfield's *The Whig Interpretation of History, Journal of Modern History,* IV (June, 1932), 278-279.

reader to enter into the "states of mind and feeling" of the pre-Revolutionary period. "The truth of such history (or whatever the critic wishes to call it) cannot of course be determined by a mere verification of references," Becker added.[81] The book was based mainly on secondary sources; but it was not froth, nor was it, necessarily, in terms of its internal logic a dead end. Although Becker never wrote another book on this area of past experience, his later, highly factual contributions to the *Dictionary of American Biography* and the *Encylopedia of the Social Sciences* concerning the lives of Samuel Adams, Benjamin Franklin, and Thomas Hutchinson[82] can be regarded as an extension of what he had learned while writing *The Eve of the Revolution.*

He had learned, among other things, how to please editors, reviewers, and the public, for *The Eve of the Revolution* was successful on every level.[83] It has sold altogether 40,000 copies,[84] although it did not make Becker into the American Macaulay — nothing ever would. There was too much irony, too much psychology, too little narrative in his writings for that; Becker did, however, have one of the qualities that he thought had marked Macaulay for success. Becker *believed* in the values of his own society, and in 1918 he was in his sophisticated way as much a "Whig historian" as Macaulay or Charles A. Beard. So much so that Charles McLean Andrews complained to Becker that he had overused the idea of *democracy* in *The Eve of the Revolution* and had in effect written history backwards.[85] "What historical research needs is a more subtle psychology," Becker thought — one that would go beneath labels such as "democracy" and "aristocracy" and penetrate into what people were really thinking.[86] The evidence indicates that he had done this with considerable success in *The Eve of the Revolution;* but it also indicates that he had written history from a democratic-liberal point of view.

The ethics apparent in *The Eve of the Revolution* were not so much

[81] *The Eve of the Revolution,* viii.

[82] See Footnote 65 above. Also, "Thomas Hutchinson," *Dictionary of American Biography,* IX (New York, 1932).

[83] Allen Johnson to Carl Becker, New Haven, Connecticut, January 11, 1918. C. H. Van Tyne called the book "profound," *American Historical Review,* XXIV (July, 1919), 734. Walton H. Hamilton cited it as an excellent example of the "new history," *The Dial,* LXVI (February 8, 1919), 137. William Roscoe Thayer, however, mistook Becker's irony for "sarcasm," *Yale Review,* VIII (April, 1919), 652.

[84] Norman V. Donaldson to David Hawke, New Haven, Connecticut, February 20, 1950.

[85] C. M. Andrews quoted by Carl Becker to William E. Dodd, Ithaca, New York, 1921. *Detachment and the Writing of History,* 79-81.

[86] Carl Becker to William E. Dodd, same as above.

like the "applied ethics" that Becker's contemporary, Charles A. Beard, was drawing from his historical reflections, as they were a statement of principles that had emerged victorious from a clash of opposing interests. It is to the principles embodied in the Declaration of Independence, Becker concluded at a time when the idealism of Woodrow Wilson and Carl Becker were one, "to these principles, for a generation somewhat obscured, it must be confessed, by the Shining Sword, and the Almighty Dollar, by the lengthening shadow of Imperialism and the soporific haze of Historic Rights and the Survival of the Fittest — it is to these principles, these 'glittering generalities,' that the minds of men are turning again in this day of desolation as a refuge from the cult of efficiency and from faith in 'that which is just by the judgment of experience.' "[87]

According to Becker, man was turning from the ethics of McKinley and from the cruder varieties of social pragmatism to a belief in transcendent values; but were not these values rationalizations and where, since God and philosophical idealism were dead in Becker's mind, could they have come from except "experience" — had they not been tested in American history, and weren't they after all Historic Rights? In *The Eve of the Revolution* Becker neither raised these questions nor suggested any answers to them. The "glittering generalities" of the Declaration of Independence had perhaps blinded him temporarily to these difficulties. This blindness is even more apparent in the second of Becker's works during this period, *The United States: An Experiment in Democracy*, which he wrote at the request of Guy Stanton Ford and the Creel Committee, and which is valuable today chiefly because of its autobiographical elements. Perhaps neither *The Eve of the Revolution* nor *The United States: An Experiment in Democracy* provided the proper occasion for Becker to question the presuppositions of liberal democracy, but the evidence also indicates that Becker failed to do so because of his strong, personal faith in these presuppositions at this time.

The Eve of the Revolution had ended on a note of near exhortation to have faith; in *The United States: An Experiment in Democracy* Becker set out to analyze certain problems that he thought were endangering that faith. In the preface to the second (and last) edition of *The United States: An Experiment in Democracy* (which was then entitled *Our Great Experiment in Democracy*), Becker described it, correctly, as a series of essays on important problems that have con-

[87] *The Eve of the Revolution,* 256.

fronted the American nation since its beginnings. These problems were more practical than philosophical, as befitted the American national character sketched by Becker; and they were of the sort that always concerned Frederick Jackson Turner. The two most significant chapters in this respect are "Democracy and Free Lands" and "Democracy and Immigration"; in these chapters Becker rephrased Turner, sharing his high valuation of the contributions of free lands to the development of American democracy and his moderate uncertainty as to the contributions that the more recent immigrants might eventually make. Becker also showed himself troubled about the effect of the growth of business enterprise upon American democracy, but on the whole the book strikes a note of optimism. The problem of the immigrant may be solved, Becker felt, by those processes that make for assimilation, and surely the government can regulate "the use of private property" without challenging private property itself. What history seems to have taught Becker is that the "best traditions" — notice the value judgment, which is perfectly legitimate, all would agree, in this type of politico-historical study — "the real 'spirit of this government' are wholly in favor of whatever governmental activity may be necessary to assure that fundamental equality of opportunity which is indispensable to true liberty and the very essence of democracy."[88]

The United States: An Experiment in Democracy was a virtuous book, but a dull one, which never caught on with the reading public. Dodd's hope that the book would bring Becker "satisfaction and influence as a scholar and a counsellor of the public,"[89] was disappointed on both counts. Becker was, however, not disappointed: "I suppose popularization of an elementary sort is worthwhile sometimes," he hesitantly reflected.[90] His teacher Turner was pleased and placed Becker's book on the reserve shelf of readings for his course at Harvard on the History of the West, "not because of my pardonable vanity over your acceptance of some of my notions, but because of your own particular contributions which I mean to study more fully soon," Turner wrote to Becker.[91] It would have taken considerable study to determine what these "contributions" were, and one would do well to follow Max Farrand, who in reviewing the book spoke of it as a popularization of the Turner frontier thesis.[92]

[88] *The United States: An Experiment in Democracy*, 322.
[89] William E. Dodd to Carl Becker, Lansing, Michigan, October 17, 1920.
[90] Carl Becker to William E. Dodd, Ithaca, New York, October 25, 1920.
[91] Frederick Jackson Turner to Carl Becker, Cambridge, Massachusetts, October 26, 1920.
[92] *Mississippi Valley Historical Review*, VIII (March, 1921), 407-409.

Becker's criticism of laissez-faire politics especially endeared the book to Charles A. Beard, who wrote the only enthusiastic review, and that probably in part because he was doing a double review and could find nothing good to say about the second book, which dealt with some of the same problems as Becker's.[93] One reviewer found that Becker's book suffered from a "fatal defect" in that it lacked the detachment we "used to expect from college professors."[94] Andrew C. McLaughlin, while recommending the volume, filled a page of the *American Historical Review* with errors that he had detected, errors ranging from faulty dates to misunderstandings of constitutional theory.[95] What was really wrong with the book was that it was too simple for the scholar, too abstract for the general reader — too much of it was devoted to the rehearsal of "well known historical facts,"[96] and very few problems were in any way solved. Beard put it as favorably as possible: "Being a historian and not a preacher he offers no simple remedies. . . ."[97]

As a historian, Becker was perhaps secretly relieved to have such a book behind him, and to turn once again to the eighteenth century, this time to the history of the "glittering generalities" of the natural rights philosophy contained in the Declaration of Independence. In *The Eve of the Revolution* he had demonstrated his emancipation from the plodding methods of Osgood and had shown that, unlike Turner, he could escape from being overwhelmed by a mass of materials, without being unscholarly or unsound. In *The Declaration of Independence, A Study in the History of Political Ideas* he established his claim to pre-eminence in the field of intellectual history; this one book alone would make him deserving of mention alongside Robinson and Haskins. It was Carl Van Doren who suggested that Becker undertake this study; he first mentioned it to Becker in a letter dated January 8, 1920.[98] On February 4, 1921, Becker promised delivery of the book within a year. As in the case of *The Eve of the Revolution*, *The Declaration of Independence* was completed ahead of schedule, on December 24, 1921; and it was published the next year.

The Declaration of Independence was divided into six parts, the most important being the first three which dealt with the natural-

---

[93] *The Nation,* CXI (October 13, 1920), 416-417.

[94] Unsigned review in *The Outlook,* CXXVI (October 20, 1920), 334.

[95] XXVI (January, 1921), 338.

[96] C. G. Haines, *American Political Science Review,* XV (November, 1921), 616-617.

[97] See Footnote 93.

[98] Carl Van Doren to Carl Becker, New York, January 8, 1920.

rights philosophy that lay behind the Declaration and with those theories about the nature of the British Empire that had led Jefferson to write the Declaration. The remainder of the volume was devoted to the drafting and the literary qualities of the Declaration, and to the nineteenth-century reaction against the philosophy embodied in that document. Becker's style in *The Declaration of Independence* was a partial throwback to the allusive, impressionistic methods of *The Eve of the Revolution*. He used the style and the words of the eighteenth century freely, and partly for this reason Becker's writing is evocative. It is a style of echoes, and its goal seems to lie not in the reconstruction of the past but in making the past reverberate in the present. In content, *The Declaration of Independence* had much more to offer than *The Eve of the Revolution;* emphasis was placed upon textual analysis, however, rather than upon the revelation of "new" facts.[99] The results were said to be lucid, scholarly, subtle, unprejudiced, and — what was unusual for a book by Becker — it was nearly called "definitive," by Frederick Ogg.[100]

Because Becker in *The Declaration of Independence* eschewed the question of whether the natural rights philosophy was true or false, Ogg felt that Becker had written "strictly as an historian, and not as a political scientist."[101] Actually *The Declaration of Independence* was history written with a distinct thesis in mind; moreover the thesis while historically valid was one that could only embarrass the believer in natural rights. It could in fact embarrass the Becker who had written *The Eve of the Revolution,* or at least its conclusion, which clearly indicated the author's own commitment, during a period of Wilsonian idealism, to the natural-rights philosophy of Jefferson. "To ask whether the natural rights philosophy of the Declaration of Independence is true or false is essentially a meaningless question," Becker wrote in the conclusion to this new book;[102] and it is clear from the context that the meaninglessness of the question arose from factors stronger than any sudden conversion on Becker's part to the ideal of historical objectivity or neutrality. "When honest men are impelled to withdraw their allegiance to the established law or custom of the community . . . they seek for some principle more generally valid, some 'law' of higher

---

[99] Schlesinger, Review of Becker's *The Declaration of Independence, Mississippi Valley Historical Review,* IX (March, 1923), 333-335.

[100] *Yale Review,* XIII (April, 1924), 600-604.

[101] *Ibid.,* 600.

[102] *The Declaration of Independence, A Study in the History of Political Ideas* (New York, 1956 edition), 277.

authority . . . to them it is 'true' because it brings their actions into harmony with a rightly ordered universe, and enables them to think of themselves as having chosen the nobler part, as having withdrawn from a corrupt world in order to serve God or Humanity or a force that makes for the highest good."[103]

This is what Jefferson (and, one might add, Wilson) had done, and on the basis of this insight Becker built his book. He inquired not whether the particulars in the Declaration of Independence were true, not whether George III was guilty as charged, but how honest men like Jefferson could think that he was. Becker saw the Declaration as deductive, stemming more from the natural-rights philosophy than from the particular grievances it enumerated.

This appears to be sound historical method, leading to valid conclusions. *The Declaration of Independence* is not, however, at all times consistent with *The Eve of the Revolution*. *The Eve of the Revolution* had been mainly a study in pre-Revolutionary psychology, and it was founded in large part upon the generalization that men are often carried by circumstance further than they had intended to go. *The Declaration of Independence* was mainly a study in pre-Revolutionary ideology, and it was based upon the idea that "grievances" and complaints about tyranny would have fallen on fallow fields, had not the minds of men been already predisposed by the natural-rights philosophy to be on the lookout for violations of liberty. Certainly in comparison with the revolutions that have most often affected European history, the American Revolution seems almost groundless — compare the "tyranny" of the British to the "tyranny" of the Turks in Eastern Europe — *unless* emphasis is given to its philosophical background. The difficulty, however, is that Becker either overstated his thesis in *The Declaration of Independence* to the effect that the most important feature of the Declaration was its philosophy and not its bill of particular grievances, or that he had exaggerated his thesis in *The Eve of the Revolution* which suggested that the force of events had made moderate men immoderate. "Not desire, but practical difficulties, forced them [the colonists] to adopt separation from Great Britain as the object of their efforts,"[104] Becker repeated in *The Declaration of Independence*. He also reaffirmed his belief that "Locke did not need to convince the colonists because they were already convinced. . . ."[105] Convinced of what and by whom? Convinced of tyranny by tyrants, or by the

[103] *Ibid.*, 277-278.
[104] *Ibid.*, 128.
[105] *Ibid.*, 72.

natural-rights philosophy? There is an inconsistency here, which ema-nates from Becker's wanting to have it both ways. Perhaps it is an inconsistency more in formulation than in fact — ideas "cause" events, and events "cause" ideas; both formulations may be right, but the specific historical priorities of the egg and the chicken aren't made clear by Becker.

Becker's imprecision on this point led to two serious and not un-related criticisms. James Truslow Adams complained in the *New Re-public* that Becker's study of the Declaration of Independence centered too much upon "purely literary sources" and that he had, in his textual analysis, neglected the "life of the common people. . . . In the study of ideas we are too apt merely to trace the lineage from author to author. A crop needs soil as well as seed," Adams complained.[106] However un-just this criticism might be — in effect it would deny the possibility of any formal history of ideas abstracted from their social context —it ties in with a criticism that Louis Hacker would make in the 1930's from a Marxist point of view — namely, that Becker was in effect a timid academician who always stopped at the *eve* of revolutions instead of following their entire course. Had Becker seen them in their entirety, he would presumably have been able to decide what comes first, the egg or the chicken; and if he had only followed Marx, he would have seen clearly the economic structure's effects upon the intellectual superstructure.[107]

Such clarity would have come at the expense of subtlety, and we can be grateful that Becker was not so omniscient as Hacker, even if it cost him the honor of perfect consistency. Actually Becker's book abounds in good judgments. In answer to the hackneyed charge that Jefferson's ideas in the Declaration of Independence were unoriginal, Becker quietly retorted: "Nothing could have been more futile than an at-tempt to justify a revolution on principles which no one had heard of before."[108] Then, despite Becker's own interest in French influences upon American culture, there are two sentences Vernon Parrington might have done well to examine closely: "But it does not appear that Jefferson, or any American, read many French books. So far as the 'Fathers' were, before 1776, directly influenced by particular writers, the writers were English, and notably Locke."[109] Here is a partial

[106] XXXII (November 22, 1922), 338.
[107] Hacker, "Historian of Revolutions," *New Republic*, XXCV (January 8, 1936), 260-261.
[108] *The Declaration of Independence*, 24, 25.
[109] *Ibid.*, 27.

negation of Parrington's sweeping generalizations about the two main currents in American thought: the democratic French current, and the liberal English one, which Parrington later presented in his famous *Main Currents in American Thought*.[110] Here, too, is an author who, if his interests in American cultural history had remained constant, could have written *Main Currents in American Thought* — the results might not have been "definitive," but such a book by Becker might well have been something more than the suggestive shambles that Parrington's work is today. Then there are Becker's penetrating remarks about Jefferson's style, which have been discussed earlier in connection with Becker's own speaking and writing. And what really good book by Becker would be complete without observations about how Jean Jacques Rousseau found the "true revelation" not in the words of Moses but "all about him in Nature, with sermons in stones, books in running brooks, and God in everything" and about how the eighteenth-century thinkers "deified Nature and denatured God?"[111]

Becker's exploration of the "common underlying preconceptions" of eighteenth-century thought is never dull because he did not subscribe to the notion that "facts" are capable of speaking for themselves. He *interpreted* the facts. " 'Tis not history who speaks, but I," Becker might have said. Becker's interpretation was in large part an elaboration of a quotation from one of his favorite authors, Pascal, which he had used on the frontispiece. "But what is nature? Why is custom not natural? I greatly fear that this nature is itself only a first custom, as custom is a second nature." What was natural, Becker inquired, and why wasn't it just as natural for George III to be a tyrant as for Sam Adams to be a lover of liberty? Reversing the position he had taken in 1912 in reviewing Robinson's *The New History*, Becker now wondered if this distinction between nature and custom, between the natural and the unnatural amounted to anything more than the "commonplace distinction between good and bad."[112] His questions about natural rights were equally damaging, even if they were almost totally lacking in originality, being little more than copies, in clever language, of the criticisms made by Hume in the eighteenth century and by the "historical school" of thinkers in the nineteenth. Actually, Becker the intellectual historian was most uncomfortable in the world of Nature, as rationalists (excepting Spinozists) tend to be. In his opinion the Nature of beautiful sunsets or natural rights is no more natural than

---

[110] I (New York, 1927), *passim.*
[111] *The Declaration of Independence*, 37, 51.
[112] *Ibid.*, 58, 60.

the Nature of disease or historic rights. Natural rights, he made clear in *The Declaration of Independence,* were not, at that time, self-evident to him; and historians who have seen mainly affinities between Becker and the Enlightenment and who have tended to regard him as a twentieth-century Condorcet moving about the salons of Ithaca had best take heed of this.[113]

The eighteenth century, according to Becker, rested its case ultimately not upon demonstrable truths but upon faith; and here he anticipated his later work, *The Heavenly City of the Eighteenth Century Philosophers:* "Thus the eighteenth century, having apparently ventured so far afield, is nevertheless to be found within hailing distance of the thirteenth."[114] Locke's or Jefferson's natural law was "essentially identical" with "right reason," as Thomas Aquinas' had been; their natural law was a priori or deductive. When Becker judged Locke's argument to be a "dreary devil . . . staggering from assumption posited as premise to conclusion implicit in the assumption,"[115] it is doubly clear why Becker found it "meaningless" to inquire into the truth or falsity of the natural-rights philosophy.

In 1918 in *The Eve of the Revolution* he had told how men were turning to the Declaration of Independence in revulsion from the "soporific haze of Historic Rights and the Survival of the Fittest," and it was clear that he had stood among them, reaffirming his faith in its eternal verities. In 1922, however, he looked upon these natural-rights verities as being as "soporific" as any of their alternatives and as being, in a sense, only "Historic Rights," historic for the English and American nations. The difference between the two books might be explained in terms of the "maturing" or developing of Becker's thought; but the maturing had in it elements of disillusionment associated, as shall be seen, with Becker's personal reaction against Wilsonian idealism.

Since Becker's personal skepticism after World War One can easily be overdramatized, mention should be made of two factors that limited it. First, while Becker "saw through" the natural-rights philosophy, he continued to treat it kindly, as one would treat a partially obsolete but dear grandparent. The natural-rights philosophy "was a humane and

[113] See Strout, "The Twentieth Century Enlightenment," *American Political Science Review,* XLIX (June, 1955), 331, where, on the basis of Becker's *Progress and Power,* he sweepingly accuses Becker of having confused "liberalism" with "technocratic rationalism." This accusation is repeated in his *The Pragmatic Revolt in American History,* 125, where Becker is described as having been "thoroughly enchanted" with technology.

[114] *The Declaration of Independence,* 61.

[115] *Ibid.,* 72.

engaging faith," Becker sighed nostalgically. "At its best it preached toleration in place of persecution, good will in place of hate, peace instead of war" — all of which is very well until one remembers what Becker had momentarily forgotten, that it was a philosophy of Revolution. "It taught," he continued, "that beneath all local and temporary diversity . . . all men are equal in the possession of a common humanity."[116] He did not think that the nineteenth-century "historical school" of Ranke, de Bonald, and Savigny, who saw men instead of Man, had been so virtuous. From these comments it is clear that Becker did not completely believe that the question of the truth or falsity of the Declaration of Independence was "meaningless." Second, it should be remembered that however critical Becker may have been of "natural rights," he chose to be their historian and not the historian of the nineteenth-century conservative reaction against them. All ideas might be rationalizations, but his position seems to have been that, not only were some ideas more deserving of study, but they might be more rational as well. Natural rights may have become unnatural to the skeptical Becker, but they seemed "right" nevertheless. Clearly Becker's quarrel, if such be the proper word, with the "natural rights" school was a family quarrel. It is equally clear that he was a twentieth-century Jeffersonian begging to differ with the master's formulation.

[116] *Ibid.*, 278.

Chapter VII

Becker and World War One: Involvement and Disillusionment

BECKER'S EARLIEST reflections on historical method presented us with the spectacle of Becker, at times the most detached of men personally, deriding detachment. His article on "Detachment and the Writing of History" (1910) had about it, however, a prophetic ring; there may come a day, Becker had said, when our very survival could depend upon qualities antithetical to those of detachment and objectivity. That day came in the form of World War One, which had the effect of ending, temporarily, Becker's emotional detachment from the affairs of other men. The detachment was broken in 1917 when, after three years of neutrality, the United States entered the war on the side of France and Britain against Germany. From 1917 until the end of the war Becker found himself cast in the rôle of patriotic historian, just as he had previously found himself cast in the rôle of literary historian, but with this difference: he now *wanted* to be a patriotic historian even at the risk of appearing before a critical posterity in company with "historians" such as Henry Cabot Lodge. If that were the end of the story, this chapter would simply tell how Becker went the way of all flesh, or of all souls sensitive to talk about a war to end all wars and to make the world safe for democracy; one could say further that the war helped Becker achieve a unity of theory and practice and thus exploded the paradox of the detached man deriding detachment.

This unity of theory and practice proved, however, to be shortlived. Following the Peace of Versailles, Becker deeply regretted having given up his detachment. His first bitter reaction was that he had been taken in by Woodrow Wilson; and he seemed at times in the 1920's perilously close to surrendering to the easy cynicism of H. L. Mencken and his admirers. Perhaps, however, Becker was too old and too traditional-minded to find cynicism anything but painful, and from his reflections on the First World War there came what Phil L. Snyder

125

has rightly termed a "Crisis for a Humane Intelligence."[1] Certainly the story of Becker's involvement in World War One is one in which hope is followed by pessimism, involvement by a return to detachment, but, most important of all, one in which bitterness is followed by compassion.

What Becker may have thought about the causes of the World War, the rights and the wrongs of the struggle when it first commenced is not known, except by indirection; it is important to note that his probing of its origins and of the question of who or what was morally responsible for it did not come until afterwards. Becker did not write about the war until after American intervention was decided upon; whether this was the result of the widespread indifference to the war that Turner so regretfully detected throughout the Mid-West[2] or whether it was part of a "let's wait and see" frame of mind is open to conjecture. Only in one essay, "German Historians and the Great War," written in 1916, did Becker touch upon the war question. In this essay, he showed himself concerned with the part that German historians had played in the development of an exceptionally strong sense of German nationalism, a question which after two World Wars is of even greater interest today.[3] Becker felt that German historians, even a good European such as Ranke, had given to the German people a feeling that history was on their side, that power and success is the reward of virtue. "The doctrine that virtue will clothe itself with power" had been transformed, Becker said, into "the doctrine that the exercise of power is necessary to maintain an alleged virtue. The Germans of today, by dint of applying the lessons of their historians not wisely but too well, have somehow managed to get ahead of schedule." In stepping ahead of the historical process which they purported to know so intimately, the German people present to the world the paradox of "professed devotees of *real-politik*" acting as "idealists and doctrinaires."[4]

So much for the German use, or misuse, of history; other nations, too, have notions of their destiny and their historic rights. What was so doctrinaire about the Germans, and what ultimately helped to

[1] *The Western Political Quarterly*, IX (March, 1956), 1-10.

[2] "I love my Middle West, though just now I am rather pained at the explanations I am forced to make for her failure to back up the President when Germany cracked the whip." Frederick Jackson Turner to Carl Becker, Cambridge, Massachusetts, March 10, 1916.

[3] See, for instance, Hans Kohn, *German History: Some New German Views* (Boston, 1954).

[4] *The Dial*, LX (February 17, 1916), 164.

defeat them, was their failure to take into account certain American ideas about history, and in particular those ideas contained in the Monroe Doctrine. This was a real failure, because as Harry Elmer Barnes would later point out in his controversial *The Genesis of the World War*, "The United States was more friendly towards Germany than towards any other major European state in 1870."[5] As late as 1913, two of Burgess's distinguished students, Theodore Roosevelt and President Nicholas Murray Butler of Columbia, sent eloquent testimonials to the Kaiser on his birthday[6] — an incredibly short time before they would pronounce him the Anti-Christ. By 1914, however, the United States was more antagonistic towards Germany than towards any other European state, partly because of British propaganda and Barnes's *bête noire,* the British press lord Northcliffe, but also because of trade rivalries and clashes in imperialistic ambitions.

The antagonism apparent in 1914 flared into open hostilities in 1917 — largely as a result of German submarine activities against "neutral" American shipping. In May, 1917, shortly after America entered into the war against Germany, Becker published an article on "The Monroe Doctrine and the War," which might serve as a classic, if perfectly respectable, example of how an American historian sought to show that, in terms of American tradition, a commitment to the Allied cause was a necessity. Becker began by giving a history of the Monroe Doctrine and ended by exonerating President Wilson's plea that we now extend the Monroe Doctrine from the Western Hemisphere to Europe as well. The Monroe Doctrine, Becker admitted, is "based upon national interests precisely as much or as little as democracy itself"; but he was somewhat less realistic in his assessment of the European situation. "Few Americans deny that a decisive victory for Germany would be an irremediable defeat for democracy." Therefore, Becker wrote, "it is the part of wisdom as well as fitting that we should do our share in making the world safe for democracy. I cannot think that in pledging our lives and our fortunes to bring about that fortunate event, the people of the United States . . . can be in serious danger of departing from their profoundest traditions."[7] Such was Becker's use of history. Among our "profoundest traditions," Becker at this stage in the game chose to find the tradition of non-intervention in the wars of Europe not relevant.

[5] New York, 1926, 642.
[6] *The New York Times,* June 8, 1913.
[7] "The Monroe Doctrine and the War," *Minnesota Historical Society Bulletin,* II (May, 1917), 68.

Becker was at the University of Minnesota when America entered the war. He wanted to enter the fray somehow, and he regretted being too middle-aged to fight. The next best thing, he thought, was to mobilize his learning and to place it behind Woodrow Wilson. Only once did he falter, and this was at a faculty meeting on "What can we do?" where it was suggested that someone, perhaps Becker, ought to do a history of what France had contributed to liberty. Becker remembered, after the war was over, that he had retorted with "some cynical remark or other, to the effect that France had imposed more liberty on others than she had ever fairly won for herself."[8] No more was said on that score.

If Becker hesitated once, he did not do so again, and in the summer of 1918 he went from Cornell to Washington to work for George Creel's Committee on Public Information. Becker's total war effort consisted of one book, *The United States: An Experiment in Democracy,* and two pamphlets that he wrote for the Creel Committee. "I find it easier to come than to get away," Becker wrote to Burr from Washington; Guy Stanton Ford had asked him to do a pamphlet on "German deviltries in Belgium, and now that that is done a new job is looming on the horizon."[9] The first pamphlet was published as *German Attempts to Divide Belgium,* and it contained the following uncharitable judgment: "But in speaking of national aspirations, we have to do with an influence of the moral and spiritual order — thus rising above the level along which the Prussian mind travels."[10] Not only was the judgment uncharitable, it was also inconsistent with Becker's previous remarks about the idealistic and doctrinaire features of the German mind; more important, it was contrary to the facts in the case, and it shows the underside of Becker's involvement in the war, the way in which even his good judgments were canceled out by anti-German passions.

Still he never went to the extreme of some American historians, such as William Roscoe Thayer, in his devil theory of history; and Becker's second pamphlet, *America's War Aims and Peace Program,* was of the peace-on-earth-good-will-to-men persuasion. Here he emphasized Wilson's peaceful intentions, the American and Allied renunciations of imperialism, and the need for "the reorganization of the world on a cooperative instead of a competitive basis." This was the last of the

---

[8] "La Belle France," Review of William Stearns Davis, *A History of France, New Republic,* XXIII (July 14, 1920), 207-208.

[9] Carl Becker to George Lincoln Burr, Washington, D. C., August 31, 1918. The George Lincoln Burr Papers.

[10] Boston: World Peace Foundation, Vol. I, No. 6, August, 1918, 340.

War Information Series — it was a suitably ironic ending — and over 700,000 copies were distributed among American schools and colleges.[11] Moreover, Becker had quoted Wilson extensively, and had made it very clear that he was totally committed to Wilson's peace program and the famous Fourteen Points; in fact, the pamphlet had had the unqualified approval of Wilson himself. "My dear Creel," he wrote, "I have taken some liberties here and there with this but send it back with my unhesitating approval. In haste, Cordially and faithfully yours, Woodrow Wilson." In his own hand, Wilson added, "I suggest holding this till after the election."[12] Wilson was plainly worried about the effects that his (and Becker's) "new international order" might have upon the Congressional elections that fall.

The rest of the story is too well known to call for a detailed recapitulation. The election in 1918 returned to Congress a Republican majority, with whom Wilson could not cooperate; the Paris Peace Conference at the end of the war showed that the victorious Allies were not so disinterested as Wilson or Becker had imagined; the Treaty of Versailles showed that Wilson, to make ironic use of the phrase he had applied to his editorial revisions of Becker's pamphlet, had indeed "taken some liberties here and there." The one thing he had got of real consequence, he felt, had been the League of Nations.[13] "His plans," as another, more recent historian has remarked, "had been hamstrung, his hopes abandoned one after another, until nothing but the League was left."[14] The question for Becker and his contemporaries to answer was whether this would be enough to insure peace, and whether, if the answer was no, the war had been fought in vain.

For Becker, the war had been worth its cost in one sense. In 1918 he had written that, although England might be self-seeking in her foreign policy, she was the moral superior of Germany. "It is certainly better to have the English principle on top than to have the German principle on top. It is better to have the Englishman on top than to have the German on top. It is better to have anything English on top than to have anything German on top."[15] There is no evi-

[11] Washington: Committee on Public Information, War Information Series, November, 1918.

[12] Woodrow Wilson to George Creel, The White House, Washington, D. C., October 26, 1918. The original of this letter is in The Becker Papers at Cornell; presumably Creel had passed it on to Becker.

[13] A conversation with Carl Becker reported by Becker in a letter to Frederick Lewis Allen, Ithaca, New York, March 19, 1933.

[14] Richard Hofstadter, *The American Political Tradition* (New York, 1955), 280.

[15] "Tender and Tough Minded Historians," Review of H. H. Powers, *America Among the Powers, The Dial,* LXV (August 15, 1918), 109.

dence that Becker ever changed his mind on that score; the British played the game better than other Europeans, Becker thought, an opinion that was strengthened by his single visit to Britain in the summer of 1924.[16] In another sense, however, the war had been disappointing; out of weakness or necessity, Wilson had sold his principles short. We were, Becker felt, left with a peace that could only promote another war among sovereign states; and the United States was left with a domestic situation from which charity, sympathy, and the Jeffersonian verities had nearly disappeared. If Becker did not fully accept Barnes's conclusion that "The intervention of the United States was an unmitigated disaster for both America and the world,"[17] he came very near to doing so.

Moreover, Becker felt a personal sense of involvement and responsibility; it was not enough to say that history was profoundly ironical, for Becker was now part of the irony, as his hopes were turned to despair. His first reaction to the Peace of Versailles was an intensely personal one, which amounted in effect to his saying that Wilson had betrayed *Becker's* War Aims and Peace Program. "I do not say," Becker would write in 1921, "that the war could have ended otherwise than it did, or that, 'all things considered,' a different peace than the Peace of Versailles could have been made. But I say that if the President was right in 1917 he was wrong in 1919. If the President changed his mind about peace without victory sometime between 1917 and 1919, it would be interesting to know why."[18]

Becker never *knew* why, with certainty; his first reaction was to blame the man who had deceived him, his second was to blame the circumstances that had deceived the man. Wilson, Becker admitted to William E. Dodd, had got "something" at Paris: "The peace is less bad than it would have been without him. But to say that the peace conforms with the 14 points is either the result of dishonesty or an egoism that enables him to see black as white." And the ridiculous thing about Wilson was his refusal to admit any inconsistency between his commitment in 1918 to a peace without victory and his commitment to the Treaty drawn up at Versailles. Wilson, Becker said, had "no humor, no objectivity, no abiding sense of a contact with reality." Wilson's refusal to accept any modifications of the Treaty also vexed Becker.

[16] Carl Becker to Betty Bohannon, New York, July 25, 1933.
[17] *The Genesis of the World War* (New York, 1926), 645.
[18] "A Chronicle of Facts," Review of John Spencer Bassett's *Our War With Germany, New Republic*, XXV (February 23, 1921), 383.

I can understand being for the treaty or against it; but I can't understand being for it to the point of refusing to accept any reservations whatever, or being against it only if these reservations are not made. The thing will be neither worse nor better by a few reservations. What does it matter anyway. It won't last; it is not being observed, and the people who made it never expected it would be. If anything ever comes of the League, Woodrow will have the credit of having launched the experiment and that will have been much; but future generations will never exalt him for having handicapped the new experiment with such a millstone as the Peace of Versailles.[19]

Becker's impressions about Wilson's having "no abiding sense of a contact with reality" had come to him firsthand when, after the Peace of Versailles and Wilson's physical breakdown, he had visited Wilson in company with Dodd, J. F. Jameson, Guy Stanton Ford, and Edward Cheyney. Wilson had given these "patriotic" historians half an hour of his time, enough for Becker to notice that Wilson's mind did not make transitions easily:

He would talk for five minutes of something — the Kaiser, or Clemenceau, or whatever: then he would drop it, and be silent, until he thought, or someone suggested some other topic. He seemed a man at bay: desperately fighting still, but now what he was fighting for was really to hold on to the conviction that he hadn't wholly failed. I recall his saying "But we've got the League — *they can't take that away from me.*"

Wilson had also talked a bit about history; he had said that people exaggerated the ability of persons in high places to know all that was happening, and that historians were prone to make the same mistake. "If he had to write history again, he would try to *know as little as possible* about what happened after the particular time of which he was writing. . . ."[20] Becker was witnessing a tragedy, he realized when his own righteous indignation against Wilson had cooled.

This indignation might never have cooled, if it hadn't been for the help of William E. Dodd. In 1920 Dodd published a biography of Wilson, and in the Preface he compared Wilson favorably with both Jefferson and Lincoln. Becker took issue with Dodd, to such an extent that their friendship seems to have been imperiled for a brief time; in an exchange of letters with Dodd, Becker worked off some of his aggressions against Wilson, so that by the time they had ceased to write about Wilson and the war question, Becker apparently was in a

[19] Carl Becker to William E. Dodd, Ithaca, New York, undated letter, written in the summer of 1920.
[20] Carl Becker to Frederick Lewis Allen, Ithaca, New York, March 19, 1933.

mood to accept the last sentence of Dodd's book if not his Preface: "It is a compelling, almost a tragic, story," Dodd had written.[21]

Dodd's comparison of Wilson with Jefferson and Lincoln, his description of Wilson as "a modern St. George," may have blinded Becker to the fact that Dodd was also pessimistic about the achievements of Wilson in foreign policy. "This book of mine is pessimistic enough," Dodd justly exclaimed.[22] He, too, had shown himself disappointed with Versailles. What was left, Dodd had wondered, but the League? "What was the League? A loose association of sovereign states that was not to infringe upon the absolute independence of any member."[23] What Dodd would not accept was Becker's growing tendency to regard Wilson as a symbol of the futility of the democratic process. This tendency of Becker's was best expressed in a lengthy letter to Dodd, written in June of 1920. The letter is a biting indictment of the idea of progress, of the politics of democracy; in short, despite Becker's suggestion that he had tended to think along these lines for some time, it is an indictment of everything Becker (and Dodd) had believed in until 1919.

> The war and what has come out of it has carried me very rapidly along certain lines of thought which have always been more congenial to my temperament than to yours. I have always been susceptible to the impression of the futility of life, and always easily persuaded to regard history as no more than the meaningless resolution of blind forces which struggling men — good men and bad — do not understand and cannot control, although they amuse themselves with the pleasing illusion that they do. The war and the peace (God save the mark!) have only immensely deepened this pessimism.
>
> It is of course easy to explain the war in terms of the sequence of events, or the conflict of interests, or the excited state of the public mind, etc. But in itself the war is inexplicable on any ground of reason, or common sense, or decent aspiration, or even of intelligent self-interest; on the contrary it was as a whole the most futile, the most desolating and repulsive exhibition of human power and cruelty without compensating advantage that has ever been on earth. This is the result of some thousands of years of what men like to speak of as "political, economic, intellectual, and moral Progress." If this is progress, what in Heaven's name would retardation be! The conclusion I draw is not that the world is divided into good men and bad, intelligent and ignorant, and that all will be well when the bad men are circumvented and the ignorant are en-

[21] *Woodrow Wilson and His Work* (New York, 1920), 352.
[22] William E. Dodd to Carl Becker, Chicago, July 15, 1920.
[23] *Woodrow Wilson and His Work*, 349.

lightened. This old eighteenth century view is too naive and simple. Neither good men nor bad wanted *this* war (although some men may have wanted *a* war); yet neither good men nor bad were able to prevent it; nor are they now apparently able to profit by their experience to the extent of taking the most obvious precautions against a repetition of it. The conclusion I draw is that for good men and bad, ignorant and enlightened (even as enlightened as Mr. Wilson), reason and aspiration and emotion — what we call principles, faith, ideals — are without their knowing it at the service of complex and subtle instinctive reactions and impulses.

Here is the negation not only of the idea of progress but of the ideas of reason and self-control as well. Becker himself continued, however, to be more rational than impulsive in that he tried to show his consistency. This, he now said, was what he had tried to say in *The Eve of the Revolution,* especially in his chapter on Adams and Hutchinson; this was what he hoped to show someday in a story he would write about the French Revolution (which he never did). It is true that Becker had always been aware of the "web of circumstances," but his awareness had hitherto been balanced, either by a belief in social pragmatism and the advantages of education, or by faith in the principles embodied in the Declaration of Independence. Now, temporarily at least, the balance had broken down, and futility held sway; the only decent things left, Becker found, lay in the private or creative realm, not in the hands of politicians:

I do not doubt that Lodge is as honest in his own mind and conscience as Wilson is. Both convince themselves that they are working disinterestedly for the welfare of their country and the good of humanity; yet neither one will or apparently can, discuss the treaty or the League or European or American politics directly, disinterestedly, or intelligently. Their talk about these things is unreal talk. It is puerile talk. In a word it is bunk.

And this is why I cannot get up any enthusiasm for or against the treaty or the League, for or against Wilson. The whole business is so saturated with self-deception and nonsense that it is only sickening when it is not merely diverting. The other night I attended a concert by your Chicago orchestra; and as I listened to these men what came over me with overwhelming force was the honesty and genuineness of what they were doing. The same is true of all genuine art, scholarship, craftsmanship, and of all human activity which has for its primary object the creation of something beautiful or useful, or the discovery of some truth, or the doing of something helpful to others. But most of politics, and much of business, has none of these for their primary object; their primary object is the gaining of some advantage over others; and hence there is a subtle taint of unreality and accordingly of dishonesty about these enterprises that warps and falsifies the minds of their followers. And so in my present temper politics strikes me as serving chiefly to illustrate and confirm the ancient saying: "The human heart is deceitful and desperately wicked."

All of which is a far cry from the Becker who had gone to Washington only two years previously to assist in the war effort, and who had believed in a war to end all wars and in a politician who wished to make the world safe for democracy, presumably of the Anglo-American variety.

> What really irritates me, I will confess to you, is that I could ever have been naive enough to suppose, during the war, that Wilson could ever accomplish those ideal objects which are so well formulated in his state papers. A man of any intelligence, who has been studying history for 25 years, and to some purpose if I am to believe your high opinion of him, should have known that in this war as in all wars, men would prefer to be fighting for justice and liberty, but in the end would demand the spoils of victory if they won. It was futile from the beginning to suppose that a new international order could be founded on the old national order.[24]

With this skepticism about politics, there also came a skepticism about whether the people ever knew what they wanted, and about the efficacy of majority rule.[25] Dodd was quick to notice this change in temper and to challenge it. "The attitudes of the masses of men seem to be what you suggest. The difference between us appears when we undertake to generalize. I am willing to let the majority rule, even determine the question of property with me," he confidently replied.[26] Becker's reconciliation with democracy took somewhat longer; ironically it took a second world war to restore the faith which the first had nearly taken away.

Becker's bitterness toward Wilson disappeared more quickly. As early as 1919 he pronounced discussions of the League's Covenant to be little more than "academic,"[27] and by 1923 his air of objectivity and detachment, one might say *virtuous* detachment, had returned. He wrote to Dodd confessing that he had had a grudge against Wilson but that more lately he had been angry with himself for having ever expected that Wilson could do more. "When he failed, I was angry be-

[24] Carl Becker to William E. Dodd, Ithaca, New York, June 17, 1920.

[25] Carl Becker to William E. Dodd, undated letter.

[26] William E. Dodd to Carl Becker, Chicago, July 15, 1920.

[27] "The League of Nations," Review of twenty books about the League, *The Nation,* CIX (August 16, 1919), 227.

cause I had failed to see that he must fail; and took it out on Wilson. But that is all over. . . ."[28]

It was not quite over, however; Becker's review of Ray Stannard Baker's *Woodrow Wilson and World Settlement,* which had appeared in *The Nation* less than two weeks previously,[29] had contained the judgment that the Treaty of Versailles was the negation of all that Wilson had professed to believe in. But in his letter to Dodd he now found it necessary to add that "Mr. Wilson was not responsible for the failure, although he was at fault for thinking that it could have been otherwise." In March of that same year Dodd wrote to Becker that, while his comparison of Wilson with Jefferson and Lincoln would have to stand, he, too, had come to see that the Wilson of the Fourteen Points was not the dogmatic Wilson of 1919 and afterward. Wilson was now "broken in mind, in spirit, and in body";[30] it was, indeed, as Becker had said, nearly all over. If, however, Wilson could be relieved of responsibility for the failure to achieve a charitable and lasting peace, where did the responsibility rest? Becker decided that it lay in the same web of circumstance and human fraility that had brought about the war in the first place.

The key to this web of circumstance lay in the "old national order," which determined beforehand the futility of Wilson's efforts, Becker thought afterwards. It was Becker's belief in the determining rôle of exaggerated nationalism that led him to minimize the question of individual guilt and responsibility and thus to approach the question, as a rule, without the passion of a hanging judge. The impersonality of Becker's approach led him also to a greater awareness of the complexity of the issues involved, as well as to a growing reluctance to state dogmatically what the "causes" of the war had been.

In reviewing Coleman Phillipson's *Alsace-Lorraine: Past, Present, and Future* for *The Nation* Becker denied that Alsace-Lorraine was, as Phillipson had said, "the proximate cause" of the war. "The immediate cause of the war," Becker countered, "was certainly the determination of the ruling caste in Germany to make use of a favorable opportunity to bring it about; but the fundamental cause was as certainly the fact that the political organizaion of the European world

[28] Carl Becker to William E. Dodd, Ithaca, New York, February 26, 1923.
[29] CXVI (February 14, 1923), 188.
[30] William E. Dodd to Carl Becker, Austin, Texas, March 1, 1923.

was violently out of harmony with its economic organization."[31] This "fundamental cause" of conflict, Becker perceived in 1919, was that in economics the European states were intimately interwoven, but that in politics they still accepted the fiction of absolute sovereignty and independence. Later that year he placed the blame for the war upon imperialism, which was profitable to a few individuals in each country if not to the masses; the "munition-makers," and the "international bankers" were the "most important and most sinister" of the groups that profited from the war, but Becker at no time attributed the causal responsibility to these groups that the Nye Committee would in the 1930's. Imperialism, too, was something terribly complex. "The problem of war . . . involves much more than the economic bearings of capitalist imperialism; it involves the far more difficult question of the State itself."[32] This question arises when we consider how to limit the powers of a national organization whose powers are regarded as absolute, until it loses these powers and hence its sovereignity in a contest of force; such was the problem confronting the League of Nations.

Becker, during the election of 1920, was fairly certain that the United States would join the League, whatever difficulties the newly created organization might then encounter. "Whichever party wins we will have the Treaty and the League, with some reservations, very shortly," he wrote to Dodd.[33] Becker failed to take into account the fact that his own skepticism toward Wilson's achievements was shared by millions, and that President Harding would disappoint even those members of his own party, such as Henry Stimson, who had been certain that, once the election was over, he would press for American entrance into the League. Since America did not enter the League, her total gain from the war was nil. It was plain, Becker later wrote, that "in 1934 the world was in a worse state than in 1914, and that the war, so far from having made the world safe for democracy, had made it convenient for dictators. . . ."[34]

In the 1920's and the 1930's Becker often wondered how this had come about, how it was that "The United States entered the war in defense of her honor and her property, and to make the world safe for democracy; she preserved her honor, lost some millions of dollars in bad debts, and helped to make the world safe for dictators."[35] Becker,

[31] CVIII (March 1, 1919), 329.
[32] "The League of Nations," *The Nation,* CIX (August 16, 1919), 226.
[33] Carl Becker to William E. Dodd, Ithaca, New York, October 25, 1920.
[34] *How New Will the Better World Be?* (New York, 1944), 38.
[35] "Loving Peace and Waging War," *New Liberties for Old,* (New Haven, 1941), 66.

like Charles A. Beard,[36] refused to blame the ills of Europe after the war upon America's failure to enter the League. Europe had been ill for some time, Becker believed; and he was no longer interested in "saving" her but in understanding why the debacle had occurred.

In this understanding Becker had to take account of the conclusions reached by Harry Elmer Barnes, whose writings became the rallying point of those "Revisionists" who wished to condemn the part that the United States had played in the war and to prove that American entry into the war had come about in part because she had failed to appreciate the fact that Germany was less guilty than certain other European powers in precipitating the conflict. "If Barnes is right," Albert Bushnell Hart indignantly exclaimed, "Roosevelt was wrong, Wilson was wrong, Ambassador Page was wrong, everybody was wrong."[37]

When Becker was asked to join in the discussion, his reply was rather laconic. Barnes was probably right, he wrote: Austria was after all more responsible than Germany, "but I also think that either statement has little to support it except a subjective buoyancy."[38] If we are going to blame Austria, why not Serbia? Because then, according to Becker, we approach the philosophical question of what is justifiable conduct on the part of a sovereign state.

Becker went on to add that he would not blame individual statesmen for the sins of the world: "Their state of mind was that of honorable gentlemen, who convinced themselves that it was their duty to wage war for the safety of their own countries, in order thereby to promote the welfare of the human race. The creature called Man is like that."[39] The same note of sympathetic understanding reappeared in his defense of Sir Edward Grey against Oswald Garrison Villard, who had in 1933 condemned Grey in *The Nation* for believing in his own (Grey's) rectitude and infallibility to an unbelievable degree. According to Becker, it was Grey's "muddleheadedness rather than any deliberate purpose" that accounted for his difficulties in 1914.[40]

[36] Charles A. Beard, *President Roosevelt and the Coming of the War, 1941: A Study in Appearances and Realities* (New Haven, 1948), especially Chapter One.

[37] "A Dissent from the Conclusions of Professor Barnes," a Contribution to a Symposium "Assessing the Blame for the World War," *Current History*, XX (May, 1924), 196. Hart was criticizing Barnes's "Assessing the Blame for the World War," which appeared on pages 171-195 in the same issue.

[38] "Assessing the Blame for the World War," *Current History*, XX (June, 1924), 455.

[39] *Ibid.*, 456.

[40] A Letter to the editor of *The Nation*, CXXXVII (November 1, 1933), 510-511. "A reply to Oswald Garrison Villard, Sir Edward Grey," *The Nation*, CXXXVII (September 20, 1933), 316-317.

Ordinarily when Becker judged a man to be muddleheaded, the judgment was delivered in a noticeably condescending way; here, however, the condescension was absent, probably because Becker still remembered his own "muddleheadedness."

This note of compassion helps to explain Becker's impressions of Harry Elmer Barnes's *The Genesis of the World War*, which Becker regarded as "the most effective" statement of the Revisionist case. Becker wrote to Barnes that *The Genesis* seemed to him "a marvellously straight, swift, cogent presentation of facts and conclusions." He found, however, that "It is perhaps an oversimplification of the psychology of individuals like Poincaire, Ed. Grey, etc.: but substantially the fundamentals are right, and this simplification will do no harm since without it you could not get the attention of many readers."[41] This was Becker's first reaction to Barnes's book. Soon after Barnes visited Cornell in 1926, where he spoke at the University Club, the editor of the *Christian Century* asked Becker to do a criticism of Barnes's position. Becker wrote to Barnes that he had declined the invitation because:

> I was in *essential* agreement. I am, so far as the brute facts are concerned and that means that it is no longer possible to lay upon Germany the responsibility for the war. Where I differ from you is in this: you are inclined to believe that some special persons are criminally responsible when he [sic] commits a murder for personal advantage, and you are inclined . . . to think that by exposing the criminals the world can be enlightened and induced to take a radically different attitude towards wars. I on the other hand can't see either of these things. It's a matter probably of temperament — some lack of vitality or glandular secretions on my part. You said yourself here that Poincaire et al no doubt were, or thought of themselves as being, honest, highminded gentlemen who were doing their duties to their countries and therefore to the H. Race — and that if we were in their positions with their training and traditions we would doubtless have done as they did. That is exactly what I think — "But for the grace of God, there go I, etc." Well, if that is the case I don't see how they can be held responsible in the sense in which you hold them so. Another point is that "we the people" are perhaps quite as responsible. A people in peace is one thing: a people in war, or under conditions in which war is imminent, is quite another set of animals.[42]

Becker went on to commend Barnes's "sledgehammer" method of jarring people and disturbing their peace, but he was constrained to

[41] Carl Becker to Harry Elmer Barnes, Ithaca, New York, undated letter, written in 1926.
[42] Carl Becker to Harry Elmer Barnes, Ithaca, New York, February 21, 1926.

add that he found Sidney Fay's *The Origins of the World War* "more judicious and water tight than yours";[43] and he told his students that Fay was "more objective" than Barnes.[44] In fairness to Barnes it must be said that behind the villainy of individuals he saw, as Becker did, the villainy of a system, which determined their conduct or at least predisposed them to regard war as an instrument of national policy. "Deeper than any national [or individual] guilt is the responsibility of the wrong-headed and savage European system of nationalism, imperialism, secret diplomacy and militarism. . . . ," Barnes wrote.[45] This is exactly the explanation that Becker would offer in 1931 in his school textbook, *Modern History*.[46]

In his *Modern History* Becker, however, displayed his usual hesitancy about specific responsibility, although he did not repeat his "we are all guilty" thesis, probably because it was too subtle for an audience of school children. "We ask but do not answer the important question, Who was responsible for the Great War?" was one of his topic headings.[47] A certain animus toward Wilson was still, however, in evidence in other topics: "The Armistice of 1918: In which it appears that President Wilson was able to keep his promises only in part"; "Why it was impossible to make the peace square with the Fourteen Points."[48] What is of interest is that as World War Two drew near, Becker came to see the First World War in a more idealistic light, as having been "something more than a conflict between certain countries for the possession of certain territories." The United States had fought for something more than the right to hold on to territories such as the Philippines — "it had to fight for the preservation of a world in which nations could be reasonably secure against unprovoked military conquest and destruction, and each nation free to live according to the ideas and institutions it preferred."[49]

This was a partial exoneration of Wilson, as well as a forgiveness approaching the point of a defense. Once again Becker, in the presence

---

[43] *Ibid.*

[44] Russell N. Chase (a one-time student of Becker's) to Phil Snyder, Cleveland, Ohio, February 16, 1956.

[45] "Assessing the Blame for the World War," *Current History*, XX (May, 1924), 194.

[46] *Modern History, the Rise of a Democratic, Scientific, and Industrialized Civilization* (New York, 1931), especially Chapter Twenty.

[47] *Ibid.* (1942 edition), 674.

[48] *Ibid.*, 724, 728.

[49] *Ibid.*, 831. It is of interest to note that Becker accepted "Revisionism" long before Beard did, only to reject it in those years just prior to World War Two when Beard, somewhat belatedly, embraced it with enthusiasm.

of a new World War, would be willing to sacrifice perfect consistency and to re-interpret the past in the light of an ever-changing present. Also, Becker had two warring dispositions within himself: one a cynical, ironic, and deterministic way of looking at man's conduct — a clinical and detached way — and the other a way of finding in man ideals transcendent over self or selfish interests — a generous and *involved* frame of mind. *Realpolitik* and the remains of Methodist idealism struggled always for the possession of Becker's soul. The outcome was that Becker was never more idealistic or noble in his interpretation of man's conduct, or at least of America's conduct, than when the United States was involved in the two World Wars. The self-sacrifice and heroism of such ventures stirred his soul in a way that peace, apparently, could not, despite his devotion to the ideal of peaceful co-existence among nations.

The years between the two wars were hard years for Becker, and for the most part they were, as shall be seen, skeptical ones. The consequences of America's entry into World War One, plus physical disability on his part, seem to have lessened his capacity for faith or involvement; and he failed to fulfill the promise of a never-ceasing productivity in the history of liberal democratic ideas such as he presented in his study of the Declaration of Independence in 1922. Vernon L. Parrington has described the post-war period as one in which liberal democracy was cast aside like an empty whiskey flask.[50] The question arises: Cast aside by whom? Certainly not by Becker, or by *The Nation* or the *New Republic*, or by Dodd, or Beard, or Becker's new friend, Felix Frankfurter, whose defense of Sacco and Vanzetti in the 1920's excited Becker's admiration.[51] If Becker did not cast aside his liberalism, he nevertheless came very seriously to question its relation to democracy or any form of majority rule, and to suspect it of being only a "way station" on the road toward a collectivism of either the right or the left.[52] Conformity, he feared, would triumph over conscience; and equality, however desirable it might be in economics, would perhaps devour liberty, or freedom of thought. All these fears, it is safe to say, emanated not from the Depression of the 1930's but from a war to make the world safe for democracy.

[50] *The Beginnings of Critical Realism in America* (New York, 1930), 412.
[51] Carl Becker to Felix Frankfurter, Ithaca, New York, 1927.
[52] "Liberalism, A Way Station," *Saturday Review of Literature*, XIV (December 3, 1932). Reprinted in *Everyman His Own Historian*, 91-100.

Chapter VIII

Becker in the 1920's and 1930's: The Social Thought of a Tired Liberal

BECKER IN THE 1920's and 1930's could best be described as a tired liberal, much aware of the fact that the communion between liberalism and democracy, liberty and equality, was neither so intimate nor so easy as his teacher Turner and the pre-World War One generation had imagined it to be. Becker's awareness of this came largely from his observations of contemporary events, which seemed to verify certain ideas entertained by Henry Adams and Oswald Spengler concerning the decline and fall of the West. The war, the wartime intolerance, the postwar cynicism, the Depression, the emergence of Caesarism of both the left and the right, all made a deep impression upon Becker's mind. But behind Becker's mental fatigue there lay a physical fatigue, brought on by painful, prolonged stomach disorders and a number of seemingly endless visits to the hospital. There is the story of how Leo Gershoy once visited Becker in the hospital, where Becker, who seldom complained of his illnesses, exclaimed wearily, "Leo, they talk a lot about a sound mind in a sound body. Hell, any kind of mind in a sound body."[1] It is small wonder, with a background such as this, that Becker in the 1920's and 1930's sometimes reminds one of Bertrand Russell's characterization of Schopenhauer: "Tired and valetudinarian, valuing peace more than victory, and quietism more than attempts at reform, which he regards as inevitably futile."[2] An even greater wonder is that this isn't the whole story of Becker in these two decades, that he still found some light in a period of darkness when it seemed that the currents of history ran contrary to his wishes.

"The values that I most cherish do not thrive well in the market

[1] Barnett Nover to David Hawke, Denver, Colorado, February 10, 1950. Another interesting comment by Becker was that his illness made him feel like Gulliver tied down by the Lilliputians. (Frederick Duncalf to George Sabine, Austin, Texas, November 4, 1945.)

[2] A History of Western Philosophy (New York, 1945), 753.

place or on the social front," Becker sadly explained on one occasion.[3] "I am afraid we are entering another period in which Liberty will be at a discount," he wrote to Burr, the historian of the ideas of liberty and tolerance, in 1933. "The liberty that we prize — liberty of thought — means little to the mass of the people and they seem duped to support any leader or dogma which promises them bread and circuses. Bread and circuses are no doubt the first necessity. Perhaps liberty is merely a function of indifference which flourishes in ages of security and plenty."[4] But often in the 1920's one could characterize Becker's own mental outlook as an indifference which is merely a function of academic liberty in a period of security and plenty — and personal ill health.

Becker's moments of indifference can be traced, of course, not only to his physical illnesses but to his disgust at the effects of World War One. No one could say of him what Sidney Kaplan has rightly said of John Dewey: "Plainly Dewey had little new to suggest and the war might never have happened for all the change it had . . . made in his former position."[5] Of course, Dewey would later conclude that "we had been deceived by propaganda" into entering World War One,[6] but the body of his thought and feeling remained largely unaffected by this catastrophe. Not so with Becker. Although Becker had little new to suggest, the war had grievously affected his former position to the point where he became at times futilitarian.

In tracing the development of Becker's sense of futility, it is instructive to contrast the wartime optimism of Turner and Wilson with the pessimism of Becker's friend Hodder. "There is only one way in which to determine how the future of the United States is going to be projected and that is by looking backward and seeing which way the lines ran which led up to the present moment of power and opportunity," Turner had quoted Wilson as saying in 1916. And Turner had gone on to ask Becker and other historians in 1917 to give "greater zest" in their teaching to problems bearing on the present crisis.[7] *Power, opportunity,* and *zest* were alien words to Becker by 1920, and probably he found occasion to recall the words of Hodder, also

---

[3] *Progress and Power,* 10.

[4] Carl Becker to George Lincoln Burr, Ithaca, New York, September 12, 1933. The George Lincoln Burr Papers.

[5] "Social Engineers as Saviors: Effects of World War I on Some American Liberals," *Journal of the History of Ideas,* XVII (June, 1956), 362.

[6] "No Matter What Happens — Stay Out," *Common Sense,* VIII (March, 1939), 11.

[7] Frederick Jackson Turner to Carl Becker, Washington, D. C., May 11, 1917.

written in 1917: "This war is very depressing. It isn't the war itself, which is a righteous war if ever there was one, but the things it brings to the surface: everything that I most dislike."[8]

There is evidence that by 1918 Becker was already coming to share Hodder's qualms. "My devotion to the cause for which the United States and her allies are fighting is as unqualified as that of any one; and if anything could shake my faith it would be the spirit of frenzied intolerance, masking under the name of patriotism, which seems to be sweeping the country," Becker wrote to Professor W. A. Hammond of Cornell.[9] In 1920 Becker contributed to *The Nation* an ironic essay directed against those who had excluded elected Socialists from the New York Assembly and Congressman Berger from the United States House of Representatives, partly as a reaction against Socialist opposition to the war effort. Becker suggested that, in the name of preserving government against liberty, the American Legion should form "a sanitary cordon" around Mr. Berger's district in Milwaukee, Wisconsin, and sweep it into Lake Michigan.[10] Becker's irony, however, was in this instance curiously ineffective as literature; it was too diffuse and gentle to be good Swift. Becker had not yet learned to hate, and when he did it would be Hitler and not the Lusk Committee that would instruct him.

Indeed, as Becker prepared to enter the waste lands of the 20's and 30's, it was more in the guise of a Lewis Carroll than a Jonathan Swift. At least, this is how he began, as the author of an allegory entitled "The King of the Beasts," which he dedicated to his son, Frederick DeWitt Becker. This allegory, written partly in verse and partly in prose, was the only full-length work that Becker ever attempted in the realm of "creative literature." Probably it represented an attempt on his part to attain the purity and genuineness of the artist, which he had commented upon in writing to Dodd of the hypocrisy of public life and the selfishness of politicians. Probably also it represented an attempt to regain a lost innocence. "The King of the Beasts" tells of how "Little Erasmus" falls asleep and dreams; in his dreams he travels among the Beasts of the Earth and asks along the way pointed, innocent questions that expose the pretenses and follies of the Beasts. The central theme of Becker's allegory is the question of why, if all Beasts have force and virtue, they persist in fighting. To which query

[8] Frank H. Hodder to Carl Becker, Lawrence, Kansas, April 22, 1917.
[9] Carl Becker to W. A. Hammond, Ithaca, New York, April 17, 1918.
[10] "A Little More Grape, Captain Bragg," *The Nation,* CX (February 28, 1920), 260-261.

the Donkey replies: "Why? Well, why not? They fight to prove that it is so. The strong fight to prove that no one has anything to fear from their virtuous force, and the weak fight to prove that the force of the virtue which is in them will always triumph over all obstacles. It has always been so." Now, however, things will be different, for a "Great Council of Force and Virtue" has been organized. At least this is what the Donkey thinks, but Little Erasmus asks, "Do you really think so?" Chapter headings such as "The Valley of Illusions," "The Council of Force and Virtue," "The Law of the Beasts," revealed Becker's intent, as does an ironic reference to the "League of Free Beasts" who are teaching the "lionly art of self-determination."[11]

"The King of the Beasts" was rejected by several publishers, and Carl Van Doren explained to Becker that the narrative element did not stand out sufficiently to carry it off.[12] Actually, the manuscript errs in style, which is sentimental where it should be savage, and in structure, for it is clearly lacking in organic unity — the transitions from verse to prose seem warranted only by the limits of Becker's limerick-making powers. Also, in comparison to a work such as James Branch Cabell's *Jurgen*, "The King of the Beasts" betrays a skimpiness of thought in its references to contemporary events; a paragraph in *Jurgen*, which is so much more universal in intent, tells us more about the World War and Wilson than all of Becker's allegory. The verse in "The King of the Beasts" did not represent all of Becker's poetic labors, however; in addition there are some lost, unpublished sonnets which Van Doren said suffered from "a certain flatness." They were "excellent verse rather than good poetry," he tactfully added, but he wondered if prose wouldn't have been better.[13] Becker took the hint, and in time the writing of interpretative essays would resume. In 1922 he published his *The Declaration of Independence,* but after this the book-making process in Becker gave way completely for many years.

It would, however, be a mistake to regard Becker entirely as an alienated man in the 1920's and 1930's, a frustrated creative artist forced back reluctantly to think once more about the tiresome topics of history and politics. The theme of alienation is important; but it is also important to remember that it was in the 1920's and 1930's that Becker really became a force to be reckoned with in his profession and that his distinctive talents acquired appreciable public recognition. In the midst of this growing public awareness, however, Becker

[11] Carl Becker, "The King of the Beasts," MS.
[12] Carl Van Doren to Carl Becker, New York, January 6, 1923.
[13] Carl Van Doren to Carl Becker, Urbana, Illinois, March 13, 1922.

remained privately apathetic. "He was doomed for many years to a kind of apathy, compounded of emotional dejection and physical tiredness," Gershoy recalls. "He was moody; and discouragement sometimes vented itself a little sharply. Of vital abundant energy it would be a mockery to speak."[14]

Twice Becker sought escape from this personal dejection in travel, once in the summer of 1924 when he traveled in Europe, and again in 1935 when he, Mrs. Becker, and their son sailed through the Panama Canal en route to and returning from Stanford University in California, where he gave the West Lectures.[15] The trip to Europe in 1924 was undertaken in company with Wallace Notestein and the Hulls, and it came as part of an attempt to recover from one of his most severe illnesses. It came also at a time when Mrs. Becker was forced to remain at home to care for her daughter Edith. There was something a little sad about the only trip that Becker ever took to Europe; it had come too late, he thought, and he (and Mrs. Becker) worried about his lack of interest in things. He kept a diary, however, on board the S. S. *Columbia,* in which he made meticulous observations about the number of miles traveled each day, barometer readings, etc., for his son. He enjoyed Notestein's enthusiasm as if "he was on his first trip over," but he couldn't share it. Only Edinburgh, where he stayed for three days, excited him; he noted that "tea was a great British institution"; he attended an Anglo-American Historical Conference in London which he found "pleasant but boring." On July 18 he visited Samuel Eliot Morison, then Harmsworth Professor of American History at Oxford, a position that Morison wanted Becker to fill someday — and which could have been Becker's in 1935 if he had only felt disposed to accept it.[16] Oxford seemed opulent to Becker — "these Oxford dons certainly live well, but rather stupid conversation." Then in August he was off to Paris and Versailles, about which he made brief, tourist-like comments in his diary.

As the trip wore on, however, some of Becker's poor spirits passed. In York on July 6, he had felt well enough to record the atrocious behavior of an American member of Congress, a "typical hustler," who sat in the lobby "talking in a loud voice, bragging about the Ameri-

[14] Gershoy, Introduction to *Progress and Power*, xxiii, xxiv.

[15] Carl Becker to Mabel Perry, undated letter telling of the voyage to California in the spring of 1935.

[16] See a confidential inquiry from Felix Frankfurter to Carl Becker, Cambridge, Massachusetts, January 9, 1935. Becker declined on the grounds that he had never taught American history and that he couldn't afford to move to Oxford.

cans and giving vent to his dissatisfactions with most things Eng-lish."[17] On July 27, 1924, he wrote to his wife that he was feeling "well enough physically" but that he still had "little zest for life. I think my mind is slower in recovering from the effects of the operation than my body. . . . I am apathetic, I dislike the idea of working, or reading anything serious, even the talk of people wearies me, and I am easily bored with everything."[18] But Paris changed much of this, temporarily at least. By August 31 in Paris Becker felt enough zest to compose some doggerel verse. "When I am in Paree / I will be glad / And feel that I am free / To be as bad / As I know how to be / I freely drink and eat / I sleep and eat / I sleep and then / I eat and then I treat / My-self again / Perchance to something neat."[19] Nearly all of which was poetic license. Then came the return home, to Cornell and to work.

Becker was too moderate or rational a man to retreat from pain and apathy into sensuality. Instead, in this period he found relief in com-posing short essays, which did not tax his strength too greatly, and took comfort in an ever-widening circle of friends, as well as in his growing reputation as the most unusual talent among American his-torians. His friendships with Robinson, Turner, Dodd, Notestein, Hod-der, Burr, and Hull remained alive, and to this group of friends he added Felix Frankfurter, Harold J. Laski, Charles A. Beard, and in the 1930's Max Lerner and Thurman Arnold.

Probably the best explanation of why Becker and his work were so well received by other historians was given, unintentionally, by C. H. Van Tyne in a letter to Becker, in which he praised Becker's *Declara-tion of Independence* as the "greatest intellectual treat" he had had in years. *"Perhaps I can be all the more generous in my appreciations of it because it is so entirely the kind of thing I cannot do,"* Van Tyne candidly explained, and he went on to add that Becker's "philosophical interpretation and charm of penetration" elevated Becker far above most members of the guild.[20] Also, Becker was too generous in his sympathies to be linked *entirely* with any single faction or school of thought within the American Historical Association. While his own point of view was well-known, he got along well with practically everyone save Homer Hockett and James Truslow Adams. "I see that you are both a classic and a 'new historian,'" his friend Hodder teased

[17] Diary. All the above quotations are taken from a small diary, which Becker kept only in the summer of 1924.

[18] Carl Becker to Maude Becker, July 27, 1924.

[19] Diary.

[20] C. H. Van Tyne to Carl Becker, Ann Arbor, Michigan, November 11, 1927. Italics added.

him. "I note with pleasure that while very unorthodox in your methods you get on with the orthodox historians very nicely."[21]

Becker was no dogmatic partisan, "no joiner of movements," as Gershoy has emphasized.[22] He was, however, a joiner of honorary societies and academies, and he never declined an honorary degree from any university. Largely on the strength of his weakest book, *The United States: An Experiment in Democracy,* he was made a Fellow of the Royal Historical Society;[23] and he was soon honored by election to the American Academy of Arts and Sciences, the American Philosophical Society, and several similar organizations. In 1932 Yale University conferred the honorary degree of Doctor of Letters upon Becker; in 1938 the University of Rochester did the same; and in 1939 Columbia University belatedly followed Yale's lead.[24] Becker was quite pleased by these recognitions, but he chose to conceal his pleasure beneath a mask of humor. "Nick Butler certainly does an expert job in the gown and cap, which makes him look like a medieval inquisitor," he confided to Merle Curti. "It was a great show. . . ."[25]

Throughout the 1920's and 1930's Becker had constantly to tell himself that it was a great show; and all the praise of students, former teachers, and discriminating contemporaries was needed at times to convince Becker that the game was worth the candle. If Becker lacked the strength or inclination for prolonged archival researches, his lectures and seminars were capable of stimulating some of his graduate students to do original research within the frame of reference he had outlined.[26] Leo Gershoy, Louis Gottschalk, Geoffrey Brunn, Robert Palmer, and many others began to produce books in the field of French history where Becker himself remained relatively unproductive. Becker took pleasure in their books and laughed when he was told, as often he was, that he was their ultimate author.[27] He enjoyed the academic

[21] Frank H. Hodder to Carl Becker, Lawrence, Kansas, July 5, 1920.

[22] Introduction to *Progress and Power,* xxvi.

[23] H. E. Malden, Secretary of Royal Historical Society, to Carl Becker, London, February 3, 1921; March 17, 1921; April 15, 1921.

[24] See Nicholas Murray Butler to Carl Becker, New York, March 6, 1939.

[25] Carl Becker to Merle Curti, Ithaca, New York, June 10, 1939.

[26] Ernest G. Schwiebert to Phil Snyder, Baltimore, Maryland, February 27, 1956.

[27] In this study I have chosen for the most part to avoid discussing the "influence" of Becker. There is, obviously, no "Becker school" among living historians; and Becker's students seem held together only by a common loyalty to the master, a common subject matter (usually eighteenth-century France) and a common concern with lucid exposition. Still Becker did continue to read his students' manuscripts long after they had left Cornell. Leo Gershoy dedicated his *The French Revolution and Napoleon* (New York, 1933) to Becker, thanking him for "his patient and meticulous criticism and his many admirable suggestions." Louis

game, placing Gottschalk at Chicago, for instance, (when Chicago really wanted Becker) and later holding his breath as Gottschalk related the most recent antics of Robert Hutchins and Mortimer Adler, both of whom Becker disliked.[28] But most of all Becker enjoyed the companionship of his students and treasured their letters, such as the one written by Brunn upon the completion of three years' graduate study under Becker. "Methods are a tricky business," Brunn wrote, "and don't always function when transplanted; but if I can retain something of the spirit and philosophy of teaching that I have come to know under your direction, I shall not worry about the future."[29]

The appreciation of students was supplemented by continued praise from Turner, Haskins, and Robinson; indeed, one of the few intellectual activities of the 1920's in which Becker was totally *engagé* lay in the writing of his essay, "Frederick Jackson Turner." The years 1925 and 1926 witnessed a long and intimate correspondence between Turner and Becker in which the master revealed himself more painstakingly to Becker than he ever did to anyone else — so much so that phrases from Turner's lengthy letters of self-analysis continually crop up in Becker's finished essay. Turner's modesty while sitting for his portrait by Becker remained as strong as ever — and he kept insisting always on his debt to *his* teachers, such as W. F. Allen, and to his students: "I was blessed with an historical progeny of which I am proud (C. L. B. among the large stars!). . . ."[30]

Becker teased Turner about his being celebrated in a book on *Masters of the Social Sciences* — "Not that there is any such thing as a Science of history, but that is no matter, Cordially yours, Carl

---

Gottschalk did the same with his *Jean Paul Marat, A Study in Radicalism* (New York, 1927), and in his *The Era of the French Revolution* (New York, 1929) he acknowledged that he owed not only his interest in the study of the French Revolution but much of his philosophy of history to Becker. Gottschalk's philosophy of history, or more accurately of historical method, is contained in his *Understanding History* (New York, 1950). For the most part, however, Becker's students have written little about either the meaning or method of history. Readers interested in pursuing Becker's influence further should consult the contributions by Geoffrey Brunn, Leo Gershoy, Louis Gottschalk, and Robert R. Palmer to *Carl Becker's Heavenly City Revisited*, where for the most part they loyally defend Becker against recent criticisms of his handling of the *philosophes*.

[28] See, for example, Carl Becker to Louis Gottschalk, Ithaca, New York, April 19, 1944. "I hope for your sake and for everyone's sake something checks Hutchins. It looks to me as if he will, if he has his way, go far to wreck the U. of C. I should think the best men, apart from those who are within sight of retirement, would be looking for jobs elsewhere."

[29] Geoffrey Brunn to Carl Becker, Ithaca, New York, September 15, 1927.

[30] Frederick Jackson Turner to Carl Becker, Madison, Wisconsin, November 23, 1925.

Becker."[31] Turner replied in a vein that showed he had in his last years recovered somewhat from the "scientism" of his youth, which may help the reader to understand Turner's subsequent appreciation of Becker's presidential address before the American Historical Association: "No, there's no science of history. Sometimes I doubt if there is a real science (in the sense that cuts out history) of anything. Nuff sed. Yours cordially, Frederick Jackson Turner."[32] Nowhere is there any evidence of the effects of World War One upon the friendship of Turner and Becker. Any strains that might have been caused by Becker's loss of faith were concealed, and Becker's brilliant essay on Turner was a labor of love. Turner thoroughly appreciated the essay, all the while protesting his unworthiness.[33] Charles Homer Haskins, Max Farrand, and Felix Frankfurter admired Becker's achievement tremendously.[34]

Frankfurter, however, wondered if Becker hadn't idealized his former teacher. Becker agreed wholeheartedly, "We would none of us be much good as teachers if our students didn't idealize us a little. Even my students perceive some wonderful thing I have done for them; when as a matter of fact all I do is to sit about and look wise and tell them they can do more than they think they can — often more than I think they can myself. Then they have a habit of going ahead and doing it. Without our best illusions life would be a poor thing. Illusion is after all the best reality; and truly the most convenient form of error."[35] For Becker himself the illusion that life is worth living and history worth writing about continued to be nurtured by a wide range of friends and admirers; most of their praise was directed at Becker's presidential address before the American Historical Association and at his *The Heavenly City*. Meanwhile Becker was finding what pleasure he could in the fact that his audience now included H. L. Mencken, Carl Sandburg, and hundreds of thousands of high school students.

If Becker did not retreat from pain or apathy into sensuality, still less did he retreat into spirituality. In 1928 when Becker visited Iowa,

[31] Carl Becker to Frederick Jackson Turner, Ithaca, New York, February 11, 1926.

[32] Frederick Jackson Turner to Carl Becker, Madison, Wisconsin, February 13, 1926.

[33] Frederick Jackson Turner to Carl Becker, Madison, Wisconsin, May 14, 1927.

[34] Charles Homer Haskins to Carl Becker, Cambridge, Massachusetts, May 23, 1927. Max Farrand to Carl Becker, New York, April 23, 1927. Felix Frankfurter to Carl Becker, Cambridge, Massachusetts, May, 1927.

[35] Carl Becker to Felix Frankfurter, Ithaca, New York, June 2, 1927.

which he described as "the very heart of the Methodist menace," he was delighted to find Methodism "gasping for breath." "Most of my relatives," he confided to a friend, "(except those who are over 80), although brought up in the faith, never enter the church except for weddings or funerals. Another generation and the thing will be dead." Four days in Iowa were enough — the atmosphere of "the reputable and the platitudinous" nearly suffocated Becker. "A good lady of 80 years told me today that she would rather bury her granddaughter than see her smoke a cigaret and that if Al Smith were elected she wouldn't wish to live any longer. Dodd of Chicago thinks Smith has a fair chance."[36]

Where religion was concerned, Becker's attitude in the 1920's and 1930's hardened considerably and approached the point of public intolerance. As his thoughts became more pessimistic and relativistic, he ran into trouble with religious reviewers, especially Catholic ones. Such trouble was nothing new; as early as 1919 the *Catholic World* had shown its distress over the alleged flippancy of Becker's *The Eve of the Revolution*.[37] In the 1930's, however, the trouble was intensified as Becker's writings tended more and more to dwell upon contemporary ideologies. Here the charge of flippancy gave way to the charge of impiety; the Catholic journal *America* even commented that Becker's extremely lucid *The Heavenly City* must have been written by a man "living in a fog."[38] This was going a bit far, and the usually amiable Becker replied in kind. In reviewing a book about Communism, Becker noted that Communism has a theological method of saving the world and he compared the Bolsheviks with the Church Fathers — "their ideology is the same" — and even their doctrinal divisions sound alike.[39] More to the point, he dismissed a Catholic history of Europe as having been seriously limited by the "Catholic bias" of its authors; and he sardonically concluded that "in understanding the world in which we live, it helps us little to be told that another one, now irretrievably lost, was better."[40]

Clearly the skepticism of the 1920's had brought out certain characteristics long latent in Becker's mind; as his own predisposition to compassion gave way to cynicism, he came, briefly, within the orbit of

---

[36] Carl Becker to E. R. B. Willis, Waterloo, Iowa, June 13, 1928.

[37] CIX (June, 1919), 405-406.

[38] XLVIII (January 14, 1933), 365.

[39] "The Writer in Soviet Russia," Review of Max Eastman, *Artists in Uniform, The Nation*, CXXXVIII (May 30, 1934), 624-625.

[40] Review of Edward Eyre, ed., *European Civilization: Its Origin and Development, American Historical Review*, XLIV (January, 1939), 346-348.

America's foremost cynic, H. L. Mencken. The first contact between the two came about because Harry Elmer Barnes had bragged to Mencken of the excellence of Becker's essay on historical facts. Mencken wanted it, sight unseen, for the *American Mercury*.[41] Becker declined on the grounds that the paper wasn't ready for publication — he never published it — but he sent Mencken a copy of his "On Being a Professor," which Mencken found "very amusing."[42] Mencken never persuaded Becker to contribute to the *American Mercury*, although Becker was a regular reader and admirer of Mencken's journal. In March, 1937, when Becker, at the suggestion of W. Stull Holt, visited Johns Hopkins to give two public lectures, he and Mencken finally met and got on splendidly. "What a man! I had long wanted to meet him," Mencken wrote after spending an evening with Becker.[43] The two apparently never met again, but one of the last letters Becker lived to receive in 1945 was from the ailing Mencken, who was delighted to find Becker still alive; he invited Becker to visit him once more in Baltimore. The letter revealed a Mencken who was a dated caricature of himself — "There was a time when I thought of launching a campaign for its [profanity's] revival, but I am now 100 old and weary."[44]

If Dionysius admired Becker, Becker was probably more comfortable in being loved by the homespun Apollo of liberal democracy, Carl Sandburg. Sandburg admired Becker's *Progress and Power* inordinately; but while Gershoy had seen fit to compare it to Condorcet's *Esquisse*, Sandburg saw certain analogies between it and Lincoln's writings. "It has much the flow of a long meditative poem, with heavy shadows crossed by a few light streaks that you fasten with grand certainty. The somberness is kin to much of Lincoln's, along with his light mockery of 'vents lacking gravity and precision,' " he wrote to Becker.[45] Lincoln's somberness and his refusal to take all events seriously had an emotional profundity and a lack of artfulness not to be found in Becker's writings; Sandburg's comparison did, however, indicate that Becker was still regarded as a friend, however critical, of liberal democracy.

It was as a friend of liberal democracy that Becker wrote two high school textbooks, *Modern History*, first published in 1931, and the *Story of Civilization*, written in collaboration with Frederick Duncalf

---

[41] H. L. Mencken to Carl Becker, Baltimore, Maryland, August 18, 1930.
[42] H. L. Mencken to Carl Becker, Baltimore, Maryland, September 4, 1931.
[43] H. L. Mencken quoted by Kent Roberts Greenfield to Carl Becker, Baltimore, Maryland, April 13, 1937.
[44] H. L. Mencken to Carl Becker, Baltimore, Maryland, March 16, 1945.
[45] Carl Sandburg to Carl Becker, [somewhere in Texas], December 7, 1937.

and first published in 1940. Sidney Fay described Becker's *Modern History* as a "most happy combination of Will Rogers, Alice in Wonderland, and the most serious and solemn books on history (like my own for instance). . . ."[46] The book had as its themes the growth of scientific knowledge, economic interdependence, humane feelings and democratic ideas, and nationalism; clearly the materials were selected with an eye to the present, and the excellence of the text lay in Becker's ability to select well from a mass of materials, as the *American Journal of Sociology* pointed out.[47] The *New Republic* commented on "its fine spirit of impartiality and detachment,"[48] and by and large the *Catholic Historical Review* agreed.[49] The *Catholic Historical Review* noted, however, that Becker seemed a bit anti-German in his account of the origins of World War One; Harry Elmer Barnes, on the other hand, wrote "I am sure that I could not have put the revisionist case half as convincingly."[50] Becker's textbook, apparently, pleased everyone, except for a few right-wing critics such as George Sokolsky. There are in The Becker Papers a good many letters from appreciative students that show their conversion to history because of Becker's *Modern History*. Certainly school boards and teachers in the high schools liked it, and he was well rewarded financially.

In the 1930's the surviving Beckers in Iowa were hard hit by the Depression; not so Carl Becker, because the *Modern History* provided him with a large measure of financial independence. His income tax returns, for example, for the year 1936 show a salary of $6,300 plus royalties on the *Modern History* of $5,581; the royalties from his splendid collection of essays, *Everyman His Own Historian*, for that year were $17.98.[51] Largely on the proceeds from his *Modern History*, Becker could indulge his taste for new cars — henceforth there was often a new Dodge in the Becker family — and speed was one of the few excesses or enthusiasms that Becker allowed himself during the 1930's. Becker was not so world weary that he could refrain from happily relating to his colleague, Professor George Marcham, the details of his mastery of the machine.[52] Leo Gershoy tells how Becker

[46] Sidney Fay to Robert O. Williams of Silver Burdett and Company, Cambridge, Massachusetts, June 24, 1929.

[47] XXXVII (January, 1932), 689.

[48] LXVIII (September 9, 1931), 107.

[49] XVII (October, 1931), 351-352.

[50] Harry Elmer Barnes to Carl Becker, Tarrytown, New York, May 21, 1931.

[51] Carl Becker, Income Tax Returns for 1936. A copy in The Becker Papers.

[52] A conversation between Professor George Marcham and the author, Ithaca, New York, July 9, 1957.

would sit behind the wheel, talking while driving, resembling a synthesis of Socrates and Barney Oldfield.[53]

Behind Becker's new-found love of speed and the automobile, a psychoanalytic biographer might detect an acting out of a phantasy in which an ailing, frustrated man exercised his will to power triumphantly, or perhaps he might find a death wish. Eros versus Thanatos is, however, too sophisticated a concept for our present purposes. In all seriousness we might yet see Becker's interest in speed and the mastery of a complex machine as the physical parallel of a growing intellectual preoccupation with the movement of social bodies, with their velocity, and with the social significance of the machine itself. Becker's interest in a "social physics" took on new dimensions in the 1920's and 1930's partly as a result of his interest in the first really modern social physicists, the *philosophes,* as a subject for historical inquiry; but also because of his interest in the direction that liberal democracy might take in a period of crisis. Was liberalism only a way station, was progress an illusion, would man continue to master the machine or would he, too, become an automaton? These are some of the questions that Becker raised in his essays, in *Progress and Power* and in *New Liberties for Old.* Just by asking them, Becker showed himself to be in the tradition of the late Henry Adams, for these were the questions that Adams had raised.

Lewis Mumford, reviewing Becker's *Progress and Power,* compared Becker's style to William James' and his thought to Henry Adams'. Becker had tried to work out a historical scale for progress in his book, had shown himself, like Adams, to be aware of the opposition of power to other instruments of intelligence, and had seen, like Adams, that "regress and power" no less than "progress and power" was a fit subject for inquiry. While Mumford may have pressed his analogy a bit far in comparing the time scales of Adams and Becker, he rightly saw the obvious parallel between the two men, their joint concern with the velocity and acceleration of movement in social bodies.[54]

Surely it was not by accident that Henry Adams came to interest Becker greatly in the 1920's and 1930's taking the place during these years of Becker's patron saint Jefferson in some respects. It might be protested that Adams was more interested in a philosophy of history, Becker more concerned — in this phase of his intellectual activity — with a philosophy of contemporary politics. Yet Becker in his review of

---

[53] Introduction to *Progress and Power,* xxv-xxvi.
[54] *American Journal of Sociology,* XLII (November, 1936), 429.

The Education of Henry Adams (1919) had shown that Adams' concern with the philosophy of history sprang in part from a personal interest in politics, that Adams' interest in the velocity of historical forces came from a keen, almost abnormal sense of personal failure to master or even to comprehend the political forces of his own day and time.[55] What a comedown for the descendant of two Presidents to be offered a consulate in Guatemala! Was Adams responsible, was his education at fault, or had history swept him aside — a useless man in an age of dynamos? Becker himself had no family history to goad him to despair at his own impotence; by the standards of *his* family he had done well, had even seen his father become reconciled to his son's vocational choice.[56] But as a son of the frontier and an intellectual descendant of Turner, Becker had, in a sense, a family history — that of liberal democracy — sufficient to trouble him deeply when he compared the present with the past. Becker, like Adams, tended at times to conceal himself where the "scribble-mad" scribes of democracy scornfully depicted by Nietzsche would have rushed into print with what we might call confessional literature. Like Adams, Becker tended to regard himself with almost perverse modesty, "as of no more significance than a chance deposit on the surface of the world."[57] Like Adams, Becker had a reputation for aristocratic standoffishness and for being something of a recluse — both men wore a mask of sardonic humor — but beneath the mask, Becker, no less than the Adams he understood so well, was "seriously seeking for the significance of his own life and the life of humanity."[58]

Adams had sought for the significance of life, according to the methods of Buckle and Darwin; he had believed that laws of evolution could be discovered amidst the bewildering mass of historical data, laws that would reduce chaos to order. Adams' hope had been the most ambitious expression of ideas entertained by the most distinguished galaxy of American historical thinkers; Andrew Dixon White, John W. Burgess, Frederick Jackson Turner, Woodrow Wilson, and James Harvey Robinson had all looked in vain for a science of history. Such a science would have been both ethical and descriptive: what our duties were would have become clear once we knew our station. This

[55] *Everyman His Own Historian,* 143-161. Reprinted from the *American Historical Review,* XXIV (April, 1919). Henry Adams could not think of success for an Adams except in terms of politics, Becker wrote to Charles A. Beard, Ithaca, New York, May 10, 1943.

[56] Jessie Becker to Phil L. Snyder, Waterloo, Iowa, November 24, 1955.

[57] "The Education of Henry Adams," *Everyman His Own Historian,* 143.

[58] "Henry Adams," *Encyclopaedia of the Social Sciences,* I, 431-432.

"historicism" has been described in Chapter Four; what is important here is to note that by the 1930's the historicist search had been fairly well abandoned. Evolution was still discussed, but relativity was the latest word from science; and the belief in the existence of historical laws was left not for liberals such as Carl Becker but for Marxists such as Louis Hacker. The liberal historian's signal of surrender was made in Becker's "Everyman His Own Historian," and the laying down of arms came in Beard's "Written History as an Act of Faith." Both men showed some confusion concerning the scientific status of historical facts, but both gladly gave up the Science of History.[59]

Where politics are concerned, it is necessary to explore how Becker in the 1920's and 1930's shared the late Henry Adams' interest in the scientific measurement of man and his velocity. The most obvious feature of such an interest is that it was not religious — as Adams knew, the belief in special acts of Providence is antithetical to the search for a social physics. Adams knew, too, that a Social Physics or Science of History would produce screams of anguish from those individuals or groups who were to be informed of their loss of momentum or of their growing obsolescence.[60] Still Adams had hoped to be objective in his reckonings; the law of entropy, for example, was much in evidence *in* the data of history, *if* one took the early Middle Ages as a fixed point from which to measure the dissipation of energy that was such an obvious feature of modern life. In *Mont-Saint-Michel and Chartres* Adams conjured up an image of medieval man most unlike the men of the nineteenth and twentieth centuries, a man blessed with a unity of thought — Catholic metaphysics — and of feeling — love of the Virgin Mary — resulting in a unity of action — the "holistic" architecture of the medieval cathedral in which every detail was an integrated part of the whole.[61] James Truslow Adams spoke of Henry Adams' work as "the clearest and most concentrated light" thrown on the medieval picture; Becker replied that, while this was dubious, the book did throw considerable light on the mind of Henry Adams.[62]

---

[59] See also Beard's highly critical review of Arnold Toynbee, *A Study of History, American Historical Review,* XL (January, 1935), 307-309; XLV (April, 1940), 593-594. Toynbee, according to Beard, made Spengler into a sciolist; still he couldn't succeed because of the nature of his subject and the faults of his method. See, too, Beard's Preface to Brooks Adams, *The Law of Civilization and Decay* (New York, 1943).

[60] Adams, "The Tendency of History," American Historical Association, *Annual Report, 1894,* 17-23.

[61] New York, 1904.

[62] James Truslow Adams quoted by Becker, "Henry Adams Once More," *Every-*

The plight of Henry Adams and his family, Becker pointed out in reviewing Adams' *The Degradation of the Democratic Dogma,* was that they had lost faith, first in God, and then in Science. Deprived of these two props, they had lost faith in progress — Becker never asked whether they had faith in man, but the historian knows that they partook of no religion of humanity, partly because of their Puritan awareness of man's depravity. In Henry Adams this doctrine of personal depravity was turned into a philosophy of public decline, much like that later worked out by Oswald Spengler. Becker, while much aware of the apparent waning of liberal democracy, refused to surrender to Adams' Science of doom. Henry Adams' fault, Becker felt, was that Adams, before losing faith in the Science of History and in his own ability to find a cosmiclike necessity in the affairs of men, had claimed too much for his Science. Despite his own interest in "social physics," Becker felt compelled to remind admirers of Henry Adams that the historian deals with changes in human beings, not in physics. Even if progress had given way to regress, the "ash-heap" foreseen by Adams for man was so far remote that no immediate preparation for it was necessary on our part; Becker made it clear that Henry Adams' Absolute End was as distasteful to him as any Christian talk about the Absolute had been. Man and his values, Becker countered, were finite in structure and in meaning. "It is the function of history, as I understand it," Becker insisted, "to deal with this [finite] meaning and these values as they are revealed in the thoughts and actions of men."[63] This was Becker's usual, modest procedure, in which he resembled Henry Adams the practicing historian but not Henry Adams the philosopher of history. Sometimes, however, Becker felt more cosmic, and the more cosmic he felt, the more he resembled Henry Adams. If we tried to see progress "an an omniscient intelligence indifferent to human values might estimate it," Becker wrote in his essay on "Progress," "then progress and the very existence of man himself become negligible and meaningless. In such a perspective we should see the whole life of man on earth as a mere momentary ripple on the surface of one of the minor planets in one of the minor stellar systems."[64]

Here, in a way, is the central dilemma in Becker's thought in the 1920's and 1930's — how to study, sympathetically, the values of man,

man His Own Historian, 163. Reprinted from the *Saturday Review of Literature,* IX (April 8, 1933).

[63] *American Historical Review,* XXV (April, 1920). Reprinted in *Detachment and the Writing of History,* 34.

[64] "Progress," *Encyclopedia of the Social Sciences,* XII (1934), 499.

as if they had value, when all the time one is reminded of how transitory and meaningless life seems to be. What does the human drama matter if there is no divine audience to applaud or condemn our actions? Is posterity an adequate substitute for God, and what if posterity is as indifferent to us and *our* progress as the universe is to man? These are some of the questions that come to mind when one reads Becker, and one can more readily understand his theoretical and practical difficulties against this background.

The most revealing of texts in this connection is probably Becker's *Progress and Power,* in which he raised grand questions only to bog down in trivial answers. *Progress and Power* was published in 1936, after having been delivered as a series of lectures at Stanford University in 1935 at the request of the Raymond Fred West Memorial Foundation. Loren Petry, Leo Gershoy, Max Lerner, and Robert Palmer had all read the manuscript before its publication, and Becker later confided to Max Lerner that the manuscript in its very first draft had read like a tract for the times.[65] What was striking about its final form, however, was that, according to Louis Gottschalk, it seemed as detached as if Becker had written it from Mt. Olympus.[66] Certainly Becker had refused to abandon his sense of proportion; even the question of whether material interests or ideas were more important failed to stir him as it did many of his contemporaries. "I do not know how men can try to satisfy material needs without first thinking about them, or how they can think about satisfying such needs unless the needs already exist,"[67] he explained. Man, according to Becker, is not a creature designed to illustrate an economic or biological law of history; nor is he the child of a divinity or the reflection of an abstract idea. What then is man, and what can be said on his behalf?

Becker knew, far better than Henry Adams, the importance of subjective feeling in determining his answer to such questions. His own answer was quite candid — by his personal standards very little could be said for man. My private preferences, Becker wrote, come under such labels as Liberty, Equality, Fraternity, Humanity, Toleration, Reason; my aversions are symbolized by words such as Authority, Compulsion, Obedience, Regimentation, Uniformity, Standardization.[68] By recreating the universe in terms of his private values and aversions, Becker knew that he, perhaps like Henry Adams, could more easily

[65] Carl Becker to Max Lerner, Ithaca, New York, October 5, 1935.
[66] Louis Gottschalk to Carl Becker, Chicago, March 29, 1937.
[67] *Progress and Power* (Palo Alto, 1936 edition), ix.
[68] *Ibid.,* 10-14.

come to grips with the question of the nature and trajectory of man. Still this wasn't what Becker wanted. "What can be said on behalf of the Human Race? Judged by my private values, very little can be said in its behalf." This would, however, be true at *any* time in history; and for those who believed in their own infallibility, or in the Absolute Idea, the Dialectic, or the Judgment Day, as processes that would validate their private preferences this would be sufficient; "a cheap ticket to salvation," Becker called it, "the price is merely that they should dismiss to oblivion the great majority for failing to enter their clean but sparsely furnished Heaven."[69]

Becker was conveniently forgetting the occasions when he excluded the majority from his sparsely furnished heaven; and he was forgetting his earlier confidence that history would some day enthrone his Turnerian-Jeffersonian-Wilsonian biases. In 1935, at least in writing *Progress and Power*, he wanted to arrive at an objective definition of man — one that would, as he said, include everyone from the Hittites to Hitler — and then to ask whether man had really progressed. Becker announced that he would, therefore, for his present purposes, "dismiss all ethical and moral *judgments*, forget about the final or relatively good end toward which man may be moving, and endeavour to estimate human progress in terms of what man has in fact done, and of the means that have enabled him to do it. . . ."[70] Such were his intentions, but if Becker's writings on historiography and his exposé of the limits of historical objectivity have *any* meaning, they indicate that not even Becker could ascend Mt. Olympus to such a height.

Becker got only to the point where he could talk with reasonable detachment about the means of progress. His lectures on "Tools and the Man," "The Sword and the Pen," "Instruments of Precision," betray a technological preoccupation. Power, one of Becker's private aversions (at least Force and Compulsion appeared on Becker's black list), had, he admitted, played a major rôle in human progress. In fact, since Becker had decided to make no moral judgments about man, he occupied himself almost exclusively with the power of man's tools, which deceived some into thinking that Becker had been seduced by technocratic dreams. Certainly in his deference to facts rather than to dreams, to "fact finding" as being more efficient than "fault finding" (which the machines seem to know), Becker lent support to this view.[71] In *Progress*

---

[69] *Ibid.*, 13-14.

[70] *Ibid.*, 14.

[71] *Ibid.*, 94. But see "Liberalism — A Way Station," *Everyman His Own Historian,* 99, where his hostility to the conformity of the Machine Age is clear, as is his fear

and Power, he was either being neutral and objective in his descriptions, or he was a technocrat, temporarily at least.

"Of social progress, ethical progress, he tells us nothing," one critic complained.[72] The truth is that Becker in trying to transcend his own liberal democratic bias succeeded only in becoming bland, and in writing but a minor treatise on the sociology of power. When he had got through his detached explorations and had descended from Mt. Olympus, he was little the wiser. One man's progress remained — perhaps still remains — another man's poison; and nothing Carl Becker or Henry Adams or Karl Marx can do will change this truth. Becker still held to the idea of progress partly because he wanted to (it is *the* religion of the secular liberal) and partly out of habit (habit, he wrote once, might save democracy,[73] and hence our faith in progress). Where the idea of progress was concerned he wrote: "Our behaviour is not unlike that of certain Protestant sects whose habit of going to Church has outlived their religious convictions: we have made a fair recovery from the Absolute, but its after-effects linger in our emotions, like an irritating cough in the bronchial tubes after influenza."[74]

In *Progress and Power* Becker's humor helped conceal his convictions, but neither his humor nor his style — whether it was Lincolnian or Jamesian — could conceal the comparative paucity of his thoughts about man and his tools, if Becker were compared either to Karl Marx with his emphasis on the class basis of technology, or to Henry Adams with his discourse on the metaphysical implications of the dynamo. Where Marx had seen an intricate dialectical development and Adams had seen a frightening regress from cultural unity, Becker saw mainly a matter-of-fact progress, although clearly Becker was worried whether this trend toward material efficiency might not some day make man the slave of his tools. Where Marx and Adams had seen evolution, Becker under the influence of a host of thinkers from William Graham Sumner to Alfred North Whitehead was most impressed by the relativity of evolution.[75] All things evolve; the evolution or velocity of one social body, however, is not to be measured in absolute terms from a fixed point but in relation to changes taking place in other social bodies.

---

that machines will kill eccentricity, idle curiosity, and other desirable qualities of mind.

[72] Wilson O. Wallis, "Progress and Power," *Journal of Social Philosophy,* II (July, 1937), 338-346.

[73] "Some Generalities That Still Glitter," *Yale Review,* XXIX (June, 1940). Reprinted in *New Liberties for Old,* 124-151.

[74] *Progress and Power,* 10.

[75] Becker, "Books That Changed Our Minds," *New Republic,* XCVII (December 7, 1938), 135.

Also, the judgments about this relativity are in themselves relative, Becker thought, since no observer could step outside of the process he was describing. A very clear implication of this, although Becker never developed it, was that we might doubt the legitimacy of Henry Adams' selecting the early medieval period as a fixed point from which to watch the movement of modern man. Becker, of course, in his *The Heavenly City* effectively compared and contrasted the climates of opinion of the thirteenth and eighteenth centuries, but here some critics have suggested that he may have been more literary than literal.[76] Also, he may have been using the thirteenth century *as if* it were a convenient yardstick. For a man who admittedly knew no science, Becker had a fairly sophisticated sense of scientific method — he was, for example, much impressed with Hans Vaihinger's *The Philosophy of As If* with its theory of fictional propositions and their functional validity in science.[77] Also, Becker's *The Heavenly City* derived much of its dramatic effectiveness from quotations from philosophers of science who stressed the limitations and relativity of twentieth-century science and compared it with the more certain and confident Newtonian science of the eighteenth century. J. H. Jeans the idealist and Bertrand Russell the empiricist became merged, in the pages of Becker's book, in their admission that we moderns know not from where we come or to where we go — we know only that we are bodies in motion, and that some day, according to the second law of thermodynamics, even our motion or activity, which is our only "essence," will cease. Until then, "Whirl is king, having deposed Zeus," Becker quoted.[78]

Actually Whirl did seem king, and Becker, like Dewey in *Individualism Old and New*, hoped earnestly for time enough for man to learn how to harmonize his social structure with his technical achievements.[79] It was this hope for time, for the adjustment of old liberal democratic habits to new modes of activity, that marked Becker as a traditional liberal given to hesitation, as Harold J. Laski[80] kindly pointed out; to timidity, as Louis Hacker[81] intimated; to stultifying "auto-analysis," as Eliseo Vivas[82] noted; and to "despair," as Stanley Pargellis[83] observed.

[76] *The Heavenly City*, 1-32.
[77] See Footnote 75.
[78] *The Heavenly City*, 14.
[79] Dewey, *Individualism Old and New* (New York, 1930), *passim*.
[80] Review of Becker's *Progress and Power* and Beard's *The Discussion of Human Affairs*, *New Republic*, LXXXVIII, (September 16, 1936), 162-163.
[81] "Historian of Revolutions," *New Republic*, LXXXV (January 8, 1936), 260-261.
[82] *The Nation*, CXL (April 24, 1935), 487-488.
[83] *Yale Review*, XXV (September, 1935), 213-214.

Some critics, however, saw a positive value in Becker's tentativeness. "They hope," Harold J. Laski wrote eloquently of both Carl Becker and Charles A. Beard, "that somehow, given time, the reason of man will prevail over his emotional drives. Their sense of the vast complexity of the social scene makes them shrink from the acceptance of a fighting philosophy which is prepared to battle for its faith. They who have studied so many revolutions are sceptical of that in which the socialist puts his trust." Yet Laski, a professed "Marxian socialist," claimed that he and these two liberal eclectics shared the same (unspecified) goal. At any rate Laski had drawn the following lesson from Becker's *Progress and Power* and Beard's *The Discussion of Human Affairs:* "When you are aware of the limitations of your knowledge you cannot dare to crucify in its name. You shrink from the affirmation of dogma; you refuse to identify your candle's little, fitful gleam with the light of the sun."[84]

Beard was often more dogmatic than Laski indicated, but the important thing here is that Laski's Beard was the same Beard Becker so admired. Becker in reviewing Charles and Mary Beard's *The Rise of American Civilization* had characterized it as being "written with verve and swift facility, with nervous, careless prodigality of phrase and epithet, with free and pungent comment, and with an occasional irrepressible sardonic sideswipe at anything smug that turns up by the way." Theirs was a Marxist interpretation in the main, Becker had noted, but it was not written to formula, and their "rapier like intelligence" was too honest to be "duped by illusions, whether tough or tender-minded."[85] In fact, Becker saw much truth in the Marxist interpretation of history, as one way of looking at modern society, although he had used it not at all in his *Progress and Power.* It was the Marxist formula for action, forceful and coercive action, that Becker, who leaned on "time" and "habit" when faith wore thin, found objectionable.[86] Becker had no magical remedy for the ills of the 1930's; and Beard despite his more obvious tendency towards radicalism — or radical talk — hadn't either. Becker's review of Beard's *Cross Currents in Europe Today,* written in 1922, epitomizes his opinion of Beard, which never significantly changed and which explains in part why Beard and Becker would remain friends even in World War Two, when Beard was

[84] See Footnote 80. Becker and Beard, along with Turner, were the cream of the crop among American historians, according to Laski. See his *American Democracy* (New York, 1948), 66, 361, 378.

[85] *The Nation,* CXX (May 18, 1927), 559-560.

[86] "The Marxian Philosophy of History," *Everyman His Own Historian,* 113-131, especially 114, 125-127.

deserted by many of his liberal but internationalist friends. "And what is the remedy [for Europe's postwar dislocations]? Mr. Beard hasn't any. In these times that is a great merit. There are plenty of people with remedies. . . . Mr. Beard is too intelligent to be taken in by ready-made formulas . . . too sophisticated not to delight in dispelling illusions; yet too humanely sympathetic to fall back into the easy cynicism of one who is content merely to observe the tragic comedy of human existence. He is an exasperating cynic and a warm-hearted friend of suffering humanity. . . . Perfectly aware of human folly, he never quite loses faith in human nature."[87]

This was Beard, and it was also Becker, although Becker at times nearly fell into the easy cynicism of the detached observer. In the 1930's Becker's loyal friend Dodd was busy with the unrewarding task of being American Ambassador to Germany,[88] and while he served to warn Becker of the "Nazi menace," he was largely out of touch with him.[89] Beard became, in a sense, a sophisticated substitute for Dodd, playing the enthuiastic lover of man and contemner of villainous men to Becker, who often tired of the game. Together Beard and Becker marched through the pages of the *New Republic* and *The Nation* as slayers of the mediocre, especially the mediocre textbook writer and the commonplace politician.[90] When pressed for specific reform proposals Beard was usually silent, except on questions of municipal government and foreign policy; and Becker was even more reticent. Their

[87] *The Nation*, CXV (November 22, 1922), 552-553.

[88] See Dodd, *Ambassador Dodd's Diary, 1933-1938*, edited by William E. Dodd, Jr. and Martha Dodd (New York, 1941). Charles A. Beard wrote an introduction to this volume in which he sadly recalled the simpler days when he and Dodd had been historians "twitting" one another about their respective Hamiltonian and Jeffersonian biases. Dodd's last entry in his *Diary*, dated September 30, 1938, reads: "The present-day world has learned nothing from the World War." But: "Democratic peoples must maintain their faiths at home. . . . ," 446-467.

[89] While at the American Embassy in Berlin, Dodd found time to write a favorable review of Becker's *Everyman His Own Historian, Journal of Modern History*, VII (December, 1935), 465-466. The two friends continued to correspond, and in *How New Will the Better World Be?* Becker listed Dodd alongside Churchill as having been among the few to understand the menace of Nazism before the war had actually begun. Certainly Becker hadn't understood Hitler at first, and in 1933 he was jesting with Dodd about whether the Germans would burn *his* books if he shipped them to Germany. (William E. Dodd to Carl Becker, Chicago, June 22, 1933.)

[90] Beard always enjoyed this more than Becker, but Becker was Beard's equal in debunking. See his review of Lucius Henry Holt and Alexander Wheeler Chilton, *A Brief History of Europe, New Republic*, XXII (May 5, 1920), 322. For Becker's irony about politicians (he had recently had to sign a loyalty oath pledging to support the Constitutions of the United States and New York), see his "In Support of the Constitution," *The Nation*, CXL (January 2, 1935), 13-14.

friend James Harvey Robinson had written, in *The Mind in the Making*, "I have no reforms to recommend except the liberation of intelligence."[91] This was, all too often, to be the formula of the liberal intellectual in the 1930's, including Charles A. Beard, Carl Becker, and John Dewey. After a while the exhortation "Be intelligent" loses its magic, as Morton G. White has shown in his *Social Thought in America, The Revolt Against Formalism*.[92] If Becker did not share Beard's or Dewey's sublime faith in abstractions such as Intelligence or Social Planning, he shared their fear of losing "the leniency and flexibility" (as White has put it) allowed by such generalities.

When in the 1930's the exhortation "Be intelligent" did lose its magic, the liberal came in for heavy criticism from people less tolerant than Sandburg or Laski. "Certain people have lately taken to calling me names," Becker complained; and he said, truthfully, that during the Depression he had been called a Communist, a timid liberal, a defeatist, and a social fascist.[93] From an intellectual point of view, the most serious criticism had to do with the charges of timidity and defeatism. Catholic and Communist critics agreed that Becker's conception of man was unrealistic. According to one Catholic, Becker in his pessimism had sold out to materialism and had forgotten that man is the son of God.[94] Becker, according to another, was a moral relativist and thus his moral exhortations, against violence, for instance, were of no consequence. "In a world devoid of fixed standards no action can be considered as being wrong; at worst it can be only socially unacceptable to certain groups," Paul Kiniery of Loyola University exclaimed.[95] If Becker was too much of a materialistic pessimist for the Catholic, he was too much of an ineffectual Pollyanna for the Marxist. According to Sam Sillen of the *New Masses*, Becker took refuge in "dreams that capitalism will reform — how he can't guess." He fears fascism, but he slanders the Soviet Union and rejects the socialist alternative to fascism. "And so he can only keep on bravely and calmly repeating his dreary formula that everything will come out right, even though he can't see how that will happen."[96] Both Catholic and Communist crit-

[91] *The Mind in the Making*, 28.

[92] New York, 1949, 180-202.

[93] *New Liberties for Old*, 96.

[94] Moorhouse F. X. Millar, Review of Becker's *Modern Democracy, Thought*, XVI (September, 1941), 409, 411.

[95] Paul Kiniery, Review of Becker's *New Liberties for Old, Thought*, XVII (June, 1942), 381-382.

[96] Review of Becker's *Modern Democracy, New Masses*, XXXIX (May 6, 1941), 22-24.

icisms were fairly effective indictments of the essays and lectures Becker produced on the Social Question in the 1930's. Certainly if one believes in Catholicism or Communism, one cannot forgive Becker his errors. Even if one believes in neither, one might still find fault, as Ralph Barton Perry did, with Becker's relativism in moral theory and with his skepticism about liberal democracy.[97]

Catholics such as Father Kiniery, died-in-the-wool Marxists such as Samuel Sillen, and philosophic realists such as Professor Perry (although Perry much less than the others) appeared willing to give up Becker for lost until he got over his moral relativism or his political pessimism. Of all the intellectuals of the 1930's who were not in some sense "relativists," only the Protestant Reinhold Niebuhr seemed really to understand Becker. Niebuhr welcomed Becker's social pragmatism and his apparent moral pessimism — probably because he regarded them as the secular equivalent of his own Christian philosophy of limited, pragmatic political action and his Christian ideas about Original Sin. Most of all, he loved Becker's irony at the expense of the "naive" and overly optimistic rationalists and democrats of the eighteenth and nineteenth centuries; indeed Becker's *The Heavenly City* seems to echo through many pages of Niebuhr's *The Nature and Destiny of Man*.[98] Becker probably would have been satisfied to be lost to Father Kiniery and Samuel Sillen, only to be saved to Reinhold Niebuhr and Becker's secular-humanist-liberal-democratic-pragmatic friends (after all, the latter were by now comparing him to William James, Henry Adams, and Oliver Wendell Holmes;[99] and Gershoy was describing his *Modern Democracy* as the most fitting last will and testament of democracy, should democracy perish).[100] The trouble was

[97] Review of Becker's *New Liberties for Old, Yale Review,* XXXI (December, 1941), 408-411. Review of Becker's *Modern Democracy, Virginia Quarterly Review,* XVII (Summer, 1941), 440-446.

[98] See Reinhold Niebuhr, Review of Becker's *Modern Democracy, The Nation,* CLII (April 12, 1941), 441; Review of Becker's *New Liberties for Old, The Nation,* CLIII (November 1, 1941), 430-431. Whether or not Reinhold Niebuhr's *The Nature and Destiny of Man* (New York, 1941, 1943) was directly influenced by Becker's interpretation of the *philosophes* and their overconfidence in man, it is clear that Niebuhr's *analysis* contributed little to what Becker had already said, even if his religious *conclusions* were quite distinct from Becker's secular ones. On the question of influence, Niebuhr could only say that he had regarded Becker as being in many ways "a kindred spirit." (Reinhold Niebuhr to the author, New York, September, 1957.)

[99] Moses J. Aronson, Review of Becker's *New Liberties for Old, Journal of Social Philosophy,* VII (October, 1941), 93.

[100] Leo Gershoy, Review of Becker's *Modern Democracy, Yale Review,* XXX (June, 1941), 839-841.

that some intellectuals wouldn't take no for an answer and were determined to save him, to convert him to their "ism," despite himself.

With the exception of a rare letter from a Protestant clergyman, most of the proselytizing was done by the left — which shows where the religious impulse of the 1930's really lay and which reminds one of D. H. Lawrence's description of the socialist passion for equality as the last genuine religious impulse left on earth. Louis Hacker, then an ardent admirer of Marx, was especially zealous. The time had come, Hacker said, reminding Becker of what he had written about the American Revolution, for every man to declare his allegiance: "The choice is not, as Carl Becker seems to think, between liberty and equality; the choice is between life and death."[101] Hacker had hopes for Becker's conversion, despite the fact that he had analyzed Becker as an example of a middle-class historian held captive by social convention. Becker tauntingly replied that he could not respond to Mr. Hacker's criticism — Mr. Hacker had used him, scientifically, as a specimen; as a specimen he couldn't react or move without affecting the precision of Mr. Hacker's observations.[102] But what could Becker say when Arthur M. Allen, a bookstore keeper, called him a logomachist who substituted, as Aldous Huxley had phrased it, "simple intellectual schemata for the complexities of reality"? The book man agreed with Becker's suggestion in "Liberalism — A Way Station" that liberalism might be a "rationalization, an intellectual by-product of democracy," but he took vigorous, intelligent dissent from Becker's judgment that "economic security is quite as much an abstraction as liberty or egalitarianism." He wrote indignantly, "You in your study, with food and warmth, with your books and the leisure to read them, with the opportunity to meet and teach your college students, seem to me to have what you and I should agree to be 'economic security for the individual.' "[103]

Becker really did not solve many problems in his thinking about politics in the 1930's, although Professor Curti thought that Becker's skepticism had helped make "liberalism functional in clarifying issues and in prompting goals which the social radicals really want."[104] This may be true of liberalism, for Becker was one of the minor contributors to the functional, pragmatic climate of opinion in which the Welfare State has evolved. One may seriously doubt, however, that he did the

[101] "Historian of Revolutions," *New Republic*, LXXXV (January 8, 1936), 261.
[102] Letter to the editor concerning Hacker's review of Becker's *Everyman His Own Historian*, *New Republic*, LXXXV (January 8, 1936), 256.
[103] Arthur M. Allen to Carl Becker, Troy, New York, December 27, 1932.
[104] Merle Curti to Carl Becker, Northampton, Massachusetts, October 19, 1935.

cause of social radicalism any great service, however much good he may have done the disposition of a few social radicals such as Harold J. Laski. The truth is that Becker was in certain respects a confused man in the 1930's. It cannot be stressed too strongly, however, that his confusion seems to have come not from a lack of intellectual clarity, but rather from his having "too much" of it, — certainly not for his readers but perhaps too much for himself in a sense that precluded him from total commitment or an "act of faith" or a "leap in the dark" so complete as to negate doubt and other "inefficient" activity.

Becker in the 1930's served as both a skeptical "countervailing force" and a seismograph. A professor, he reminded his Marxist critics, is "a man who thinks otherwise,"[105] and in his refusal to give up liberal democracy at a moment's notice he certainly countervailed against a small but vocal minority that apparently was willing to do so. He was also, however, a seismograph in that his writings recorded with unbelievable fidelity the hopes and confusions of all tired liberals. At times, as Charles E. Merriam wrote to George Sabine after Becker's death, it was hard to know what Becker's philosophy really was, and whether he was a cynic or an idealist: "His 'values' seem historically derived, and yet he conjures up 'eternal verities.' Sometimes he sounds like James and Dewey; sometimes like an 18th century rationalist — sometimes like a determinist . . ."[106]

Becker was all these things. His values were historically derived; they did come from eighteenth-century rationalism. They were Jeffersonian, as Harold J. Laski rightly recognized;[107] and while Jefferson's program was obsolete, Becker thought as a rule that Jefferson's sympathy toward man was not. Nor was Jefferson's "assumption that human conduct and custom should be based upon the disinterested interpretation of the most exact and comprehensible knowledge attainable."[108] The obsolescence of Jefferson's program was apparent to everyone, save possibly the Southern Agrarians — "Experience has taught us, or surely will teach us," Becker wrote, "that the eighteenth century solution for social ills will no longer serve."[109] Liberty had not brought equality, and now the demand for equality — or security — threatened

[105] "The Marxian Philosophy of History," *Everyman His Own Historian*, 131.

[106] Charles E. Merriam to George Sabine, Chicago, November 9, 1945.

[107] Review of Becker's *New Liberties for Old*, *New Statesman and Nation*, XXIII (April 11, 1942), 244-245.

[108] Becker, "Thomas Jefferson," *Encyclopedia of the Social Sciences*, VIII, 378. Written in 1932.

[109] "Freedom of Speech," *Everyman His Own Historian*, 106. Reprinted from *The Nation*, CXXXVIII (January 24, 1934).

to destroy liberty. Democracy, which to Jefferson had been "a placid stream flowing between green banks," had become for de Tocqueville "a devastating flood," Becker remarked once;[110] and for Becker, too, it would be a devastating flood if it destroyed liberty and free speech.[111] Only "the disinterested interpretation of the most exact and comprehensible knowledge attainable" could save us, but James and Dewey had shown, apparently to Becker's satisfaction, that disinterestedness is often either unattainable or uninteresting. Freud had proved to Becker that so much of what passes for thought is *determined* by non-rational wishes; and if this is so, what is the value of liberty or freedom of discussion, when by Jeffersonian standards there is nothing rational to be discussed or no man rational or dispassionate enough to discuss it if there were? Even Becker's love of free speech could be interpreted as being no different from the capitalist's love of economic laissez-faire — everybody has a "vested interest," if one only searches for it hard enough. And this was what Becker did, especially in parts of *New Liberties for Old.*

New Liberties for Old, published in 1941, consisted of articles that Becker had been writing for the *Yale Review* since 1936, shortly after he was elected to the Advisory Board of that journal. There is no need to summarize its contents or to assess its permanent worth, if any, although certainly it is more of a contribution to our knowledge of the psychology of politics than his *Progress and Power* had been to our awareness of the basis of power. For present purposes *New Liberties for Old* can simply be used as one illustration of the confusion Merriam and others have noticed. Part of the book can best be read as simply a reformulation of Pareto's proposition that "A person often accepts a proposition for no other reason than that it accords with his sentiments."[112] This applies to Becker's discussions of "ideology," "rationalizations," "deep seated sentimental responses," reason "as a function of the animal organism," the force of habit and custom, the average man's disinclination to reason, and man's love of a fight solely for the satisfaction of fighting.[113]

Life, if this be all, is truly nasty, brutish, and short; but, as Becker recognized in his Preface, when World War Two drew closer, he came

[110] Review of Gilbert Chinard, *Jefferson et les Idélogues, American Historical Review,* XXXI (April, 1926), 585-586.

[111] See Footnote 109. Also, "The Marxian Philosophy of History," *Everyman His Own Historian,* 125-126.

[112] Vilfredo Pareto, *The Mind and Society, I, Non-Logical Conduct* (New York, 1935), 43.

[113] *New Liberties for Old,* 34, 48, 72, 93.

to place more and more emphasis upon the values of democracy and of liberal, rational habits. At first his renewed deference to democracy and liberty and reason was a qualified, pragmatic one. We must, he said, undertake the writing of new political constitutions, and we can only hope man's intelligence is up to this task. These new political constitutions "will be shaped by an experimental and pragmatic rather than by an absolute conception of rights. . . . They will be based less upon universal principles than upon statistical tables, will be concerned less with invariable natural law and more with temporary but insistent concrete needs."[114] This in 1938 was pragmatism, utilitarianism, and experimentalism, all over again. But a year later Becker showed himself very critical of President Franklin Roosevelt when Roosevelt applied the criterion of utility to his critics. Criticism of the American government was not "useful," the President had said; and Becker in his protest against Roosevelt's judgment acted as if he regarded free speech as a thing right in itself, independent of pragmatic, utilitarian, or experimental considerations.[115]

By 1940, however, Becker was finding more serious matters than the President's choice of language to reflect upon. In an essay, "Some Generalities That Still Glitter," he bitterly attacked what he called "anti-intellectualism," "activism," and even "relativism":

> It was most readily supposed that if reason was an instrument biologically developed to serve the interests of the organism, its pronouncements could never be disinterested; that if truth was relative, nothing could be really true; that if morals varied with the customs of time and place, any custom that got itself established was moral, and one system of morality as good as another. . . .[116]

Here Father Kiniery and Professor Perry were probably right in not letting Becker off the hook so easily. Becker never really got off the hook, and it is difficult to see how any pragmatist could, logically speaking, verify his Jeffersonian tastes, without dragging in a theological or natural-rights argument — which might save his Jeffersonian belief in the rights of man but at the price of negating the distinctive parts of his pragmatic philosophy.

What had happened to Becker, as he acknowledged in the Preface to *New Liberties for Old*, was that the negative examples of Hitler and fascism had rekindled some of his faith in liberalism and democ-

---

[114] "Afterthoughts on Constitutions," *New Liberties for Old*, 95.
[115] "When Democratic Virtues Disintegrate," *New Liberties for Old*, 119-120.
[116] *New Liberties for Old*, 137.

racy.[117] Politics always affected Becker's theory of knowledge, and the uses made by Fascists of anti-intellectualism, activism, and relativism reminded Becker anew of Pascal's judgment that thought makes the whole dignity of man. Current events also reminded him that democracy was kinder to free thought than fascism, and that the liberal must for this reason strive to preserve democracy. Becker made this into one of the basic arguments of his Page-Barbour Lectures, which he delivered at the University of Virginia in 1940.[118] How, Becker asked the totalitarian philosophers in 1941, could they have convinced themselves that man is not rational without the aid of reason?[119] Only a few years earlier one might have asked the same question of Becker. Certainly there is no logical consistency between the Jeffersonian concept of a disinterested reason and those modern philosophies which teach that the wish or the circumstance is father to the thought. Nor is it enough to say that James and Dewey at least had good intentions in regard to liberal democracy, and that Becker did, too. Becker by 1941 had not so much solved a problem as he had moved away from one.

Becker, moreover, knew he hadn't solved any basic problems, although he had pleaded in vain for time, enough time for liberal democracy to solve the problem of what Dewey and others called the "cultural lag" of ideas and institutions behind inventions, and thus to answer in a practical way questions that Becker at least could not answer theoretically.[120] In every book that Becker wrote on current problems there is a revealing note of apology which surely came from something more than modesty on his part. Becker's awareness of not having answered significant questions may help account for the fact that throughout the 1930's, at least in comparison to more dogmatic contemporaries, he especially resembled, until the eve of World War Two, his beloved Benjamin Franklin, whom he described as having been "never wholly committed" to any human endeavour.[121] Becker was never wholly committed because he could not be sure as to what was

---

[117] *New Liberties for Old*, xvi.

[118] *Modern Democracy* (New Haven, Connecticut, 1941), 100.

[119] Review of José Ortega y Gasset, *Toward a Philosophy of History*, *Yale Review*, XXX (June, 1941), 815-817. Becker didn't think Ortega was himself totalitarian, but he suspected him of an anti-intellectualism similar to that employed by totalitarian thinkers.

[120] *Modern Democracy*, 91-92. Nor did Becker have any "particular measures" in mind. "It is for the experts to suggest the particular measures," he wrote. He didn't identify the experts, but perhaps they were an elite of Deweyite social scientists.

[121] *Encyclopedia of the Social Sciences*, VI, 420-421. See also his sketch done for the *Dictionary of American Biography*, VI, 586-598, later republished in book form as *Benjamin Franklin* (Ithaca, New York, 1946).

deserving of total commitment. Into all of Becker's topical writings there crept a note of detachment, and while he was capable of being unusually detached, he was never, except during wartime, capable of being wholly involved.

Becker was, however, undeniably sympathetic toward much of the advanced political thinking of the 1930's. He had voted for Norman Thomas in 1932 more out of dissent than from conviction,[122] but still he was an attentive student of democratic socialism. He looked with favor upon the National Industrial Recovery Act *if* it were truly the beginning of "a planned economy"; he hoped that profits would be taken from "the control of a few private persons" and distributed more equally.[123] He noted the socialistic tendencies of George Soule's *The Future of Liberty* kindly but without endorsement in a review essay called "Journey to the Left."[124] The journey to the left was one that Becker, however, would not make; and he remained in practice a liberal democrat. The new liberties he would substitute for old ones were really the very old liberties idealized in the slogan of the French Revolution, "Careers open to talent." Economic laissez-faire had allowed such large concentrations of wealth to accumulate in private hands that this had, according to Becker, the effect of limiting economic opportunity. Becker was in no sense a "trust-buster" in the Wilsonian tradition, but a believer in the "social regulation of economic enterprise" as a means of bringing about "that measure of equality of possessions and of opportunity" without which genuine democracy cannot survive. He was then on the side of government-regulated private business, and to protect property he would limit its rights.[125]

Property rights were to be relative to over-all social needs; but what of the other "natural rights" of Locke and Jefferson? One reason why Becker would not give up entirely the ideal of private property was that he regarded property as a check upon the despotism of numbers and thus as a safeguard of life and liberty. Of all the liberties Becker cherished, "freedom of thought" ranked highest. He knew that an unrestricted democracy might destroy liberty, and he often warned more optimistic friends such as Max Lerner of this possibility: "Unrestrained majority rule carries with it a danger of dictatorship and suppression of civil liberties. You can have majority rule without periodic

---

[122] See Footnote 42, Chapter 1.

[123] Carl Becker to Fred Rodkey, Ithaca, New York, November 27, 1933. Becker warned that any attempts to plan the American economy would be more successful if no mention of Russian collectivism was made.

[124] *Saturday Review of Literature*, XV (November 28, 1936), 6.

[125] *New Liberties for Old*, 112.

voting. There is majority rule in a real sense in Russia, Germany, Italy," he wrote. From his World War One days Becker knew that individuals, while "good fellows" in their private capacities, could turn into a great beast on civic occasions. To protect minorities from such a beast, Becker would even protect some of the rights of privileged economic groups, however much he disliked them personally.[126] Because of his fear of unrestrained democracy, Becker was not excited by President Roosevelt's "court packing" plans for the Supreme Court. "I am not opposed to the Court as an institution," he wrote to his student Val Lorwin, "or to its powers: because I think civil liberties are safer in the hands of 9 or 15 jurists than in the hands of elected legislators." As a plan for improving the *quality* of the Court, Roosevelt's proposals for increasing the number of judges and discouraging the presence of senile judges on the bench seemed acceptable to Becker. Only preserve the Court, he warned, as a safeguard against extremists of the left and of the right.[127]

Becker's belief in civil liberties was stronger than it was philosophically deep. Despite occasional, Jeffersonian-natural-rights outbursts, such as the one he had made against President Roosevelt's idea of utility, Becker tried throughout the Depression to believe that in practice truth will eventually out; and like J. S. Mill he stressed the social utility of toleration more often than he pointed out its intrinsic worth. Communism should have a free hearing, he wrote, because it cannot survive in the open market place[128] — although with Becker, as with J. S. Mill, one wonders why "false" ideas will necessarily fail if so many people are so often as mistaken or foolish as Becker (and Mill) thought them to be.

Becker's willingness to allow free speech to Communists, however, did not incline him to join the octogenarian John Dewey in his journey to Mexico City to give Leon Trotsky a "fair hearing" against Stalin's charges of betraying the Communist cause. Becker and Beard, too, declined to sit on Dewey's Commission; Dewey was reported as "particularly" regretting Becker's inability to serve in view of Becker's experiences with historical documents and the weighing of evidence. It can be inferred that Becker, like Beard, regarded the issue between Trotskyites and Stalinists as a family dispute in which he wanted no part.[129]

[126] Carl Becker to Max Lerner, Ithaca, New York, March 25, 1938.
[127] Carl Becker to Val Lorwin, Ithaca, New York, February, 1937.
[128] Carl Becker to Mrs. Norman Spitzer, Ithaca, New York, May 10, 1933.
[129] Becker was asked to sit on Dewey's Commission by George Novack, Secretary of the American Committee for the Defense of Leon Trotsky, New York,

Becker could not, however, avoid the Communist question altogether, since his textbook, *Modern History,* came under fire on several occasions during the Depression for its alleged Communist sympathies. The *American Legion Magazine* for September, 1940, carried an article "Treason in the Textbooks," and Becker's book was placed under suspicion.[130] That spring in *Liberty Magazine* George Sokolsky had criticized *Modern History* along similar lines.[131] Later both the Legion and Sokolsky apologized, privately, to Becker's publishers for their criticism of Becker.[132]

Actually, far more serious trouble had threatened in 1935 when the Committee of the Federation of Citizens' Associations had petitioned the Board of Education in Washington, D. C., to grant a hearing concerning the "desirability of eliminating" Becker's *Modern History* and similar, unspecified works from the public school system.[133] Becker's publishers were fearful of the nationwide consequences of such an act, and Becker was prepared to go to Washington to defend his book against the charges of undue sympathy toward Communism. This proved unnecessary, and soon the Board of Education completely cleared Becker and found his *Modern History* to be "fair, impartial, and scholarly."[134] But not before the Hearst *Washington Herald* had joined in the attack against Becker.[135] Mencken's old paper the *Balti-*

March 23, 1937. Becker wrote declining in a letter dated March 25, 1937. Felix Morrow, Acting Secretary, replied to Becker, telling him of Dewey's regret. (Felix Morrow to Carl Becker, New York, undated letter.) Included in The Becker Papers is a typed letter from Charles A. Beard to George Novack, Washington, D. C., March 19, 1937, in which Beard questioned the value of the "trial." Beard and Becker exchanged notes on this matter and were in essential agreement. (See Charles A. Beard to Carl Becker, brief undated letter in The Becker Papers, written sometime in 1937.)

130 O. K. Armstrong, "Treason in the Textbooks," *American Legion Magazine,* XXIX (September, 1940), 8-9, 51, 70-72. Becker's book was placed on a list that included the works of George Counts and Charles Beard, under the label "Are These Books in Your School?"

131 XVII (May 4, 1940), 41-42.

132 J. F. Barton, Director of Publications for the American Legion, quoted by Burr L. Chase of Silver Burdett to Carl Becker, New York, October 2, 1940. George Sokolsky's apology was made to the Editor in Chief of Silver Burdett, Robert Williamson. Robert Williamson to Carl Becker, New York, November 29, 1940.

133 Memorandum submitted by the Committee of the Federation of Citizens' Associations to the Board of Education in Washington, D. C., November 12, 1935.

134 Report of special committee to Board of Education, December 18, 1935. On page eight of this report Becker was quoted as having written to Mr. George J. Jones, Head of the Department of History for Divisions 1 to 9: "I am not, have never been, and never expect to be a Communist."

135 *The Washington Herald* attacked Becker repeatedly in November, 1935, but especially on November 21.

more Sun had come to Becker's defense and had quoted from his "The Marxian Philosophy of History" a passage which begins "I refuse to join the Communists because. . . ."[136] And the *Ithaca Journal* ran a column in which Becker proclaimed "I am not a Communist. I do not and never have advocated revolution as a means of solving social problems, and I much prefer the American system of government to any dictatorship, whether Communist or Fascist."[137] Among his friends, Becker treated the matter as being all part of a day's work, and he refused to take it seriously; he now made it a point to refer to himself in private as "a well-known Communist writer."[138] A man more vulnerable than Becker, unaided by the *Sun* or by other historians,[139] would, however, have suffered considerable loss both in terms of reputation and royalties. H. L. Mencken's reaction to this incident is unknown, but he, too, would probably have treated it lightly. Sometimes we laugh to keep from crying.

[136] *Baltimore Sun,* November 22, 1935.

[137] November 27, 1935.

[138] Becker described his contemners as "a bunch of patrioteers." Carl Becker to Merle Curti, Ithaca, New York, [November or December, 1935].

[139] Merle Curti and a host of major historians had sent telegrams to the Washington Board of Education on Becker's behalf. So had Felix Frankfurter and Alvin Johnson.

Chapter IX

The Heavenly City *and Historiography: A Nearly Absolute Relativism*

THE PREVAILING "climate of opinion" in the 1920's might best be described as one of cynicism, and in the 1930's as one of commitment; part of Becker's difficulty lay in the fact that he was too committed for the 1920's, too cynical for the 1930's. Another part of his difficulty lay in his inability to square logically the Jeffersonian tradition with the pragmatism and relativism current in these two decades. It is true, as Gershoy has observed, that Becker's acceptance of Jefferson's philosophy had from "the very beginning" been "tinctured by his pragmatic attitude,"[1] but the World War and the Depression had shown him that man is neither as rational nor as good as Jefferson and the liberal pragmatists had believed. Anti-reason and evil had been seen to function pragmatically, so that Becker's Jeffersonian philosophy and his pragmatic method were shown to be two separate and distinct things. It was conceivable that what Becker regarded as the cruder varieties of social pragmatism might turn upon the Jeffersonian tradition and destroy it, over the protests of Becker and Dewey. Certainly the continued progress of liberal democracy was very much in doubt, and Becker in *Progress and Power* had been unable to define progress at all, except in terms of technology.

Becker was trapped in the pragmatic web he had spun for himself in the more confident pre-World War One days. As a pragmatist, he could not escape the "cultural naturalism" of Dewey, which sees man as bound closely to his present circumstances.[2] Although Becker was interested in the prophetic type of mind, whether Henry Adams' or

---

[1] Gershoy, "Invitation to Learning," A Discussion of Carl Becker's *The Declaration of Independence* on the Columbia Broadcasting System, February 22, 1948.

[2] See Dewey, *Logic: the Theory of Inquiry* (New York, 1938) for the best development of this cultural naturalism. Chapter Twelve of this work has an almost point-by-point similarity to Becker's presentism. The cultural limitations that bind the historian inescapably to the ideas of his class, group, or nation, receive exactly the same treatment given them by Becker, which shows how easily pragmatism shifts into a kind of relativism.

174

H. G. Wells', he could but reject Adams' pessimism and endorse, cautiously, Wells' optimism.[3] But under no circumstances could he be as futuristic as Wells, who had described himself as "more interested in tomorrow than he is in today, . . . the past is just material for future guessing. To the prophetic mind all history is and will continue to be a prelude."[4] Nor could Becker retreat, in either a literal or a romantic way, into the past. Logically speaking, he could not have accepted Lord Acton's dictum: "For History must be our deliverer not only from the undue influence of other times, but from the undue influence of our own, from the tyranny of environment and the pressure of the air we breathe."[5] Becker did, however, think that it is "often very difficult to avoid the notion that one could easily, by turning round, walk back into the country of the past."[6]

Becker, if he could have had his way, would, I think, have turned around in the 1920's and the 1930's and walked back into two periods of history. First, he would have gone back to his "age of innocence," when he had studied under Turner — and in a sense this is what he did do in his essay on Turner — and then he would have gone back into the eighteenth century, which is the principal source of all liberal democratic innocence. The abiding fascination of the eighteenth century for Becker must have lain in his having a feeling of personal identity with it, as a kind of first home, or home away from home. In this way, the eighteenth century was to Becker what the Middle Ages often is to the Catholic, a source of solace if not always of inspiration. I take it for granted, Becker once wrote, that we are interested in the past "for our own sake and not for its sake. . . ."[7] This was Voltaire, James Harvey Robinson, and H. G. Wells speaking; and Becker, while stressing the fact that this mode of thought is also a matter of faith, was always more attracted to the secular rationalism of the eighteenth century and its modern derivations than to the faith of Christian historians such as Lord Acton. By an act of imagination, Becker partly succeeded in doing what his own theories about historical inquiry would not have allowed — he escaped from the tyranny of the 1930's into *his* Golden Age, the age of the eighteenth-century *philosophes,* and finally, standing with one foot in the twentieth century and one in the eighteenth, he wrote his best book, *The Heavenly City of the*

---

[3] "Mr. Wells and the New History," *Everyman His Own Historian,* 169-196.
[4] H. G. Wells, *What Is Coming? A European Forecast* (New York, 1921), 2-3.
[5] John Dalberg Lord Acton, *Lectures on Modern History* (London, 1952), 33.
[6] "What Are Historical Facts?", *Detachment and the Writing of History,* 41.
[7] *Ibid.,* 43.

Eighteenth Century Philosophers, in which he compared the climates of opinion of the thirteenth, eighteenth, and twentieth centuries. *The Heavenly City* was a work of both historical imagination and present-mindedness, which, as Max Lerner said, reminds one of Maitland's remark that the best history is written backward.[8]

The Heavenly City is then partly autobiographical, as many good histories somehow are. It is, however, not obviously so; the casual reader would be struck more by Becker's lively detached curiosity than by Becker's personal involvement in the story. At any rate, the book is not so revealing as Professor David Noble thinks it is, at least not in the way he imagines. Professor Noble notwithstanding, *The Heavenly City* is not an indictment of the presentism that Becker had endorsed prior to World War One, nor does it *necessarily* commit Becker to any modern philosophy of science as distinct from eighteenth-century philosophies of science.[9] Becker could be most detached even when examining himself, and *The Heavenly City* is not confessional literature in the sense that *New Liberties for Old* sometimes is. Primarily it is an attempt at historical understanding — not in understanding for the sake of the eighteenth century, but for the sake of Becker's audience and for the sake of Carl Becker, who would like to know his own intellectual ancestry — and himself — better.

Certainly Becker and the *philosophes* shared an interest in what might be called the philosophy of science, in the uses of history, and in the verdict of posterity. Perhaps Becker was himself virtuous for the same reason he attributed to Diderot and the *philosophes,* namely that he would prove *contra* the Christians that he could be good without being God-fearing.[10] But, while Becker is of *philosophe* descent, he most often in the actual text of *The Heavenly City* would remind us that the eighteenth century is closer in many ways to the thirteenth century than to the twentieth.[11] And if the "Heavenly City" of the eighteenth century is to him a "Garden of Eden," it is also a "Paradise Lost," lost forever and as surely as the Middle Ages is lost to the Catholic. Becker, as we know from sources other than *The Heavenly City,* could not accept the deism, the belief in the rationality of the universe, and the moral optimism of his intellectual predecessors, the *philosophes,* any more than he could accept the theism, the belief in

[8] *Yale Law Journal,* XLII (May, 1933), 1143.
[9] "Carl Becker: Science, Relativism, and the Dilemma of Diderot," *Ethics,* LXVII (July, 1957), 242.
[10] *The Heavenly City,* 81.
[11] *Ibid.,* 27-29.

Divine Providence, and the Methodism of his physical parents, although he did share with the *philosophes* a community of common intellectual interests, a love of reason, and a qualified belief in social reform and progress.

Becker could, however, seldom speak of any past without a trace of condescension; and in *The Heavenly City* he emphasized the important gap that separated the, in his opinion, naive *philosophe* from the sophisticated modern. Becker, the intellectually sophisticated if tired modern,[12] could not resist emphasizing the *faith* of the eighteenth-century rationalist, just as Becker scholars cannot resist a discussion of the ebb and flow of Becker's own faith. If there was, as Becker insisted, a hangover of Christianity in the moralizing of the eighteenth-century "philosophers," there was at least a remnant of this Christianity in Becker's own "philosophy." And if scholasticism had been modernized and adapted to the eighteenth century by the *philosophes*, Becker even in his pragmatic theorizing had modernized and adapted rationalism, however perversely, to the twentieth century. On the one hand, in his books on politics, he could not desist from explaining rationally the limits of reason; on the other, in his writings on historiography, he could not attach too much importance to the rôle of the historian's own reason in shaping his stories about the past, even if, in Becker's opinion, this reason was often influenced by nonrational, environmental factors.

Becker's apparent deference to the world of "brute fact," which appears in *The Heavenly City*, is in a sense misleading; actually it was not so strong as his love of a logical analysis that was not without its own scholastic or rationalistic overtones. Historical "facts," he had told Turner in 1910, were to him dull things; and his *The Heavenly City* shows that this remained so. *The Heavenly City* is for better or worse an interpretation of historical "facts" rather than an exposition of them. As such it presents a problem to the philosopher of history concerning the relationship between interpretation and facts: How can an interpretation of the spirit or preconceptions of an age be "true" when some of its supporting facts are slipshod or false? On the other hand, as critics sometimes complain, books can be factually accurate but still "false." This suggests that the dualism between historical analysis and historical synthesis or interpretation persists despite Becker's own efforts to overcome this dualism in his theoretical writings.

[12] "For my part, I have been fed upon so many philosophies that none of them makes any great impression." Carl Becker to Charles A. Newhall, Ithaca, New York, April 14, 1919.

The Heavenly City was composed in a short time, as all of Becker's books apart from his doctoral thesis were; and like most of his later works, it was written on order. It was delivered as the Storrs Lectures at the Yale University Law School in April of 1931 and published the following year. It had been written in a rare period of good health, and it was the first really new book that Becker had written in ten years. "I've felt better and more like work than for ten years past," Becker wrote to Dodd in January of 1931, telling him that he was "trying to do something" with the social philosophy of the eighteenth century: "I am enjoying writing it more than I supposed, and I believe it won't be too bad."[13] When delivered at Yale, Becker's Storrs Lectures were exceptionally well attended, and the Dean of the Law School wrote to Becker that he had heard "expressions of pleasure" on all sides.[14] If *The Heavenly City* had been written swiftly and if Becker had worn his learning lightly, as befitted a man who was coming to be known as "a gentleman and a scholar," it was obviously the consummation of considerable thought, going back to Becker's own "The Dilemma of Diderot" and his *The Declaration of Independence*, as well as to recent studies in the history of the eighteenth century.

Some reviewers of *The Heavenly City*, especially Adrian Coates, pointed out that there was nothing especially surprising or original in Becker's interpretation.[15] The truth of this can be seen by taking each of the four Storrs Lectures separately and mentioning its chief sources, apart from those left behind by the *philosophes* themselves. The first lecture on "Climates of Opinion" has, as Becker acknowledged, its sources in what A. N. Whitehead was writing about climates of opinion and the philosophical implications of the theory of relativity.[16] The second lecture, "The Laws of Nature and of Nature's God," is very similar to those parts of Becker's earlier *The Declaration of Independence* in which he had related how the *philosophes* deified Nature and denatured God. The third chapter, "The New History: Philosophy Teaching by Example," comes in part from Becker's own absorption with historiography and from his contact with *philosophes* such as James Harvey Robinson and Andrew Dixon White;[17] but it also prob-

---

[13] Carl Becker to William E. Dodd, Ithaca, New York, January 29, 1931.
[14] Charles E. Clark to Carl Becker, New Haven, Connecticut, undated letter.
[15] *Philosophy*, VIII (October, 1933), 495-496.
[16] *The Heavenly City*, 5.
[17] See *ibid.*, 90, where Becker noted that the *philosophes* and Robinson spoke nearly the same words in the same accents. Burr wrote to Becker that Andrew Dixon White was the only *philosophe* he had ever known. George Lincoln Burr to Carl Becker, Ithaca, New York, October 23, 1932.

ably owes something to J. B. Black's *The Art of History: A Study of Four Great Historians,* which Becker had favorably reviewed in 1927. Black, according to Becker, had demonstrated how the *philosophes* had written history with a subjective purpose in mind; they had even boasted that such was their intention. Their subjective purpose had been that of the social reformer intent on demonstrating that man was by nature good until corrupted by Christian institutions and metaphysics.[18] The fourth and final Storrs Lecture, "The Uses of Posterity," reflects Becker's own preoccupation with the question of how posterity will judge us and our ideas of progress; but it also calls to mind Becker's review of a life of Madame Roland, which, along with Becker's own study of Madame Roland, had led him to write in 1930 that "In the eighteenth century posterity had its uses."[19] Also, while writing *The Heavenly City,* Becker had paused to review F. J. C. Hearnshaw's *The Social and Political Ideas of Some Great Thinkers of the Age of Reason,* and he had been especially impressed by Hearnshaw's treatment of Rousseau. Rousseau, according to Hearnshaw, had merely translated the Christian story into language more agreeable to the eighteenth century.[20] Whether Hearnshaw "influenced" Becker at all cannot be clear, but what Hearnshaw had said of Rousseau is what Becker said of all the *philosophes;* and it was the thesis of all four Storrs Lectures.

Before stating his principal thesis, Becker had to overcome a common fallacy in our conception of medieval and eighteenth-century thought. The medieval period is often characterized as an Age of Faith; the eighteenth century as *the* Age of Reason. As a student of James Harvey Robinson's, Becker knew how much modern thought including modern science actually owed to the "superstitions" and "faith" of the Middle Ages. Becker showed that the Middle Ages, or at least the intellectuals of that period, were "remorselessly rationalistic," seeking always "to press" the "irreducible brute facts" of existence into the "neat categories prescribed by the faith," but so too was the eighteenth century, or its *philosophe* intellectuals. Wherein lay the difference? Becker suggested that it lay in the fact that the thirteenth century and St. Thomas had a reason in faith, whereas the eighteenth century and Voltaire had a faith in reason. As for the twentieth century, it had

---

[18] *American Historical Review,* XXXII (January, 1927), 295-296.

[19] Review of Madelaine Clemenceau-Jacquemaire, *Vie de Madame Roland, American Historical Review,* XXXV (July, 1930), 854.

[20] *Journal of Modern History,* III (March, 1931), 116-118. Becker also noted that there was more Christian mythology in the eighteenth century than "has yet been dreamed of in our philosophies."

neither of these so much as it had a deference to scientific and historical analysis.[21]

The principal idea in *The Heavenly City* is that the *philosophes* were not so modern in many respects as we had supposed, that actually they "demolished the Heavenly City of St. Augustine only to rebuild it with more up-to-date materials."[22] Becker defended the title of his book as being "a peculiarly happy one," when the Yale University Press asked him to change it;[23] and Becker, of course, was right. In *The Heavenly City* he showed successfully that the *philosophes* gave themselves away by the passion with which they attacked the established order. In psychoanalytic terms, which Becker did not employ, one might see in their attack upon the Authority of the Church something like the rebellion of son against father — it is not so much that the father is at fault as it is that his authority *must* be challenged. All this is done in the name of a disinterested love of man, which of course compares favorably with the venial sins of the father; but actually it is not a simple struggle between good and evil but one in which the question of mastery is involved. Becker's picture of the warfare between *philosophes* and orthodox Christians also reminds one somewhat of his earlier description of the American Revolution as having been fought not so much over the question of home rule as over the question of who shall rule at home. Most *philosophes*, along with orthodox Christians, accepted the necessity of God, just as the American colonists had accepted the necessity of government; but the *philosophes* were determined to divorce the government of God from the earthly rule of the Church and the *ancien régime*, just as the American revolutionaries were determined to free the abstraction *civil government* from its institutional embodiment in the British government. Once this was accomplished the *philosophes*, like the American revolutionaries, could establish the authority of right reason over wrong institutions at home. The son could supplant the father, without destroying the symbols of all authority — the *philosophes* like the American revolutionaries were in many respects quite conservative, fearful of anarchy and nihilism.

What Becker himself said was that the *philosophes* stopped fearing particular acts of Providence, and came to see all the universe and all the laws of nature as provident in the sense of having been rationally designed by a deity for the benefit of mankind. They threw out the

---

[21] *The Heavenly City*, 9, 30, 27.
[22] *Ibid.*, 31.
[23] Carl Becker to Norman V. Donaldson, Ithaca, New York, January 15, 1932.

Garden of Eden, but they found in republican Rome or in the primitive savage something like a perfect state of innocence. They rejected the authority of the Bible, but worshiped reason and nature. "They courageously discussed atheism, but not before the servants. They defended toleration valiantly, but could with difficulty tolerate priests. They denied that miracles ever happened, but believed in the perfectibility of the human race."[24] In the last article of their faith they were, according to Becker, the "victims of their own common sense." Their faith in a heaven on earth in preference to "pie in the sky," in immortality in the memory of man rather than in the heaven of God, had received many cruel disappointments, Becker explained, especially in the events of the French Revolution. Becker avoided the question of the actual influence of the *philosophes* on the French Revolution, but he intimated that there was a close connection between the two: "It was more especially in France, where social discontent was most acute that the doctrine of progress, of perfectibility, became an essential article of faith in the new religion of humanity."[25] But unlike Edmund Burke, who saw mainly an excess of *philosophe* Reason in the French Revolution, Becker seems to have seen a grand debauch of *philosophe* Sentiment. "Men rarely love humanity more fervently than when they are engaged in deadly conflict with each other,"[26] Becker wrote; and perhaps he was thinking about man during World War One as well as during the French Revolution.

In fact, Becker, like the *philosophes,* was thinking of all men; he was, as Marjorie S. Harris observed in another connection, guilty of the very over-rationalization he sometimes saw in the *philosophes.*[27] But in *The Heavenly City* at least Becker's over-rationalization appeared to be nearly the reverse of the optimistic over-rationalization of the *philosophes.* Toward the end of the Storrs Lectures, Becker wondered if he, too, did not after all see a pattern in history. If this pattern were correct, Becker was right in paying less attention to the legacy left to liberal democracy by the *philosophes* and more attention to the similarities between the French and Russian Revolutions. He wondered if the religion of humanity would not always express itself thusly, whether the religious part of the story would not always be expressed in new secular myths reminiscent of the Christian picture of man's fall and redemption, and whether the religion of humanity would not

[24] *The Heavenly City*, 31.
[25] *Ibid.*, 139.
[26] *Ibid.*, 144.
[27] *Journal of Philosophy*, XXX (March 16, 1933), 190-193.

always be a harsh and fanatical one. Becker asked what would happen to liberty in another hundred years, and whether by then Communism might be as respectable as Republicanism is one hundred years after the French Revolution: "Are we to suppose that the Russian Revolution of the twentieth century, like the French Revolution of the eighteenth, is but another stage in the progress of mankind toward perfection? Or should we think, with Marcus Aurelius, that the man of forty years, if he have a grain of sense, in view of the sameness has seen all that has been and shall be?"[28]

The Heavenly City was, to say the least, a provocative book, containing reflections that would please *and* offend almost everyone, philosophers and partisans alike. What struck the philosophers most was Becker's style rather than his logical analysis; Adrian Coates was especially incensed by Becker's description of logic "as a hocus-pocus designed to give formal validity to conclusions we are willing to accept if everybody in our set will too."[29] If Becker was cavalier toward logic and the things done in the name of Reason, others were suspicious of Becker's logic or reasoning about the *philosophes*. Practically everyone was aware of a certain dramatic emphasis when Becker wrote of the persistence of Christian formulas in *philosophe* thinking, and we are all aware of the oversimplification necessarily involved in so short a survey of *philosophe* thinking. What makes *The Heavenly City* so distinctive is its impressionistic style — Becker moved from thinker to thinker, from thought to thought, as an artist moves from color to color. Inevitably, however, the colors sometimes ran together, and we are then reminded of one of Becker's favorite quotations from Napoleon: "Over-simplification is the enemy of precision." Certainly there is something wrong, as Marjorie S. Harris claimed, with a schemata that makes no mention of Roger Bacon in the thirteenth century or Immanuel Kant in the eighteenth.[30] Also, as recent critics have suggested, if Becker had read Ernst Cassirer's *The Enlightenment*, he would not have characterized so much of eighteenth-century science as Newtonian; then, too, he might have noted the positive contributions of the *philosophes* to modern social science.[31] Finally,

[28] *The Heavenly City*, 168.

[29] Coates, Review of *The Heavenly City*, *Philosophy*, VIII (October, 1933), 495-496. The quotation is taken from page 25 of Becker's book.

[30] See Footnote 27.

[31] These are, I think, the best of the criticisms contained in *Carl Becker's Heavenly City Revisited*, which is the result of a symposium held at Colgate University in 1956. The reader should, however, be aware that Peter Gay, Walter Dorn, and other contributors to this volume would reject Becker's thesis concern-

as Joseph S. Ullian has pointed out, Becker might have seen that the eighteenth century's tendency to intertwine historical science and ethics is not radically different from the twentieth century's attempt to construct a "descriptive science of ethics" in which anthropological, sociological, and linguistic "facts" about language are used to provide us with "normative" judgments.[32]

Where academic philosophers or philosophical historians found fault with Becker's Reason or Sense of History, interested parties could not help but delight in the way Becker had spoken of their opponents at the same time that they protested Becker's treatment of their own intellectual heritage. The Catholic complaint has already been noted; despite Becker's detachment about Catholicism and his exposé of its enemies, it was clear that he was detached to the point of not believing one word of St. Thomas'. Becker's liberal colleague Preserved Smith was pleased to report a rumor that Becker's *The Heavenly City* had been put on the *Index Librorum Prohibitorum*.[33] The rumor turned out to be false, but some liberal secularists were even less pleased with Becker's treatment of their "mystique" than the Catholics had been with his treatment of theirs. Othon Guerlac, while admiring the book tremendously, refused to confuse the believers in progress with the believers in the Jewish and Christian "mythology."[34] T. V. Smith enjoyed the book aesthetically, but he, too, refused to confuse Hume with the Christian: "If there was such a little difference between Hume and those early woe-begoners, then that little difference is more precious to me than

---

ing the identity of basic preconceptions in the thought of the eighteenth century with those of the thirteenth. My own feeling is that Becker established this complex point rather well, despite the inaccuracy of some of his supporting data; my opinion is shared by Leo Gershoy and Louis Gottschalk in their contributions to the Colgate reassessment. While Becker's book deserved a critical reappraisal (as what book does not?), a large number of criticisms, as Gottschalk complained, seem aimed at Becker for not having done what he had in fact done. He had, for instance, seen the significance of the empiricism expounded by the *philosophes,* and he had stated his awareness of the *discontinuity* between Voltaire and St. Thomas. Becker was, however, interested in the *residues* of Christian thought and feeling in the Enlightenment, a topic that, in his opinion, had been neglected by other historians. Certainly he did not mean to deny the importance of the anti-Christian feelings of the *philosophes,* but rather to show that "it is true of ideas, as of men, that they cannot fight unless they occupy the same ground." (*The Heavenly City*, 122.)

[32] Joseph S. Ullian, "Becker and His Heavenly City," unpublished paper written at Harvard University in 1953.

[33] Preserved Smith to Carl Becker, Washington, D.C., November 21, 1935.

[34] Othon Guerlac to Carl Becker, Ithaca, New York [1932]. Guerlac also wrote that if Becker had been a Frenchman he would have been asked to join the French Academy.

ever before."[35] Surely, this is a good if limited criticism. Becker's preoccupation with the psychology of the *philosophes* and the climate of opinion sometimes did cause him to slur over differences in the *content* of opinion. Reconciling opposites, showing that we are all Christians, we are all rationalists, is one way to write history, but we must not expect the opposites to want to be reconciled in our neat categories. Not only did Catholics and secularists refuse Unity in Becker, but capitalists and communists did, too. Max Lerner, while seeing similarities between capitalism and communism, refused to admit any meaningful analogy between the "strength" of the Soviet and the "compromises" of Hume and Diderot.[36]

Only the student of myths or persons not wholly committed to some dogma could appreciate *The Heavenly City* as being something more profound than a well-written if perverse historical exercise. Thurman Arnold wrote from the Yale Law School, first telling Becker that he could not think of any book greater than *The Heavenly City*, and then a year later telling him that his own *The Folklore of Capitalism* was consciously modeled upon Becker's *The Heavenly City*.[37] Joseph Wood Krutch was chilled by what he took to be Becker's belief in the Idea of Eternal Recurrence,[38] but Charles A. Beard believed that Becker had ended his book with a question mark rather than with a doctrine. Beard, who wrote Gottschalk that no American had ever written a better book than Becker's *The Heavenly City*,[39] thought that Becker had been a consistent relativist in refusing to commit himself either to the idea of man perfecting himself or man stumbling around in a circle.[40]

It remained, however, for Harold J. Laski to see that the book was truly liberal in attitude if not in doctrine. Laski admired Becker's learning and his style, but most of all he loved Becker's "sense of compassion for high aims mingled with a fine detachment from all dogmas, an ability to explain the battle without feeling it necessary to pass a moral judgment on . . . the combatants. That spirit is what I mean by liberalism; and I think it the rarest, as I think it the most exquisite of human qualities."[41]

[35] T. V. Smith to Carl Becker, Chicago, October 26, 1932.

[36] *Yale Law Journal*, XLII (May, 1933), 1143-1148.

[37] Thurman Arnold to Carl Becker, New Haven, Connecticut, 1937, January 5, 1938.

[38] *New York Herald Tribune Books*, December 18, 1932.

[39] Charles A. Beard to Louis Gottschalk, April 29, [1940].

[40] *American Historical Review*, XXXVIII (April, 1933), 590-591.

[41] Harold J. Laski to Carl Becker, London, January 21, 1933.

One use of *The Heavenly City* for the student of Becker is that it tells something about the "climate of opinion" in which Becker's own thoughts about historiography emerged. When Becker wrote about the "New History" of the eighteenth century he deliberately modernized it by comparing it with the New History of James Harvey Robinson and H. G. Wells.[42] The similarity between the "New History" of Voltaire and that of the moderns lay in the fact that they all tried to turn upon the past and exploit it in "the interests of advance." Becker quoted Voltaire's cynical witticism that history is only a pack of tricks we play upon the dead, and commended the "profound truth" of it. "It is unlikely," Becker continued, "that these tricks do the dead any harm, and it is certain that they do us much good. At best they help us to master our own difficulties; at worst they help us to endure them by nourishing the hope of a more resplendent future. The kind of tricks we play is therefore likely to depend on our attitude toward the present."[43]

Becker, of course, saw that between the eighteenth and twentieth centuries the nature of historical study had changed greatly; indeed, as his critics suggest, he may have neglected some of the virtues of eighteenth-century historical scholarship in order to achieve a more effective contrast between the historical thinking of the nineteenth century and the natural-rights thought of the eighteenth century. Even with their imperfect historical understanding the *philosophes* had, however, a greater attraction for Becker than a master of historical technique such as Leopold von Ranke had. While Becker had been influenced by nineteenth-century historicist thought, it is important to insist upon the "romantic" nature of the historicism accepted by his teachers, Turner and Burgess, and thus to distinguish between the tradition to which Becker was exposed and the technical historicism of men such as H. B. Adams and later C. M. Andrews, who accepted what might be called the "scientific" side of Ranke's thinking. Both Turner and Burgess had believed in scientific objectivity in historical inquiry but not simply for the sake of the past; they had written history with higher purposes in mind, the encouragement of national self-consciousness, for example. In this they of course resembled the Ranke who had not been so detached as his American admirers liked to imagine. In another of Becker's teachers, Robinson, one wing of American historiography had emancipated itself from the romance of nationalism, only to return to the romance of humanity of the eight-

---

[42] *The Heavenly City,* 88-90, 111.
[43] *Ibid.,* 88-89.

eenth-century *philosophes*. Science was still sacred to Robinson, but it was not the science of fact piled upon fact but the science of theoretical constructs, of the *philosophe*-social scientist who would understand the past to improve the present. This was the creed of the "New Historians" such as Robinson, Beard, and Barnes; of the three only Beard would later be guilty of a Crocean deviation from the idea of science at the same time that he held fast to the idea of progress.

In Chapter Five it was shown that Becker had developed as early as 1910 a philosophy of historical method which fitted in with the pragmatism of Robinson's teacher William James and with Robinson's own pragmatic ideas concerning social betterment. If Becker was more of a "New Historian" than Dr. Smith has imagined,[44] it is surely paradoxical that in the 1920's and 1930's Becker, while more than ever skeptical of progress, still held to much of the historiography and, by habit, to the liberal democratic convictions of his teachers Turner and Robinson. Reason, Becker could have said with Eugenia in Henry James' *The Europeans*, can be terribly flat, like a bed with the mattress removed[45] — unless there is a pillow of faith.

Becker's support of the "New History" was not, of course, an uncritical one; he was never wholly committed. To Merle Curti, Becker once confided that while Harry Elmer Barnes referred to him as a "New Historian" Becker wasn't always sure why this was so. "I don't claim to be new or old or anything that a label can be attached to. . . . ," he wrote in a nominalistic vein.[46] To J. F. Jameson, Becker admitted that he had "a good deal of sympathy with Barnes and Robinson and their School (I am supposed to be a Newer Historian you know), but they, especially Barnes, hit my thumb a great part of the time."[47] We must not, however, be blinded by these statements; an understanding of the context in which they were written shows them to be the product of an irritation with Harry Elmer Barnes and James Harvey Robinson for their continual demands for a New History that they themselves seemed reluctant to write. Becker in his review of Barnes' *The New History and the Social Studies* in 1925, as well as in his review of Robinson's *The Human Comedy* in 1937, showed his disappointment on that score. "I waited hopefully for the appearance of one of these new histories," Becker complained, and he still hoped that Barnes would write "a new history, instead of writing more

---

[44] See Footnote 86, Chapter Five.
[45] *Selected Novels of Henry James* (New York, 1954), 444-445.
[46] Carl Becker to Merle Curti, Ithaca, New York, October, 1935.
[47] Carl Becker to J. F. Jameson, Ithaca, New York, May 10, 1927.

articles and books telling us how to write the new history."[48] In 1937 Becker reviewed Barnes' *A History of Historical Writing*, and while he inquired as to the meaning of words such as *new* and *orthodox* in Barnes' description of historians, he expressed a somewhat ironic pleasure at being listed among the "new." In all seriousness he spoke approvingly of Barnes as "a learned crusader . . . passionately interested in the application of scientific knowledge to the task of creating the good society" and convinced that history should be brought to bear upon this problem.[49]

While waiting hopefully for the appearance of a really "new history," Becker never forgot that it is a question not of whether you have a philosophy of history, but of whether the one you have is good for anything. He, therefore, continued to applaud those historians who wanted to write useful history. Personally he at times doubted the utility of anything in the 1920's and 1930's: "No doubt the truth shall make you free. But free to do what? To sit and contemplate the truth?" Still one had to bring the past to bear on the present: "Certainly nothing else has been, or ever can be, done with it. The past is gone. It can never be recovered as in itself it really was."[50] Of those who actually tried to write "new histories," H. G. Wells was well received by Becker, although Becker wondered, *contra* Wells, if man ever admitted of being so radically different in the future from what he had been in the past. Mr. Wells, he said further, is biased, but he indicated quite clearly that he approved Wells' bias, which was to look upon man from the "human" rather than the "cosmic" point of view and to write history "in the light of a definitely conceived theory of progress."[51] Becker in his own *Progress and Power* would appear more cosmic than human; and he failed to define progress as simply as Wells. For that matter, he did not define moral progress at all. Still Becker had a sympathy for Wells that he could not possibly have for the profoundly pessimistic Henry Adams. Adams was more fascinating, but Becker seemed to think that the good intentions of Wells' heart made up for the bluntness of his mind.

James Harvey Robinson read Becker's "Mr. Wells and the New

[48] Review of Harry Elmer Barnes, *The New History and the Social Studies*, *Saturday Review of Literature*, II (August 15, 1925). Reprinted in *Detachment and the Writing of History*, 35-40. Review of Robinson's *The Human Comedy*, *The Nation*, CXLIV (January 9, 1937), 48-50.

[49] "What Is Historiography?", *Detachment and the Writing of History*, 65-78.

[50] "A Usable Past," Review of William E. Barton, *The Life of Abraham Lincoln*, *New Republic*, XLIV (October 14, 1925), 207-208.

[51] "Mr. Wells and the New History," *Everyman His Own Historian*, 181-183.

History" with "the greatest pleasure and naturally with entire approval." Robinson, in his rôle as the armchair Moses of the New Historians, felt that Wells could do more than anyone for the New History in the eyes of the public. He was shocked that so few historians, apart from Becker and himself, really understood Wells; he believed that the second edition of Wells' *Outline of History* could be far superior to the first, if only professional historians would help instead of scoff: "I will see that he gets hold of your books. I hope that you will see him."[52] Robinson's enthusiasm was as usual largely a bright bubble, but one that somehow refused to burst. Wells and Becker, so far as is known, did not meet or correspond — in the Becker Papers there is only a two-sentence letter from Wells: "Dear Sir: Many thanks for your most friendly notice of my book. The way historians & scholars have stood me is wonderful. Yours sinc. H. G. Wells."[53] Five years later Becker reviewed the revised edition of the *Outline*, in which Wells spoke less of the future and more of the past, as "a special achievement," although he felt that scholars would continue to discover much that was amiss in it.[54]

Becker himself found much amiss in heroic ventures such as Wells', but he continued nevertheless to encourage them. In 1919 he reviewed Frederick J. Teggart's *The Processes of History* in a sympathetic fashion. Teggart's scientific method, Becker thought, might some day, if persistently applied, explain the "*universal processes* of historical change." While Becker insisted that his own approach was to study "the concrete doings and sayings of particular Europeans,"[55] he emphasized both here and in his later review of Ellsworth Huntington's *The Character of Races* that history was for him, as for Robinson, a house with many rooms: "Although a historian, I gladly run out to welcome any strange, interesting looking generalizations that appear at the gate."[56] Even when these generalizations went beyond the "facts" of scientific history, Becker could appreciate, perhaps doubly, their worth. In reviewing a book on the French "idea" of America in the eighteenth century, Becker advised the reader to call it psychology or history; no matter which label was applied such investigations were deserving of encouragement.[57] As Homer Hockett would critically suggest in his

[52] James Harvey Robinson to Carl Becker, New York, November 16, 1921.
[53] H. G. Wells to Carl Becker, Dunmow, England, [undated].
[54] *American Historical Review*, XXXII (January, 1927), 350-351.
[55] *American Historical Review*, XXIV (January, 1919), 266-268.
[56] *American Historical Review*, XXX (April, 1925), 571.
[57] Review of Bernard Fay, *L'Esprit Revolutionnaire*, *American Historical Review*, XXX (July, 1925), 810-812.

review of Becker's *Everyman His Own Historian, psychologist* might be a better word than *historian* for Becker himself.[58] Becker, to judge from his Preface to *The Eve of the Revolution*, wouldn't have cared. The essential thing was for a man to write a book on any subject that interested him, and to get on with the business of finding something to say about it that would be read by an audience wider than that of professional historians.[59] When professional historians, such as Charles Oman, spoke of history as only "a series of interesting happenings," Becker felt the need to remind them that it is very difficult for historians not to have an interpretation or set of generalizations stored somewhere in their minds, and he quoted Turner to this effect.[60]

Dr. Smith has written that Becker was "substantially consistent" in his theories of historiography over a period of forty years.[61] Probably he was substantially consistent in his pragmatic conception of history, in his belief that history should be useful, and in his emphasis upon the importance of ideas or insights over "facts." But he was not consistent, I maintain, in two fundamental ways: he was not internally consistent, I think, because pragmatism as a theory of knowledge is, logically speaking, self-negating in its search for truth; and furthermore, he was not at all times clear on the question of whether history can be in some sense scientific. The first of these "inconsistencies" may be "a matter of opinion." The second is, however, a matter that can be verified by textual analysis. Although I shall analyze Becker's "Everyman His Own Historian" later in some detail, it is certain that throughout this address Becker regarded the historian as either the maker or the caretaker of myths more than as a scientist of any sort. As Becker's friend, the philosopher George Sabine, remarked, the address in its logical implications "hadn't left history a leg to stand on."[62] Becker, without in any way rejecting the New History's emphasis upon presentism and utility, had often seemed willing to give up the ghost of Historical Science; and he talked more and more often about historical study as an imaginative understanding.

Historical myths seemed at first to be harmless tricks played upon the dead, as he had pointed out as late as 1932 in his *The Heavenly*

[58] *Mississippi Valley Historical Review,* XXII (September, 1935), 332-333.

[59] Review of Barnes' *The New History and the Social Studies, Detachment and the Writing of History,* 39-40.

[60] Review of Charles Oman, *On the Writing of History, American Historical Review,* XLV (April, 1940), 591-593.

[61] Smith, *Carl Becker: On History and the Climate of Opinion,* 107.

[62] George Sabine to Carl Becker, Ithaca, New York, November 26, 1941.

City; Fascist and Marxist mythologies, however, soon convinced Becker that the liberal democratic brand of mythology needed all the support that Truth and Science could give it. Whether history and the social sciences are really sciences, Becker said in 1940, depends on how you define science; and even then it is a matter of degree, of "more" or "less." "The aim of all science (that is to say, knowledge)," he then wrote in a distinctly unpragmatic vein, "is to find out what is true as distinct from what is practically useful or aesthetically satisfying or morally justifiable. That the task of finding out what is true is more difficult in one branch of science than another is not a valid reason for abandoning the task."[63] Here in the above quotation, apart from the beginning in which Becker regarded science as depending upon how you define science, is an anti-relativistic conclusion to more than a decade of intense relativism. (Notice his Greek definition of science as knowledge.) Surely this runs contrary to the idea that Becker was "substantially consistent" in his views on historiography.

The question of why Becker, by the end of the 1930's, would speak more in the name of Truth, Knowledge, and even Science than on behalf of Mythology is easily answered, just as is the question of why he came to talk more of the lasting truths of liberal democracy. The immediate menace of Fascism and the more distant specter of Communism scared him, as it did John Dewey, back to within calling distance of the Absolute, in the secular liberal sense. A far more difficult question to answer is why Becker had ever become such a thoroughgoing relativist in the first place. One might argue that the kind of pragmatism endorsed by Becker in "Detachment and the Writing of History" necessarily terminates in extreme relativism; that is, such logic ultimately reduces itself to an instrumentality of the will to believe. By virtue of showing the importance of judgments of value in shaping our judgments of fact, pragmatism compels all judgments to hinge ultimately upon James' famous "Will to Believe," which had originally been restricted to questions for which, according to James, no factual answers are yet at hand, such as those involving religious decisions. Becker, in his emphasis upon the importance of value judgments in historical studies, clearly had it two ways: if you wrote history from a Marxist or Fascist point of view, you were guilty of abusing or over-using your evidence; if, on the other hand, you tried to steer clear of value judgments, you produced no historical synthesis at

[63] Review of Gaetano Salvemini, *Historian and Scientist: an Essay on the Nature of History and the Social Sciences, American Historical Review,* XLV (April, 1940), 592.

all, only a melee of information, as Becker complained of A. M. Schlesinger's *The Rise of the City*.[64] Either you weren't accurate enough or you were too faithful to the "evidence," but what after all was "evidence"? Here one might ask Turner's question of what was the "good" of looking at history from this point of view. What was the utility of such an impasse, and was it necessary?

Becker felt it was necessary, and he did so partly on the authority of some of the best minds of the 1920's and 1930's, which appeared to demonstrate absolutely the relativity of both reason and value. The philosophy of pragmatism, and the social science of Sumner and Freud, had long predisposed Becker to see the relativity of moral codes; and if Becker saw rightly the importance of moral judgments in shaping our judgments of fact, it followed that social science might itself be as parochial or provincial as the codes it purported to describe. This is what the Marxist means when he speaks of *bourgeois* science; and in a way this is what A. N. Whitehead and J. B. Bury meant when they talked of the relativity of the idea of progress, and what A. N. Whitehead meant when he pointed to the relativity of historical science (the very science, one might add, that had permitted him to see the relativity of the idea of progress). Becker admired Bury and especially Whitehead. Whitehead's *Science and the Modern World* and his *Adventures of Ideas* had helped him, he recalled, to understand how "social thinking is shaped by certain unexamined preconceptions current at the time."[65] In 1933 in reviewing Whitehead's *Adventures of Ideas,* two years after his own "Everyman His Own Historian" had been written, Becker applauded Whitehead's characterization of "objective history" as reflecting "provincialism." He delighted in quoting Whitehead's judgment that "Observational discrimination is not dictated by impartial facts. It selects and discards, and what it retains is arranged in a subjective order of prominence."[66]

Becker had it on the authority of Whitehead that the scientific objectivity of the Rankeans might be so much nonsense. At least some historians agreed with Becker and Whitehead, so that Becker's "Everyman His Own Historian" could scarcely be regarded as a daring manifesto, but as the most literary, articulate summation of a distinct body of sentiments already felt by a distinguished handful of historians who

[64] Carl Becker to A. M. Schlesinger, Ithaca, New York, February 14, 1933.

[65] Review of J. B. Bury, *The Idea of Progress, American Historical Review,* XXXVIII (January, 1933), 304-306. "Books That Changed Our Minds," *New Republic,* XCVII (December 7, 1938), 135.

[66] *American Historical Review,* XXXIX, (October, 1933), 87-89.

were still interested in the philosophy of history that C. M. Andrews had dismissed as "vague" and "unsubstantial."[67] Becker's former teacher Frederick Jackson Turner applauded the address: "Not only is it a characteristically fine piece of writing, but I can agree with the ideas contained in it," he wrote to Becker.[68] Turner had probably been most impressed by Becker's exceedingly democratic conception of the historian's relations with Mr. Everyman; in any event he was not disturbed by the skepticism that troubled Sabine and William E. Dodd. W. Stull Holt of Johns Hopkins saw the skepticism, only to pronounce it a "grand" and "glorious" "treason," "a sacrilege against the deity, Scientific History, who has been enthroned so long."[69] Preserved Smith of Cornell and Ferdinand Schevill of Chicago were delighted that Becker had killed the notion that facts have any meaning in themselves, apart from that shed upon them by our own minds. "They are dark objects, invisible and intractable . . . ," Smith wrote, until they are made to shine in the light of our ideas.[70] Schevill saw the address as exploding the "hookum of 'scientific method' and 'historical truth'"; he saw it as a release from servitude to social scientists.[71] Neither Smith nor Schevill paused to wonder whether the "dark objects" known as facts had not been forever darkened by the implications of Becker's address or whether the negation of Science was not also the negation of Truth.

Only Charles A. Beard could be said to have grasped fully the implications of Becker's address; he and Becker had spent "jolly hours" together in Minneapolis, Minnesota, when Becker had delivered the address in 1931.[72] Beard rejoiced at Becker's position and he would in his presidential address in 1933 follow Becker in doubting Historical Science; he, too, would see that relativism reduced history to an act of faith. Doubtless Beard's faith — or bias — was stronger than Becker's, although I fail to see the "crucial though apparently slight differences" between the relativism of the two men that Dr. Smith does as being anything but "slight."[73] Actually the principal difference lay in the fact that Becker concentrated more on the problem of knowledge; Beard, on the problem of historical process or movement. The ques-

[67] Andrews, "These Forty Years," *American Historical Review*, XXX (January, 1925), 246.

[68] Frederick Jackson Turner to Carl Becker, San Marino, California, January 14, 1932.

[69] W. Stull Holt to Carl Becker, Baltimore, Maryland, January 13, 1932.

[70] Preserved Smith to Carl Becker, Atlantic City, New Jersey, January 15, 1932.

[71] Ferdinand Schevill to Carl Becker, Chicago, February 9, 1932.

[72] Charles Beard to Carl Becker, Pasadena, California, January 11 [1932].

[73] Smith, *Carl Becker: On History and the Climate of Opinion*, 111.

tion for Becker's biographer is whether Becker was consciously influenced by Beard or any of his contemporaries in their discontent with "scientific" history. The answer is caught in the brambles of "influences," but it seems safer to infer that Becker influenced men such as Beard more than he was influenced by them. At least he was the first to come forth with his relativism; as we have seen, his "Detachment and the Writing of History" had anticipated in 1910 much that he developed in more detail in the 1920's and 1930's. Apparently he had also read Whitehead and Croce before Beard did; and he seems to have read them more perceptively.

Beard's only recorded reaction to Whitehead occurred in an aside made while reviewing Toynbee's *A Study of History*, where he contrasted Toynbee's attempts at scientific objectivity with Whitehead's efforts "to push mysticism into every area of common sense"; apparently Beard disapproved of both thinkers.[74] Beard's enthusiasm about Croce's ideas on historiography helped to shape his presidential address in 1933;[75] but even here Beard's reflections on historiography and the impossibility of scientific objectivity were probably influenced more by his reading of Karl Heussi and other German idealists, none of whom Becker seems to have read. Becker had reviewed Benedetto Croce's *History: Its Theory and Practice* for the *New Republic* in 1922, and he later wrote that Croce helped to shape his ideas about history, as these ideas were expressed in his "Everyman His Own Historian."[76] Several letters by Beard and Becker show that they had come to share much of Croce's aversion to the idea of a Science of History, although neither of them gave up the Philosophy of History in favor of Croce's idea that history *is* philosophy. Becker in 1943 wrote to Beard congratulating him on his Introduction to Brooks Adams' *Law of Civilization and Decay*, and in this letter he complained that Adams' concepts such as *civilization, concentration, force, energy,* were all lacking in that precision so essential to sound physical science. He also re-stated a proposition that he used many times: "Fortunately for the physicist, the electron cannot acquire a knowledge of physics. If it could, every law of the electron discovered by the physicist up to date could be used by the electron to modify its

[74] Review of Toynbee's *A Study of History, IV-VI, American Historical Review,* XLV (April, 1940), 594.
[75] "Written History as an Act of Faith," *American Historical Review,* XXXIX (January, 1934), 219-231.
[76] "Books That Changed Our Minds," *New Republic,* XCVII (December 7, 1938), 135.

behavior in the future, and so dish all the laws of physics. The subject matter of the sociologist, which is man, can do just that."[77]

If this be true, it certainly curtails the predictive possibilities of any science of history; and it was chiefly for this reason that Beard had rejected the Science of History in 1933. Neither Beard nor Becker paused to consider whether their idea of science did not reflect more of the nature of physics and less of other natural sciences in which prediction plays a smaller part; but both Becker and Beard proceeded as if the limits of Adams' or Marx's procedures had proved the unscientific nature of any "historical prophecy." They themselves believed that history moved in a given direction, towards collectivism and, they hoped, toward democratic collectivism; but this belief was, they felt, more an act of faith than of science. In many of their questions about the Science of History it is possible to see the hand of Croce, as one might see it in Beard's exclamation: "I just hate the sight of physical and biological analogies in historical writing. . . ."[78]

One significant thing in Becker's and Beard's surrender of the idea of a Science of History in the 1930's (which for Beard at least was a complete about-face from the positivistic hopes of his earlier years) is that the surrender was a practical rather than a theoretical one. It stemmed not from Croce's condescending estimate of science as an expression of "the practical will" or of utilitarian impulses, but from what they, especially Beard, regarded as the failure of the Science of History to yield practical results in the way of accurate predictions. Even with the surrender of Robinson's dream of a Science of History, Becker and Beard held fast to the idea of a useful history; and here I think David Noble is right in saying that the relativism of Beard and Becker owed more to American instrumentalism (pragmatism) than to European idealism.[79] Further proof that this is so can be seen if one examines Croce's writings for *dissimilarities* from, as well as for similarities to, the ideas of Becker and Beard, and if one studies what Becker actually said about Croce's *History: Its Theory and Practice*, which he reviewed along with Robinson's *The Mind in the Making*.

Croce, to begin with, had seen, grudgingly enough, that a case could be made for practical history as a practical act, but he dogmatically asserted that practical history is not "pure" history. It fails to see the *identity* of philosophy and history, and it identifies history more with

[77] Carl Becker to Charles A. Beard, Ithaca, New York, May 10, 1943.
[78] Charles A. Beard to Carl Becker, New Milford, Connecticut, May 15 [1943].
[79] *Ethics*, LXVII (July, 1957), 248.

activity than with thought. Pure history, according to Croce, sees that history is the predicate, or the individual, coupled with the subject, the universal supplied not by science but by philosophy.[80] Both Becker and Beard were silent on this point, and Becker always defined history not as the history of thought but simply as the memory of things said and done.[81] Croce chose to neglect the identity of history with practical life in favor of the identity of history with abstract universals; Becker (along with Beard) felt strongly that "it is impossible to divorce history from life," and he meant from *practical* life.[82] Croce believed, however, that history was either "*living*" history or mere antiquarianism. Becker agreed, and in his "Everyman His Own Historian" he mentioned Croce as the authority behind his own belief that history is part of the present.[83] Living history to Croce lay in what he called "the eternal present."[84] To Becker (as well as to Beard) nothing was eternal, not even the all-important present; and Becker appeared at times to consider the present, as did William James, to be "a specious present," one which is mainly a mixture of a past we hold to with a future we reach out for.[85] Croce rejected the "pseudo-concepts" of social science;[86] Becker (and Beard) only questioned them. Croce denied that history could be reduced to "a classification and statistical table of reality."[87] Becker, who had read all of Croce in translation, agreed that history "cannot be reduced to a verifiable set of statistics or formulated in terms of universally valid mathematical formulas."[88] Like Croce, Becker saw the nature of historical inquiry as consisting of "imaginative creations,"[89] but he (along with Beard) saw also something that Croce did not; namely, that psychology and social science might assist the historian in these creations.

Where Croce and Becker really revealed their basic differences was in the treatment of the Enlightenment. Croce regarded the Enlightenment as being the closest thing to a regress in historiography that historical development ever allows. The rationalism of the Enlightenment,

[80] Croce, *Theory and History of Historiography* (London, 1921), 43, 60-61. This book appeared in America as *History: Its Theory and Practice.*
[81] "Everyman His Own Historian," *Everyman His Own Historian,* 239.
[82] *Ibid.,* 242.
[83] *Ibid.*
[84] Croce, *Theory and History of Historiography,* 60.
[85] "Everyman His Own Historian," *Everyman His Own Historian,* 240.
[86] Croce, *Logic as the Science of the Pure Concept* (London, 1917), 34, 179-180, 338-339.
[87] *Ibid.,* 305.
[88] "Everyman His Own Historian," *Everyman His Own Historian,* 243.
[89] *Ibid.*

he thought, had no idea of historical imagination; it was a kind of prelude to latter-day positivism; its reason was that of science rather than philosophy; and it *moralized* about the past.[90] Becker said pretty much the same thing in his *The Heavenly City*, but he said it more respectfully, as befitted one, who like his *philosophe* predecessors, would have turned on the past and used it for the interests of advance — if only he could have learned how.

Not only did Croce pass moral judgment upon the Enlightenment (and any moral judgment on Croce's part would seem to be a negation of his own ideal of a pure history), but he spoke scornfully of all radicals and sensitive souls who would fly into the face of historical reality. Beard, who was always quick to point to the limits of Ranke's objectivity and to show that his historiography was influenced by his political conservatism, remained strangely silent when Croce spoke contemptuously of radicalism, so silent that one wonders how thoroughly Beard had read Croce. Becker, however, took Croce up on this point from the very beginning; he seemed to sense the incompatibility of Croce's detached idealism and the pragmatic historiography designed for "Mr. Everyman." In 1922 Becker compared Croce's detachment with Robinson's social commitments, and despite the limits of his own commitment he decided in favor of Robinson. Becker inquired why, if history was what Croce believed it to be — namely, the creation of mind — wasn't Robinson's mind, or approach to history, as good as anyone's? Croce might have replied that mind is in a state of process; Becker impatiently asked whether the mind can't speed up its own process: "But let us give Robinson the last one: at least one mind can poke another. Perhaps it can. Who knows?"[91]

Always Becker was in the main committed to the idea of exploiting the past pragmatically; surely Becker's defense of Robinson against Croce showed that Becker's differences with the New Historians, as we said in Chapter Six of his differences with the Jeffersonian school of thought, were *family* differences. Becker's inconsistencies and ambiguities on the question of the nature of history, even his agreement with Croce on several points, should not conceal his lasting belief that history is useful, or ought to be, in a moral sense that was alien to Croce's historiography. The New Historians may remind us in a way that Becker seldom does, at least after World War One, of Coventry Patmore's comparison of the rejoicing of people like Lord Macaulay

[90] Croce, *Theory and History of Historiography*, 243-263.

[91] Review of Benedetto Croce, *History: Its Theory and Practice*, James Harvey Robinson, *The Mind in the Making*, *New Republic*, XXX (April 5, 1922), 174-176.

over mankind's progress with that of "a prosperous shopman" speaking of an increase in his business.[92] Becker was throughout most of the 1920's and 1930's too skeptical to play the part of Lord Macaulay, but he was never too skeptical to defend the Whig historians against their enemies, whether the Whigs were Macaulays or Robinsons. The idea of progress lingered on, as Becker remarked in *Progress and Power;* and it informed Becker's reflections on historiography, even when it could not assist his reflections on contemporary politics.

As was suggested earlier, Becker's reflections on historiography may be said to have commenced with his youthful questioning of the tenets of Christianity, of whether we should believe the testimony of witnesses who report facts or ideas that we suspect. This kind of problem took on new dimensions for Becker in the 1920's and 1930's partly because he had felt deceived by the testimony of others in World War One, but mainly because of the Zeitgeist of the Depression Era, which calls to mind W. B. Yeats' remark that the best lack all conviction, while the worst are filled with passionate intensity. Here the question of the reliability of testimony, the question of what is fact and what is value, was of the utmost importance. Also, the fact that Becker's best efforts in the 1920's and the 1930's (apart from those he put into *The Heavenly City*) went into a study not of history but of historiography, coupled with his own lack of intense social or political conviction, reminds one of Lecky's controversial judgment that in periods of intellectual poverty, the study of logic or the methods of reasoning takes on a greater interest than it otherwise would. There is a simpler explanation written by Becker himself, which, however, does not preclude other possibilities: "Now that I am old," Becker would write in 1937, "the most intriguing aspect of history turns out to be neither the study of history nor history itself . . . but rather the study of the history of historical study."[93]

Whatever the reasons, Becker's preoccupation with historiography did increase in his later years, only to diminish when the coming of World War Two re-engaged his interest in the questions of politics, of war and peace. By Becker's preoccupation with logic in the 1920's and 1930's we mean not a concern with formal logic but with operational logic and with historical changes in this logic. Critics might feel inclined to apply to Becker Morton G. White's verdict against Beard,

[92] Coventry Patmore quoted by E. J. Oliver, *Coventry Patmore* (New York, 1956), 200.

[93] "What Is Historiography?," *Detachment and the Writing of History,* 65.

namely that he confused the logic with the psychology of historical writing;[94] but we must bear in mind Becker's own refusal to distinguish between the two approaches in a rigorous way. We must also remember that Becker's position in historiography, while pragmatic in origin, is also reminiscent of that taken much earlier by F. H. Bradley. "It is a very common and most ruinous superstition to suppose that analysis is no alteration," Bradley had written.[95] Becker seemed predisposed to believe that historical inquiry is not an alteration of the past which actually happened, but that it is an alteration of our memories of that past. With his teacher Turner, he believed that "Each age tries to form its own conception of the past" and that "When . . . we consider that each man is conditioned by the age in which he lives and must perforce write with limitations and prepossessions, I think we shall all agree that no historian can say the ultimate word."[96] Here the alteration of opinion or memory is continuous, and it is clear that the emphasis of Turner, and of Becker, is upon changes not in the logic of inquiry but in the psychology of the inquirer, his conditioning processes, and the effects of this upon his logic. With his teacher Robinson, Becker would have said that we do not think enough about thinking; and behind his concern with the psychology of the inquirer lay a lifelong curiosity on Becker's part about the psychology of the historian's subjects, with why the subjects felt or thought as they did.

It is from this point of view, from Becker's refusal or inability to separate logic and psychology, that his two papers, "What Are Historical Facts?" and "On Historical Evidence," can best be read. In a sense, they contain the reasons behind the position taken by Becker in his famous "Everyman His Own Historian," which is more literary than philosophical. "What Are Historical Facts?" was written in 1926 and "On Historical Evidence" in 1937, but despite the difference in time the two are essentially consistent both with one another and with what Becker had said about facts and evidence earlier in "Detachment and the Writing of History." Together these two essays form the pillars which support the arch, "Everyman His Own Historian"; the three together comprise the most significant (if sometimes mistaken) American contribution to the analysis of the historian and his craft. Certainly there is a similarity to Beard's relativism and to the position developed by John Dewey in his *Logic: The Theory of In-*

---

[94] White, *Social Thought in America*, 231.

[95] *The Principles of Logic*, I (London, 1932), 95.

[96] Turner, "The Significance of History," *The Early Writings of Frederick Jackson Turner*, 52, 55.

quiry (1938); but in depth and texture of thought, as distinct from originality (or rightness) of thought, Becker's is by far the superior work. One can only regret that he did not write the book on historiography that he intimated he someday might, and I for one regret this far more than the other book that Becker did not write, his history of the French Revolution.

"Pragmatism is uncomfortable away from facts," William James once wrote.[97] Actually both James and Becker were a priori as often as they were factual in their reflections, and Becker did not as a rule share James' zest for as many facts, as many pluralities, as possible. He did, however, want to know what a fact is, and in his essay "What Are Historical Facts?" he attempted to answer this question. A fact, he maintained, is a symbol, or a generalization, about thousands of other facts or symbols. It is a statement about events not to be confused with the events themselves. "Of a symbol it is hardly worthwhile to say that it is cold or hard," Becker wrote, although he himself spoke often in other contexts of "brute facts." He went on to say that "It is dangerous to say even that it is true or false. The safest thing to say about a symbol is that it is more or less appropriate."[98]

The most glaring deficiency of Becker's essay is that he did not say what the symbol was appropriate to. It would be hard to deal with symbols that do not represent something outside of themselves, except in formal logic or pure mathematics; it would be even more difficult to reconcile the above quotation with Becker's discussion, in the same essay, of "illusions." In his discussion of illusions such as the "German Mark," Becker asserted that this "illusion" was "nevertheless an historical fact." By this he meant that the illusion itself existed, but this was to beg the whole point; the point being, to use Becker's own phrase: is the symbol "corresponding to reality"? In this one phrase lies the central problem of how symbols relate to what it is they are supposed to symbolize. "The popular notion," William James had written, "is that a true idea must copy its reality."[99] Such is our bias — although, because of thinkers such as James and Becker, this notion is not so popular nowadays. In the philosophy of history when we give up the time-honored question of how an idea copies or describes or symbolizes some reality, surely we leave logic altogether and start talking about the psychology or the sociology of knowledge.

[97] William James, "What Pragmatism Means," *Essays in Pragmatism* (New York, 1955), 151.

[98] "What Are Historical Facts?," *Detachment and the Writing of History,* 47.

[99] "Pragmatism's Conception of Truth," *Essays in Pragmatism,* 160.

This is a judgment of fact, as well as a criticism, because the very next question Becker sought to answer was: "Where is the historical fact? I will say at once, however brash it sounds, that the historical fact is in someone's mind or it is nowhere."[100] Then Becker asked, "When is the historical fact? If the historical fact is present, imaginatively in someone's mind, then it is now, a part of the present."[101] If no one thinks a fact, then it is not a fact, although Becker does not say what it is, only that it is not. Continuing this line of thought, Becker, while noting certain differences between the scientist and the historian, paraphrased Eddington's description of scientific inquiry and concluded by saying that "When their minds [the scientists'] all rest satisfied they have an explanation, what is called the truth."[102]

Here in Becker's thought there is a linking of the ideas of truth and satisfaction, in a way that is more reminiscent of James than of Eddington. This linking of the two ideas has often had unfortunate consequences in the history of thought. Even if one tries to restrict the idea of "satisfaction" to a purely intellectual kind of satisfaction, it still entails considerable difficulty. In Becker's case two undesirable results seem to follow from the idea of satisfaction: first, the satisfaction of the experts is to be taken as a sign that the truth has actually been found out, insofar as this is possible; second, in view of Becker's own distinctions between science and history, there is always the danger that the idea of "satisfaction" (so vaguely defined by Becker) might get out of hand and degenerate into a question of whether the expert — or even Mr. Everyman — is "satisfied" by what the scholar has said. In the first instance, as Becker took repeated pleasure in pointing out, so many scholars have been satisfied too soon; and if this is so, it might be that satisfaction is not the most relevant consideration to associate with truth-finding. In the second instance, it is not clear whether the satisfaction is really a logical criterion or simply a consequence that in some cases correlates with the discovery of truth. The latter possibility is potentially the more dangerous, since in the hands of a pragmatist who believes that things *become* true in terms of their consequences, the consequence of satisfaction might be permitted to stand as proof of the truth, indeed as the only proof.

Becker in this paper on historical facts showed himself to be displeased with the effects of historical scholarship. Science at least

[100] "What Are Historical Facts?," *Detachment and the Writing of History*, 47-48.
[101] *Ibid.*, 50.
[102] *Ibid.*, 60.

had made it possible, he complained, for the war to be a *World* War, but what had historical scholarship done? "Has it done anything to restrain the foolishness of politicians or enhance the wisdom of statesmen?"[103] Did this mean that historical scholarship was therefore any the less sound or true? Clearly Becker did not think so, but it is equally clear that by his own logic and by his ideas about satisfaction he should have at least entertained such possibilities. Actually, Becker himself was uncertain about what to do with this paper on historical facts. To Carl Van Doren he confided that the paper was "intended to provoke discussion rather than to be an exact expression of my own ideas."[104]

Harry Elmer Barnes found Becker's essay far more destructive of Ranke's *wie es eigentlich gewesen* school of thought than any other attack had been, more so even than Beard's "That Noble Dream."[105] In his *History of Historical Writing*, Barnes spoke eloquently of Becker's "brilliant" paper that had been delivered over a decade earlier in Rochester, New York. If ever published, Barnes was certain, it would "probably come to have the same place in historical science that the theory of indeterminacy occupies in contemporary physical science."[106] Becker politely refused to publish the paper,[107] perhaps because he thought its indeterminacy to be too great. However, in terms both of content and implication it fitted in with everything that Becker would say in "On Historical Evidence" (1937) and "Everyman His Own Historian" (1931). "Always keep this in mind," he wrote as late as 1940, "a fact is not something objective and material in the outer world — but only something the mind is convinced is true."[108]

Becker's paper "On Historical Evidence" is, if anything, more sweeping in its relativism than "What Are Historical Facts?" Having explained facts, or explained them away, as symbols, Becker turned in this paper to the question of "how much evidence is required to establish, as we say, the historical fact." He continued to distinguish rigorously between "the fact that" and the event which it symbolized. He asked whether Bernheim's "two independent witnesses not self-deceived" were sufficient to establish the "fact that" such and such an event ac-

---

103 *Ibid.*, 62-63.
104 Carl Becker to Carl Van Doren, Ithaca, New York, February 28, 1934.
105 Harry Elmer Barnes to Carl Becker, Auburn, New York, February 26, 1936.
106 *A History of Historical Writing* (Norman, Oklahoma, 1937), 266-268.
107 This was the same paper H. L. Mencken had wanted to publish after talking with Barnes.
108 Carl Becker to Carl Horwich, Ithaca, New York, June 11, 1940.

tually occurred.[109] Clearly it wasn't, because historians looked upon reports of miracles with a skeptical eye, even if there were hundreds of witnesses to such events. Here, as was noted earlier, the question was whether we should follow Hume or De Maistre on the possibility of miracles. Which the historian follows depends, Becker believed, not so much on the nature of the miracles or even the validity of Hume's or De Maistre's logic as upon preconceived ideas held by the historian. If the historian hasn't a preconceived idea as to what must have happened, Becker argued, he at least has preconceived ideas as to what could not have happened. "The preconceived idea, which thus comes into conflict with testimony as to the particular fact, is determined by the climate of opinion in which the historian lives," Becker believed.[110] Some people have tended to regard Becker's "climate of opinion" as a vague, nebulous cloud; here, however, the climate of opinion is clearly a strategic, causal factor in history, or at least in the writing of history — despite Becker's own skepticism about the category of causality.

Climates of opinion change "so that the testimony which a competent historian of one age will readily accept, may as readily be rejected by a competent historian in another age."[111] What is a miracle for the Middle Ages, Becker implied, is only a belief in miracles for the modern mind. The particular way in which Becker interpreted such changes in the standards or criteria for truth seems to be a nearly classic statement of relativism: "The validity of human testimony to establish the fact is in the last analysis fixed by the historian's settled convictions as to the nature of the universe and the kind of fact that can occur in it. In this sense history is, as Charles Beard says, 'an act of faith,' but then no more so than all experiences."[112]

In returning to Becker's original questions concerning the nature of historical evidence, it is clear that, according to Becker, evidence is whatever the historian calls evidence. The original event cannot be reproduced, so the evidence is left to be used or rejected as the "expert" historian sees fit: "For practical purposes we have to draw the line (between what is and is not evidence) somewhere; and so I will just cut it short by saying that any event is a historical fact if all competently trained persons who have examined the evidence are sure it did occur."[113] On the face of it, this is highly encouraging and

[109] Becker, "On Historical Evidence," MS. 1.
[110] *Ibid.*, 6.
[111] *Ibid.*, 7.
[112] *Ibid.*, 15.
[113] *Ibid.*, 1.

practical; we leave the question to the experts. But what if the experts disagree? — and surely a "competently trained" Christian historian might take exception to Becker's tendency to follow Hume in his skepticism concerning the authenticity of miracles. It would, of course, be hard to establish the validity of any *particular* truth which experts do not *now* accept as being true — this is rather like asking the Platonist for an example of an Idea that exists apart from the mind of man. Here we must reply upon the historical method to show that what we now consider as being true was often rejected by competently trained persons in the past. Forgeries have been accepted by experts for centuries, only to be exposed by latter-day experts; some hypotheses valid for mechanical physics are in a sense "false" for modern quantum physics. Such instances at least suggest the possibility that truth is often different from what we or the experts assume it to be; still further it suggests that the truth is "out there" somewhere, perhaps in the Platonic Ideas, or for our purposes in the archives, waiting to be discovered. It might, *contra* Becker, be wise to insist that the idea that "man creates truth" is conceived in the language of metaphor, and that such ideas, if taken literally, lead not to the discovery or even the creation of truth but to the negation of truth and the creation of myths. Here we can either take the side of Becker the scholar, who discovered certain interrelations of fact and put forth several "true" hypotheses about the eighteenth-century mind, the American Revolution, *et cetera*, or we can take the side of Becker the historiographer, who, as Sabine put it, hadn't left history a leg to stand on and who in "Everyman His Own Historian" described the historian primarily as a "keeper of useful myths."

It is, of course, necessary to add that the myths that Becker himself would preserve are, from the liberal democratic point of view, harmless ones; the "tricks" he would play on the dead are only the old Turnerian ones. In his reflections on historical inquiry, he had attempted to answer the questions Turner had asked of his seminar at the University of Wisconsin: "Is that a fact or only a plausible inference? What is an historical fact? Can you prove an inference?"[114] Now in thinking of the social rôle of the historian Becker rethought the ideas of Turner, as Turner had expressed them in his essay on "The Significance of History." Becker, Merle Curti complained in his review of *Everyman His Own Historian,* tended to be rather too conservative

[114] Frederick Jackson Turner quoted by Becker, "Frederick Jackson Turner," *Everyman His Own Historian,* 202.

in his definition of the historian's task:[115] according to Becker, "We are
. . . of that ancient and honorable company of wise men of the tribe,
of bards and story-tellers and minstrels, of soothsayers and priests, to
whom in successive ages has been entrusted the keeping of useful
myths."[116]

Becker went on to add that it is the historian's duty to conserve
myths rather than to create them; but this was clearly inconsistent with
the view he sometimes expressed to the effect that the historian
"creates" his facts, as well as with his sympathy for the "New Historians"
who wished to create useful myths for a collectivist democracy. This
came out later in the address when he emphasized that "Our proper
function is not to repeat the past but to make use of it, to correct and
rationalize for common use Mr. Everyman's mythological adaptation
of what actually happened."[117] Becker here is not a priest but a pragmatist in his emphasis upon using the past; he is a Turnerian democrat
in his belief in the *common* use of history. He has also, inadvertently
perhaps, revealed the presence of ghosts in his ideas about history.
What is a Rankean phrase like "what actually happened" doing in an
address which purported to show that history is useful myth, which
stated that: "We are surely under bond to be as honest and as intelligent as human frailty permits; but the secret of our success in the
long run is in conforming to the temper of Mr. Everyman, which we
seem to guide only because we are so sure, eventually, to follow it"?[118]

Becker in "Everyman His Own Historian" was struck by two things:
(1) the need for useful historical knowledge (he prefaced the address
with a long story about how Mr. Everyman makes use of a kind of "historical document" even to pay his coal bills); (2) the relativity of the
historical knowledge we think we have to the needs which fashioned it
(the historian must keep Mr. Everyman's coal bills up to date). The historian is then, according to Becker, a man of myths, but of myths that
should "harmonize, as well as ignorance and prejudice permit, the actual and the remembered series of events. . . . Let not the harmless,
necessary word 'myth' put us out of countenance," he advised.[119]

The word *myth* might, however, easily put one out of countenance
because Becker did not provide criteria for distinguishing useful myths
from useless ones, or for knowing when we have succeeded in harmo-

[115] *American Historical Review*, XLI (October, 1935), 117.
[116] "Everyman His Own Historian," *Everyman His Own Historian*, 247.
[117] *Ibid.*, 253.
[118] *Ibid.*
[119] *Ibid.*, 247.

nizing the "actual and the remembered series of events." Becker, it is commonly thought, had two histories — history as it happened, and history as it is remembered.[120] Actually it would seem that he had four histories: (1) history as it happened; (2) history as it is remembered by Mr. Everyman; (3) history as it reflects the historian's efforts to improve upon Mr. Everyman's memory; and (4) history as it ultimately proves to be useful and acceptable because and *only* because Mr. Everyman likes the way in which the historian keeps his accounts for him.

History, the present author feels, surely *ought* to be useful. If it enables us to understand others or ourselves better, to see the hopes and despairs of "the human predicament," or even to anticipate in a limited way the drift of certain social currents, almost everyone would applaud. There is, however, a world of difference between a useful truth (and, as Becker repeatedly pointed out, many truths, or academic exercises, *are* useless) and a truth that "becomes" true simply because it is useful. What Becker accomplished in his comments on historical facts and evidence amounted to the rejection of the correspondence theory of truth in historical inquiry. More accurately, he had set up a new correspondence theory in which the old ideal of a correspondence between the report and the reported is of necessity surrendered to a correspondence between the reporter (the historian) and what his reader (Mr. Everyman) regards as useful. If useful and necessary, then true, Becker had said in 1910 in his essay "Detachment and the Writing of History"; and this he simply repeated in the 1930's.

There is evidence that Becker was less than satisfied with his criteria of satisfaction and utility, which probably accounts for his not publishing either of his essays on Historical Facts or Historical Evidence, although both were highly polished and subtle pieces of reasoning. Certainly a note of dissatisfaction and of doubt is revealed in his reaction to the responses to his presidential address. He had received a standing ovation at Minneapolis in 1931, and one that was richly deserved in view of his catholic attainments. He had written political history, intellectual history, biographical sketches, and reviews, which had established his eminence as a scholar, a historian, and above all a writer. Simply from a literary point of view, Becker's "Everyman His Own Historian" ranked at the very top of presidential addresses before the American Historical Association. Even people outside Becker's profes-

[120] See, for instance, Zagorin, "Carl Becker on History, Professor Becker's Two Histories: A Skeptical Fallacy," where Zagorin tries to reduce these two histories to one at Becker's expense.

sion, including Felix Frankfurter[121] and Oliver Wendell Holmes, admired it greatly. The aging Holmes thanked Becker for an off-print and wrote, "I have heard you called the finest historian in the country . . . and I readily believe it."[122] Holmes, who had done as much as anyone to make American jurisprudence "pragmatic," may have noticed Becker's pragmatism as well as his style.

How then could Becker be less than satisfied? Perhaps the enthusiasm of some of his admirers made him doubt himself. To W. Stull Holt he admitted that there was "some dynamite" in his address. Most people, Becker said, admit that history needs re-writing "because of the appearance of new 'material' or a more expert technique." Such people see historiography as the record of constant progress toward knowledge and "sound" interpretation; but, Becker wrote: "Of course the implications of my address are far more radical than that." He then complained, however, that Dodd of Chicago had been reported as saying that the address made historical research seem futile: "Misunderstanding could hardly go farther than that."[123] He was sufficiently worried to sit down and write a three-page letter to Dodd in which he stressed the need for more and better historical research into the records left by the past.[124]

A careful comparison of Becker's presidential address with his letter to Dodd shows, however, important differences in the tone and emphasis of these two documents. While it is true that Becker had in his presidential address spoken approvingly of the historian's efforts to improve upon Mr. Everyman's memory, the tone of the address had been exceedingly skeptical and the emphasis had been overwhelmingly upon the historian's dependence upon Mr. Everyman and the "climate of opinion." Dodd was surely right when he replied that, while agreeing with much of what Becker said, he still thought that younger scholars had come away from Becker's address with "a certain feeling of futility."[125] Becker answered that, on the contrary, a belief in the possibility of definitive histories would make research futile: "But my thesis that nothing can ever be finally settled makes the effort to settle it ever necessary and useful."[126] Here Dodd might well have said: I fail to see the necessity.

---

[121] Frankfurter called it "the swellest piece of writing" he had read for a long time, and he described Becker as a poet as well as a thinker. Quoted by A. M. Schlesinger to Carl Becker, Cambridge, Massachusetts, February 9, 1932.

[122] Oliver Wendell Holmes to Carl Becker, Washington, D.C., February 7, 1932.

[123] Carl Becker to W. Stull Holt, Ithaca, New York, January, 1932.

[124] Carl Becker to William E. Dodd, Ithaca, New York, January 27, 1932.

[125] William E. Dodd to Carl Becker, Chicago, January 29, 1932.

[126] Carl Becker to William E. Dodd, Ithaca, New York, February, 1932.

Becker further revealed his doubts as to how far relativism should carry him in his review in 1939 of a book written by Maurice Mandelbaum, *The Problem of Historical Knowledge,* in which Mandelbaum had attacked the "historical relativism" of Croce, Dilthey, Mannheim, Rickert, Beard, and Becker.[127] Becker wrote to Beard in December, 1938, that his first impression of the book was very unfavorable.[128] In January of 1939 Becker read a paper before the Circle at Cornell criticizing Mandelbaum's attempted refutation of relativism, and from the interchange of ideas with his colleagues Becker thought he had got a better "notion of what Mandelbaum is really driving at."[129] Still he found Mandelbaum confusing; the net effect of reading Mandelbaum, however, was that Becker toned down the relativistic implications of his own ideas on historiography. Becker insisted that Mandelbaum had admitted the legitimacy of what Becker meant by relativism — namely, that new histories replace the old, that what is included or stressed in the new histories "depends in no small part upon the social situation" of the historian, the *Weltanschauung.* "If relativism means more than this — if it means that a considerable body of knowledge, an increasing body of knowledge, is not objectively ascertainable, if it means a denial that the *ideal* of objective historical knowledge is possible of at least *partial* attainment — then I am not a relativist."[130]

Once before in this chapter the reader has been cautioned not to take at their face value Becker's own words, not to take out of context some of his criticisms of the New Historians. Now the author must be even more drastic and insist that Becker did not fully understand his own relativism, or at least did not see in it the implications that are objectively there. If what Becker said about facts and evidence and Mr. Everyman means anything, it means not only that the historian ultimately must cater to Mr. Everyman or perish — this is an existential necessity — but that *because* he is part of the same "climate of opinion" as Mr. Everyman he could do nothing else — this is a logical necessity. The evidence or the facts are only what competently trained people say they are — no one can resurrect Caesar and ask him to cross the Rubicon while Fulbright students take notes. We are at the mercy of the historian, just as he is at the mercy of Mr. Everyman. Furthermore, judgments of fact are inevitably at the mercy of judgments of value — a man's belief in miracles becomes only the historian's belief that he

[127] Maurice Mandelbaum, *The Problem of Historical Knowledge* (New York, 1938).

[128] Carl Becker to Charles A. Beard, Ithaca, New York, December 27, 1938.

[129] Carl Becker to George Sabine, Ithaca, New York, February 5, 1939.

[130] Review of Maurice Mandelbaum, *The Problem of Historical Knowledge, Philosophical Review,* XLIX (April, 1940), 363.

believes in miracles, nothing more or less. By this logic of implication, Becker, despite himself, would have had to equate fact with
fancy, to concede that Methodism may be as respectable intellectually
as agnosticism, to say that no age knows any age except itself, to doubt
really that the present can know even the present but only its own
ideas about the present, to confess that no man knows another but only
his own ideas about another, and to admit finally — bringing in Freud
— that he may be suffering from self-deception.

Solipsism is the minimum consequence of a relativism that started
out modestly, bravely enough only to insist that the Absolute Truth has
perished and that what remains must be relevant or perish, too. Hara-
kiri, as Becker pointed out in his essay on "Progress," is the maximum,
but logical, consequence of a relativism that has outlived its relevance
or the needs to which it was related.[131] World War Two saved Becker
from paying the maximum, even figuratively speaking; it rescued
him from relativism. As the war drew near he gave up the relativist
argument almost entirely, which proved that he was after all a good
relativist, a good pragmatist, and a good citizen.

Becker remains, however, a poor but exciting epistemologist. He has
taught us that much of what passes for disinterested, "detached" history is often an uninteresting product of an uninterested mind; this is
what was meant by the earlier reflection, made in connection with
Becker's *The Heavenly City*, that "good" history is often in some sense
autobiographical. He has reminded us, as F. H. Bradley had done long
before,[132] that presuppositions are important in historical inquiries and
interpretations, and if he has not told how truth is possible he has at
least recalled for us what bias is and why a certain amount of it is
inevitable. In the place of a coldly neutral approach, he himself often
but not always practiced an intuitive, sympathetic act of imaginative
understanding in his historical studies. His method, I feel, was useful,
while his theory was hopelessly wrong. Ultimately, the success of intuition, sympathy, imagination, and understanding depends upon there
being something independent "out there" in the evidence left by the
past upon which we can exercise these faculties. Intuition, sympathy,
imagination, and understanding are at best devices that are employed
to interpret the facts that historians have garnered from the evidence
which, *if* they are really facts, symbolize some event or idea that actually happened, or appeared at least once before the here and now.
This sounds possibly naive and old-fashioned, so perhaps I should end

[131] "Progress," *Encyclopedia of the Social Sciences*, XII, 499.
[132] *The Presuppositions of Critical History* (London, 1874).

by having recourse to Bertrand Russell: "Nevertheless, it is plain . . . that the truth or falsity of a given judgment depends in no way upon the person judging, but solely upon the facts about which he judges."[133]

[133] Russell, "On the Nature of Truth," *Philosophical Essays* (London, 1910), 173. Becker had learned something about the philosophy of science from Russell and had quoted from his "A Free Man's Worship" in *The Heavenly City*, 14; but where epistemology was concerned he behaved as if Russell had never existed. Empiricism for Becker was David Hume's or John Locke's monopoly. There is no evidence that he read Moore, Ayer, Carnap, Wittgenstein, or a host of other modern philosophers.

Chapter X

Becker and World War Two: The Recovery of Faith

WE ARE HAPPY, Goethe once said, when for everything within us there is an equivalent outside. By this criterion the last five years of Becker's life were reasonably happy, and surely no man as "remorselessly rationalistic" as Becker could ask for more than reasonable happiness. As Becker found, during World War Two, that the barricades of opinion against the liberal democrat had been temporarily lowered by both conservatives and radicals, he could take comfort in the apparent unity and purposefulness of American democracy. Along with a host of other writers, ranging from Sinclair Lewis to Louis Hacker, Becker rediscovered the virtues of a middle-class culture in which everyone was free "to shoot off his mouth";[1] and he allowed the theme of reconciliation to take the place of partial alienation in his thoughts and feelings.

Becker's sense of unity and his feeling of well-being also had, however, a more matter-of-fact physical origin; his renewal of faith was accompanied by a renewal of physical health. In 1940 he underwent drastic surgery that removed three-fourths of his stomach and relieved him from ill health for the rest of his life, until his unexpected death of uremic poisoning in 1945. He must have had a strong constitution to have survived at all in the 1920's and 1930's the wearisome effects of prolonged though not critical illnesses. While Becker lay in the hospital undergoing surgery in 1940, his colleague Wolf Laistner wrote to Mrs. Becker expressing the hope that her husband's "fine constitution once again stands him in good stead,"[2] and this hope proved warranted. By the next year it was apparent that the operation had been a marked success. "I will soon be back to normal (although as the years pass 'normal' is always something less than it was)," Becker wrote to a former student.[3]

Actually, "normal" proved to be something more than it had been.

[1] Becker, *How New Will the Better World Be?* (New York, 1944), 124.
[2] Wolf Laistner to Mrs. Carl Becker, Ithaca, New York, July 23, 1940.
[3] Carl Becker to Betty Bohannon, Ithaca, New York, April 24, 1941.

210

Within the few remaining years of his life Becker wrote three books, one of which was in its way equal to his better books such as *The Eve of the Revolution* and *The Declaration of Independence*, if not to his masterpiece *The Heavenly City*. This was his history of Cornell, which was based on "original" research in the Cornell archives. In addition to this he wrote a book on foreign policy and one on domestic problems. He was almost everywhere well received, and Wolf Laistner, his successor to the Stambaugh Chair of History, wrote that "If you will be a Lion, you must expect to be lionised."[4] This was a reference to Becker's position in 1942 at Smith College, but one that could also be applied to Becker's steadily increasing popularity as a lecturer (rarely available), essayist, author, and book reviewer. Editors and publishers assured him of a ready market for his every word;[5] anthologists wanted his essays for their treasuries of modern literature. Thomas Costain, after talking with Becker at Cornell, advised him to do a book on Thomas Paine. It would "be good for Cornell," Costain thought, and after talking with some "motion picture people" he was fairly certain that the book might become a film. Becker was a conscientious frequenter of the movies, but he felt constrained to refuse celluloid immortality for himself and Paine.[6]

"You may have lost part of your stomach, but you have not lost any of your wisdom or your ability to say things clearly and charmingly," Olin Templin wrote from Kansas, and he reported that twenty-two friends of Becker's had gathered at the Templin home to hear one of Becker's articles read.[7] Templin's attitude by and large was that of the intellectual, socially oriented middle class. In the 1940's Becker's audience tended to become wider and more "middle-brow," although he at no time reached a mass audience in the way that a Civil War historian or a Winston Churchill sometimes does. Veteran historical scholars, according to Becker's friend Guy Stanton Ford, sometimes disappointed their readers by writing about "all manner of problems far removed from their previous competence, but never Carl Becker."[8]

Never had Becker been a better citizen than during World War Two. Indeed, the last few years of Becker's life have a familiar quality

[4] Wolf Laistner to Carl Becker, Ithaca, New York, May 16, 1942.

[5] Herbert Blum of the *Journal of Sociology* to Carl Becker, Chicago, January 14, 1942. Alfred Knopf to Carl Becker, New York, January 5, 1942.

[6] Thomas Costain to Carl Becker, New York, June 24, 1941, and November 5, 1941.

[7] Olin Templin to Carl Becker, Lawrence, Kansas, April 13, 1942.

[8] Review of *New Liberties for Old, Mississippi Valley Historical Review,* XXVIII (March, 1942), 623.

about them. Much of the optimism of Becker's World War One days had been lost forever, but in comparison with the Becker of the 1920's and 1930's, the Becker of the 1940's abounded in faith, hope, and charity, at least for those who shared his position. Becker was never happier in a sense than when he could witness a struggle between good and evil and watch democracy vindicate its spiritual virtues by a physical trial at arms. A democracy fighting for its life was purged of many of its defects in Becker's eyes; its neuroses were resolved — or suspended — in a common faith. For both democracy and Becker, war was a catharsis. As it became evident that democracy would triumph over fascism, Becker could rejoice, cautiously, that he and the currents of history were once more moving in the same direction. Whether he would have gone through the unhappiness in the post-World War Two period that he had experienced after the first war is, of course, unknown, but it is doubtful. Becker in the 1940's appears to have learned from history, his history, how to countervail against extreme optimism and extreme pessimism.

Becker in the 1940's was freer to write and to play the good citizen-at-large than he had ever been before because of his retirement from teaching in June, 1941. One year prior to his retirement he had been appointed to the newly established John Wendell Anderson Professorship and his salary had been raised to $8,000.[9] In February of 1941 he was appointed University Historian by his friend President Edmund E. Day. He accepted,[10] and wrote to Gottschalk that this now made his retirement salary satisfactory. At a later date he planned, in his capacity as University Historian, to give the Messenger Lectures on the history of Cornell and to show the importance of Cornell in the growth of the modern preoccupation with History and Science,[11] a concern he had discussed earlier in his *The Heavenly City*.

Although Becker had never attained the popularity as an undergraduate lecturer that his teacher Robinson had, his courses had been for some time crowded; and this was especially true toward the end. Indeed, Becker achieved an immortality at Cornell that even Robinson could not have had for long at a city university such as Columbia. Robinson, Turner, Burgess, Osgood, and Dodd were dead by now; and so too were friends and colleagues such as Charles Hull, George Lincoln

---

[9] R. B. Meigs to Carl Becker, Ithaca, New York, October 26, 1940.

[10] Carl Becker to Edmund E. Day, Ithaca, New York, February 9, 1941.

[11] Carl Becker to Louis Gottschalk, Ithaca, New York, July 18, 1941.

Burr, Preserved Smith, and Othon Guerlac.[12] It comes as a shock to realize that Becker was no longer middle-aged, that he was now one of the elder statesmen of his profession and university. One had expected the stream of ironic, lucid, detached remarks to continue forever; so had his former students who wrote to him of their gratitude for his exemplary influence upon them and of their hope that he would continue to teach through his writings. Francis Wormuth voiced the opinion of many when he said that Becker had been responsible for a higher level of intellectual activity among the graduate history students at Cornell than he had witnessed at any other university.[13] Louis Gottschalk movingly wrote that no one had influenced his character or affected his outlook so much as Becker: "Cornell meant Becker to me; Cornell is now in retirement as far as I am concerned."[14]

If Robespierre was Rousseau's ape, then I am yours, Gottschalk fervently proclaimed.[15] In the case of Becker's teacher Turner the enthusiasm of students could be in part explained as the result of Turner's personality; with Becker it must have come simply from the quality of his intellectual processes. Perhaps also it was related to the fact that Becker and the Cornell graduate program in history seemed committed to the idea that an exhaustive program of course and thesis work was more apt to turn out exhausted than creative minds. As Marshall Knappen has observed, Cornell graduate students were sent out free and eager to keep on writing; and this in turn was credited to the master. On his oral examination for the Ph.D., Knappen had missed several questions asked by Becker. The next day Knappen apologized, and Becker replied, "Well, if we're sending you away with the idea that you still have something to learn, maybe we have done our job."[16]

The letters of appreciation that Becker received at the end of his career were to him "a consolation and a great reward for all the effort a teacher puts in to what often seems a futile business." Such letters convinced him that "little as I can understand what it is, there must have been something valuable that I did for many people."[17] He had, however, no regrets that his teaching was nearing the end. After forty-

[12] Becker wrote the obituary for Othon Guerlac for the *Necrology of the Cornell Faculty* in 1934 and the obituary for Preserved Smith for the *American Historical Review*, XLVI (July, 1941), 1016-1017.

[13] Francis Wormuth to Carl Becker, Bloomington, Indiana, June 5, 1941.

[14] Louis Gottschalk to Carl Becker, Chicago, July 15, 1941.

[15] Louis Gottschalk to Carl Becker, Chicago, October 5, 1944.

[16] Carl Becker quoted by Marshall Knappen to Phil Snyder, Ann Arbor, Michigan, February 18, 1956.

[17] Carl Becker to Louis Gottschalk, Ithaca, New York, July 18, 1941.

two years of talk and study even the subjects of God, freedom, and immortality might grow stale — let alone Robespierre, Danton, and St. Just — and one can well understand a letter he wrote to Max Lerner: "I am not sorry to be done with it, but sorry only that I have reached the age when one is not sorry to be done with it."[18] On June 10, 1941, there was a dinner in Becker's honor at Cornell, and it was all over, except for a term spent as Neilson Research Professor at Smith College in the spring of 1942. Becker was through with what he fondly, cynically referred to as the teaching "racket."[19]

Now there was more time for his family. Time to watch first the publishing career and then the wartime naval career of his son who, after graduate work in English at Cornell, had joined the publishing house of Silver Burdett. Time to enjoy visits from his son and daughter-in-law, and after 1940 to delight in being a grandfather. Time to write more often to his sister Jessie, recalling the Fourth of July and firecrackers and growing up in Iowa.[20] Also, there was more time for Maude, who had been in the hospital in 1942 for the first time in her life.

Following his return from Smith College, there was time, too, for one last service to Cornell, in the form of his Messenger Lectures, which were published in 1943 as *Cornell University: Founders and the Founding*, a work in which piety and perspective went hand in hand in such a way as to please both Cornell graduates and critical scholars. There were twelve Messenger Lectures, scarcely enough to allow for a "definitive" history, but sufficient to show that Becker had recovered some of the appetite for facts which had not been much in evidence since the publication of his doctoral thesis, as well as some of the exuberance that had not often appeared since his "Kansas" days. The style was felicitous and the judgments sound, except for occasional howlers such as when, in his chapter on "Life and Learning in the United States," he spoke of Francis Lieber's "stimulating lectures" at the University of South Carolina, something by most accounts impossible to imagine.[21]

Becker's method was to fit Cornell into the history of higher education in the United States in the last half of the nineteenth century, to show that it had been "deliberately designed to meet the three cardinal demands of the time — the demand for liberalization of the college of

[18] Carl Becker to Max Lerner, Ithaca, New York, May 9, 1941.
[19] *Ibid.*
[20] Carl Becker to Jessie Becker, Ithaca, New York, June 26, 1942.
[21] *Cornell University: Founders and the Founding*, 16.

arts, for the promotion of scientific research, and for advanced professional training in agriculture and the mechanical arts."[22] With the assistance of his friend E. R. B. Willis, Becker had gone through the manuscript sources in the "vault" of the university library and had traced the details of how Ezra Cornell and Andrew Dixon White had created a university that was neither entirely a state university nor a privately endowed one, but a curious, and successful, combination of both. Aided by the research of his colleague P. W. Gates, Becker related the history of the Morrill Land Grant Act, and he told of the way in which Cornell, falsely charged with fraud, had used the university's Western land grants for the ultimate good of the university which bore his name.[23]

Some of the circumstances that had made possible the success of Cornell University had been a matter of chance, according to Becker; and he was pleased to relate the story of the conjunction of fortuitous circumstances with exceptional individuals. He chose not to deal with Fate or Providence or the laws of probability or with man reduced to "a pawn of higher forces such as the clash of economic interests";[24] he chose in short to deal with Ezra Cornell and Andrew Dixon White. He described Ezra Cornell as a self-made man with a Quaker conscience, a flair for successful dreaming, and an inability to fill in the details of his own schemes. Cornell, as presented in Becker's finely drawn vignette, was "a rich but honest man who could make a case of conscience out of the prosaic fact that he had five hundred thousand dollars more than he thought his family would ever need."[25] With this he had endowed the University on condition that the state of New York equal his contribution. As members of the New York Senate, he and the future first President of Cornell University, Andrew Dixon White, had worked successfully toward that end.

White as a young state Senator must have seemed, Becker imagined, like a Matthew Arnold who had dropped in to deliver a "lecture on sweetness and light." As a matter of fact, however, he had a practical flair that stood his ally Cornell in good stead. As President of the new University, White protested repeatedly that he was a scholar, not a man of business or public affairs, but Becker refused to take him at his word. When, he inquired, had White, the gentleman and the scholar, ever declined a prominent public post, and had he ever been happier

[22] *Ibid.*, 22.
[23] *Ibid.*, 29-40.
[24] *Ibid.*, 41-42.
[25] *Ibid.*, 42.

than while on a leave of absence from the University to serve as Ambassador to the Germany where he had gone many years before as a graduate student of history?[26] Becker spoke kindly of White, but with just a tinge of envy at his versatility and the certainty of his liberal democratic creed: "In the intellectual, no less than in the financial sense, Mr. White always lived in easy circumstances. There is no evidence that he ever experienced, even in the mildest form, any intellectual or spiritual crisis, or even that he was ever seriously troubled by doubt or disillusionment. He exercised in the happiest unconscious way the will to believe."[27]

Becker, as has been pointed out, had experienced something approximating an intellectual or spiritual crisis in reaction to the consequences of World War One, and in the post-war period, he suffered from doubt, disillusionment, and ill health in a way that would have been as alien to Andrew Dixon White as the broodings of Franz Kafka would have been to the liberal-democratic Becker. In the interwar period Becker's will to believe had been mainly a will to persist in democratic habits, or to hope that American democracy would somehow muddle through without destroying liberty.

Becker was not an isolationist in the 1930's, but he did believe that Americans could best solve the problems of democracy at home. He was not a pacifist, but in 1938 he still believed that war was unlikely and that in the event of war the United States had best remain neutral: "I do not think there will be, in the near future, a European war involving Great Britain, France, Germany, and Italy," he wrote. "If there should be one, the consequences for us would be almost equally disastrous whether we went in or kept out. The place to save democracy is at home. If we can put our people to work, democracy will be safe enough here, and we can't save it in Europe by fighting for it there."[28]

What changed Becker's mind between 1938 and the attack on Pearl Harbor in 1941 cannot be fully known. In the first place, however, there was in his mind a growing conviction as to the demonism of Hitler, which came in part from books such as William L. Shirer's *Berlin Diary*, but mainly from the fact that in 1939 Hitler disturbed Becker's prophecy of peace in Europe. By 1941 Becker's will to believe in the intrinsic worth of liberal democracy was back in operation; and he was predisposed to think, as Walter Lippmann might have put it, in terms

[26] *Ibid.*, 121-122.
[27] *Ibid.*, 77.
[28] "How to Keep Out of War," *The Nation*, CXLVI (April 2, 1938), 378.

of "the Atlantic community." In reviewing Shirer's *Berlin Diary* in September, 1941, he spoke contemptuously of Charles Lindbergh and Burton Wheeler for their inability to see the menace of Hitlerism; and he expressed the belief that "the United States can best defend its peace and safety by giving all aid, and not merely all aid short of war, to Great Britain in freeing Europe from German domination."[29] Exactly what Becker meant by the phrase "and not merely all aid short of war" wasn't spelled out, but it was clearly the antithesis of his neutralist sentiments of 1938.

Temporarily it looked as if Becker might be caught between two extremes, as he had been in the Depression. The isolationist extreme was represented by a reader who, incensed by Becker's treatment of Lindbergh, wrote to Becker to remind him that Samuel Johnson had defined patriotism as the last resort of scoundrels.[30] On the other hand, Becker found that his *New Liberties for Old*, which had appeared in 1941, made him suspect for a time among the most ardent believers in an aggressive, vital democracy. After the Japanese attack upon Pearl Harbor had conveniently resolved the debate between neutralists and interventionists, Becker found his *New Liberties for Old* reviewed as "An untimely volume for public reading in these days of national stress." The reviewer for the *American Political Science Review* noted that Becker had, towards the end of this volume, repented of his sins of skepticism, but she was certain that he would not win "a friendly popular reception."[31] She was proved right, and the volume sold only about two thousand copies.[32]

Becker watched the course of the war intently from Smith College and then from his retirement in Ithaca. Speaking before a defense luncheon in Northampton, Massachusetts, on March 11, 1942, Becker set forth the basic theme of his speculations on the course of war and post-war developments. We should, he felt, be more optimistic about an Allied victory but more pessimistic about the post-war settlement.[33] He expected Germany to pass her peak in 1942 and to be defeated in 1943.[34] In December, 1944, he had to confess that even his prediction that the war would have ended by then had been proved overly opti-

[29] *Yale Review*, XXXI (September, 1941), 176.
[30] Irving Benning to Carl Becker, St. Joseph, Michigan, December 19, 1941.
[31] Elizabeth A. Weber, *American Political Science Review*, XXXVI (June, 1942), 596-597.
[32] Norman Donaldson to David Hawke, New Haven, Connecticut, February 14, 1950.
[33] Carl Becker to Max Lerner, Northampton, Massachusetts, March 11, 1942.
[34] Carl Becker to Max Lerner, Northampton, Massachusetts, May 2, 1942.

mistic.[35] In one respect, however, he had been proved correct. In the fall of 1943 he had served with Louis Gottschalk and others on the Army Air Force Committee of Historians to draw up a report on the merits of strategic bombing. Becker had reported to a "somewhat impatient" General Arnold that the Committee found less merit in strategic bombing than the Air Force did.[36] And, Becker wrote in 1944, Germany was still functioning despite all the strategic bombing she had undergone.[37] When victory did come, however, he hoped the Allies would forego the short-lived pleasures of a vindictive peace, such as had followed World War One. He spoke out emphatically against Rex Stout of the War Writers' Board for speaking of the "utter hatefulness" of Germans, and he cited Edmund Burke to the effect that he did not know how to draw up an indictment of an entire nation.[38]

Becker's own bitter hatred of Hitler during the Second World War did not drive him into an intolerance of all Germans, any more than Burke's hatred of the French Revolutionaries had prejudiced Burke against all Frenchmen. Burke as a name to be conjured with in Becker's thought actually made his first appearance during the Second World War. Then in *How New Will the Better World Be?* Becker revealed a distinctly Burkean conception of politics, as both Louis Gottschalk and Charles Merriam noticed.[39] He found "solace" in Burke, Merriam reported critically; but perhaps Becker did so in order not to believe that the new world would be much different from the old, and to save himself from a second seduction by Wilsonian utopianism or its equivalent.

How New Will the Better World Be? was published in 1944. It was an extension of two articles written for the *Yale Review* in 1942 and 1943, which had shown Becker to be a Burkean in his definition of society and a "realist" in his estimate of power politics.[40] Society, Becker quoted Burke, is a partnership between the living, the dead, and those yet unborn; to Becker this was both a source of strength and

[35] Carl Becker to J. Duane Squires, Ithaca, New York, December 22, 1944.

[36] J. Duane Squires to Carl Becker, New London, New Hampshire, December 18, 1944. Arnold may have been impatient, as Squires remembered, but see Major Clayton Bissell to Carl Becker, Washington, D. C., December 29, 1943: "General Arnold desires me to express his appreciation of your contribution to the Army Air Forces."

[37] Carl Becker to Louis Gottschalk, Ithaca, New York, September 3, 1944.

[38] Letter to the editor on Rex Stout and the Writers' War Board, *Commonsense*, XIII (June, 1944), 211.

[39] Gottschalk, "Carl Becker: Skeptic or Humanist," *Journal of Modern History*, XVIII (June, 1946), 160-162. Merriam, *American Political Science Review*, XXXVIII (June, 1944), 556-557.

[40] "Making Democracy Safe in the World," XXXI (March, 1942), 433-453. "How New Will the Better World Be?," XXXII (March, 1943), 417-439.

a confession of weakness. We can be thankful, he maintained, for the force of habit, for the very conservative elements in our thinking and society that seem to defy right reason; if we think realistically, we can see that they save society at the same time they hamstring some of our pet projects. Although he did not say so explicitly, here was the good part of the "cultural lag" which had caused him and Dewey such worry in the 1930's, the part that conserves what we have created. From this definition of society, Becker proceeded to a defense of power politics and even of "imperialism," at least of the British variety. Never had Becker been more of a countervailing force, for he wrote at a time when power politics and British imperialism were especially unpopular among American liberals including the President himself.[41] It would be two years before Churchill's Fulton, Missouri, speech, and six years before George Kennan outlined a policy of "realism" and of "containment" against the Soviet Union.

In a sense Becker countervailed even against himself in *How New Will the Better World Be?* Political power would be as necessary for any new world as it had been for the old, he warned;[42] and the personal aversion to power that he had expressed in *Progress and Power* was not mentioned. Power vacuums caused by the collapse of fascism would have to be filled, and it was clear that Becker relied upon the British Empire to do a good bit of this filling in. He did not foresee a withdrawal of Britain or France from their Asian possessions;[43] nor did he anticipate the outburst of nationalism in Asia and Africa or the collapse of Nationalist China. Most important of all, he did not see international Communism as the force which would most affect his "better world." He did, however, hint at this possibility when he warned that Russia might have different ideas from Great Britain and the United States as to what a "democratic" German government should be.[44] Despite the fact that Becker's book was obsolete within two years of its publication, we must remember that prophecies have a high mortality rate and that Becker was in a sense outlining a sensible *real-politik* solution to the kind of problem that had occurred after the *First* World War.

If Becker was soon to be a victim of the cultural lag of ideas behind events, he would only be confirming his own judgment that "our ideas are usually 'behind the times.'" It is often said of military men that they

---

[41] See, for example, Elliott Roosevelt, *As He Saw It* (New York, 1946), *passim.*
[42] *How New Will the Better World Be?*, 86.
[43] *Ibid.*, 99-100.
[44] *Ibid.*, 197.

'are always fighting the last war.' "[45] More seriously, if he did not qualify as the prophetic type in the significant sense that De Tocqueville or Lord Acton had, he did make sense for many of his contemporaries. For them, he successfully combatted the notion that the war was a crusade for democracy; here again he had to countervail against the liberal's Wilsonian hope that this would be the final step or push into the Promised Land of green pastures and freedom. The war to Becker himself had been a crusade, but one to save democracy not to expand it. "The primary purpose of this war, unless I am completely mistaken," he wrote, "is to preserve the status quo in its fundamentals, even if that involves preserving its superficial defects." By the status quo Becker meant the Bill of Rights, the Constitution, and "free enterprise tempered by such social legislation as from time to time seems essential."[46]

What appeared to Charles Merriam as a piece of unwarranted "pessimism" was welcomed as wholesome "realism" by most readers. *How New Will the Better World Be?* was purchased by the Book-of-the-Month Club, and 18,000 copies were sold.[47] Becker's picture appeared on the cover of the *Saturday Review of Literature,* along with the caption "Carl Becker . . . pricks some unwholesome bubbles." Sir Norman Angell, the least realistic of men, commended Becker's realism in regard to the good done by the British Empire, although like Merriam he regretted parts of Becker's pessimism.[48] Hans Kohn regarded the book as an excellent antidote to the belief in utopias, which inevitably ends in disillusionment;[49] and the reviewer for *Foreign Affairs* saw the book as deflating "starry-eyed Utopianism, but without surrendering to pessimism or defeatism."[50]

Edmund Wilson, who criticized the book severely, admitted that Becker had "a kind of abstract political realism but no very immediate sense of what is going on in the world. . . . The only real distinction of the book," he wrote, "lies in the fact that contemporary platitudes have been endowed by Mr. Becker with a patina that gives them the dignity of museum pieces."[51] Wilson was annoyed at Becker for giving a "misleading" account of Marxism and for stressing the "accidental" nature of the Russian Revolution. The Catholic magazine *Thought,*

[45] *Ibid.,* 23.
[46] *Ibid.,* 128.
[47] Alfred Knopf to David Hawke, New York, January 31, 1950.
[48] *Saturday Review of Literature,* XXVII (March 18, 1944), 8-9.
[49] *New York Times Book Review,* March 19, 1944.
[50] Robert Gale Woolbert, *Foreign Affairs,* XXII (July, 1944), 655.
[51] *New Yorker,* XX (April 15, 1944), 68-74.

however, saw nothing abstract or misleading in Becker's realism but compared it to the "down-to-earth" manner of *The Federalist Papers*. For once, a Catholic reviewer could say that "The realism of Carl Becker has no affinity with cynicism or negativism."[52]

Becker's *real-politik* program involved the division of the world into spheres of influence, and in actual practice he felt that this meant letting Russia have her way in Eastern Europe. There were bound to be differences, he wrote in a letter in 1945, in respect to Poland and Greece; but he saw no reason "to suppose there need be any irreconcilable differences such as would make an international organization useless." Russia had an interest in Eastern Europe comparable to the United States' interest in South America, and all would go fairly well if only the West recognized this. Here Becker allowed his reputation as a "realist" with pessimistic overtones to suffer when he observed that "In general I am not too pessimistic about the future in respect to international affairs. The prospects seem to be better than we have any right to have supposed, three years ago, they would be."[53] To at least one reader, Becker's realism and new-found optimism suggested the ugly word *appeasement*. "On page 36 [of *How New Will the Better World Be?*] you apparently disapprove of the appeasement of Germany at Munich, but on pages 192 and 3 you recommend what appears to me to be an appeasement of Russia," she wrote to him.[54] Thus there was established in microcosm one of the major issues in the approaching debate as to what American policy in regard to "free elections" in Eastern Europe ought to be, and the word *appeasement* was on the way to being eventually transferred, however unjustly, from Munich to Yalta.

Becker's limited optimism on the international scene was based in part on the hope that the United States could provide at home the "150 billion income and the 60 million jobs that are said to be necessary."[55] Saving democracy at home was really Becker's first concern, and here his secular evangelicalism, or what was left of it, found a more natural expression. The Burkean emphasis upon the wisdom of compromise and realism had been forced upon Becker by his own experience in two wars; but there was too much constraint and not enough faith in

[52] Robert C. Hartnett, *Thought*, XIX (September, 1944), 495.
[53] Carl Becker to Mrs. M. M. Kesterson, Ithaca, New York, January 26, 1945.
[54] Mrs. M. M. Kesterson to Carl Becker, Grand Rapids, Michigan, February 12, 1945.
[55] Carl Becker to Mrs. M. M. Kesterson, Ithaca, New York, January 26, 1945.

man in Burke's thought for Becker ever to become a Burkean in the sense that New Conservatives such as Peter Viereck and especially Russell Kirk have. Burke's ideas about politics, custom, and society were taken over by Becker, but the principal feature of Becker's political thought in the wartime period lay in his renewed faith in the "eternal verities" which Thomas Jefferson had outlined in the Declaration of Independence and which Becker had endorsed in 1918 in *The Eve of the Revolution.*

Becker, with his usual eclecticism, did not bother about the possible need for reconciling Burke with Jefferson. Of course, both Burke and Jefferson were heirs to the Revolution of 1688 and to Locke's political philosophy; indeed, Burke had defended the position taken by Jefferson and the American colonists. Still Burke's conception of society was more organic than Jefferson's literal rendering of Locke had allowed for, and Burke in a sense cared less for the will of the people than Jefferson ever did. Becker, like Burke, conceived of society in organic terms, but he could employ Jeffersonian language such as "The Will of the People" without any Burkean fears. At least he could do this in speaking, not of the people in Eastern Europe, but of the American people who had proved their loyalty to the democratic heritage in time of war. In his last published article Becker would tell, with evident approval, of how the American people had turned their electoral college to democratic ends alien to the conservative instincts of the Founding Fathers.[56] A consistent Burkean might have told the story differently.

Despite Becker's eclecticism it is, however, possible to discern some fundamental unity in the positions he took during the 1940's if we single out three areas of experience and characterize his predominant attitude in each: (1) In foreign policy Becker was a "Burkean" in his gradualism and realism and in his defense of the old order. (2) In domestic affairs he was a Jeffersonian, with what George Sabine has called "a very substantial background of democratic faith."[57] (3) In the practical aspects of both foreign and domestic policy, he bridged the gap between (1) and (2) by practicing something called social pragmatism, and by behaving in general, despite his occasional criticisms of Roosevelt, as "a philosophic New Dealer."[58] To speak of a New Dealer as being, in any way, Burkean and/or Jeffersonian may offend some, until we realize that Roosevelt really sought to preserve the existing

---

[56] "The Will of the People," *Yale Review,* XXXIV (March, 1945) 385-404.
[57] George Sabine to Charles E. Merriam, Ithaca, New York, November 14, 1945.
[58] Thomas P. Peardon, Review of *Freedom and Responsibility in the American Way of Life, American Political Science Review,* XL (February, 1946), 138-139.

social structure and to respect the traditions — in part, the Jeffersonian traditions — prescribed by the wisdom of the past.

Becker's final synthesis or expression of these ideas was scarcely an original contribution to the philosophy of politics, nor was it intended as such. In 1943 he answered briefly the question, "What Is Still Living in the Political Philosophy of Thomas Jefferson?", in the form of the Penrose Lecture before the American Philosophical Society in Philadelphia. In 1944 he delivered a fuller but less theoretical exposition of these ideas in the William Cook Lectures on *Freedom and Responsibility in the American Way of Life* at the University of Michigan. The positions he took, while perhaps internally consistent, could not easily be squared with his pre-war skepticism or relativism. Becker thus remains of greater interest as an example of the different tensions and emphases felt by a humane, liberal democrat than as a thinker who reconciled the ideas of liberty and equality, the individual and society, will and reason, or freedom and responsibility.

Becker's lecture on Jefferson involved a recanting of his earlier skepticism concerning the discrepancy between the democratic ideal and the democratic practice. "Indeed, the incredible cynicism and brutality of Adolf Hitler's way of regarding man and the life of man . . . has forced men every where to reexamine the validity of half-forgotten ideas, and to entertain once more half-discarded convictions as to the substance of things not seen," he wrote. "The substance of things not seen" has a suspiciously metaphysical ring about it, and Becker confirmed this in the very next sentence: "One of these convictions is that 'liberty, equality, fraternity,' and 'the inalienable rights of man' are generalities, whether glittering or not, that denote realities — the fundamental realities that men will always fight and die for rather than surrender."[59] While Becker believed that Jefferson had been guilty at times of a facile optimism in his belief in the efficacy of reason and in man's ability to secure his rights in simple, institutional forms, he insisted that "in essentials the political philosophy of Jefferson is our political philosophy; in essentials democracy means for us what it meant for him." He went on to list certain "self-evident" truths that a modern Jeffersonian might accept, and these included "fraternal good will," "the love of truth," and the belief that "the individual man has dignity and worth in his own right."[60]

In *Freedom and Responsibility* he restated these principles and dis-

[59] "What Is Still Living in the Political Philosophy of Thomas Jefferson," *Proceedings of the American Philosophical Society*, LXXXVII (1944). Reprinted in *Detachment and the Writing of History*, 238.
[60] *Ibid.*, 238-240.

cussed them in relation to practical problems such as freedom of speech and economic security. He characterized "freedom of the mind" as being that fundamental freedom without which all other freedoms lose their meaning,[61] and he defended in particular academic freedom. He spoke contemptuously of a learning that was unrelated to the problems of society, and of that kind of research which, "carried on by professors secure in their tenure and under no obligation to concern themselves with the social significance of learning and teaching, tends to run into a barren antiquarianism, as harmless and diverting, and just about as socially useful, as crossword puzzles or contract bridge."[62] Teachers who spoke out on public questions had to be protected, but Becker's justification of their freedom of speech was in emphasis more Deweyite than Jeffersonian: "We can justify it, if at all, not by reference to its antecedents, but only by reference to its consequences."[63] Apparently the tension between self-evident and socially workable truths was still in Becker's mind; only he, like Dewey in *Freedom and Culture,*[64] had shifted his emphasis back to the "eternal verities" that were antecedent to the emergence of American social pragmatism in the twentieth century.

Where freedom of economic activity was concerned, Becker argued that some degree of collectivism or of a managed economy was necessary, and he would not give to the business community anything like the degree of freedom that he would allow the academic community. There is "no use," he wrote, "in saying we do not want any sort of governmental regulation of private economic enterprise. We already have a good deal of it; and it is about as certain as anything can be that we shall have more."[65] Doubtless this was true, but it reminds one somehow of Justice Brandeis' definition of the irresistible as that which we don't want to resist. As for what the American people actually needed, Becker was vague to the point of being platitudinous. "We need more intelligence. . . . We need more integrity. . . ." but most of all we need a greater sense of individual and collective responsibility. With both Burke and Jefferson, Becker saw that the endurance of responsible political organs, and of the tradition of liberty under law, depended in the long run upon the virtue of the people.[66] Here, his atti-

[61] *Freedom and Responsibility in the American Way of Life,* 26.
[62] *Ibid.,* 64.
[63] *Ibid.,* 53.
[64] *Freedom and Culture* (New York, 1939), *passim.*
[65] *Freedom and Responsibility in the American Way of Life,* 118.
[66] *Ibid.,* 134-135.

tude seems to have been, if this be a platitude, let us make the most of it; and this was his legacy to liberal democracy.

A man does not attain immortality during his own lifetime, and it seems unlikely that Becker will ever achieve such a high estate in the eyes of posterity. Since his death on April 10, 1945, it has, however, become clear that he will long remain a significant figure for students of American culture. He founded no school of thought, and he seems to have attracted only the most undogmatic disciples. His "skepticism" and "relativism" were exhausted during his own lifetime; and before his death he had returned almost completely to the Faith of the Fathers, which for an American usually means a return to the natural-rights philosophy of the eighteenth century. As a thinker he is, therefore, significant not for the conclusions he arrived at, but for the journey he made.

In the course of his life he was, as has been shown, both a weather-vane and a countervailing force, a man of paradox torn between skepticism and faith, between pragmatism and a belief in the intrinsic worth of certain principles and modes of life. In all these frames of mind he served, often unintentionally, to record the hopes and fears of thoughtful liberals. Although in terms of originality or influence he was negligible in comparison with men such as John Dewey or Reinhold Niebuhr, he is of value to the scholar because he is in many respects a "typical" or "representative" thinker, not in the sense of being ordinary or average but in the sense of exemplifying the crises of his times, of making explicit philosophical difficulties that were implicit in the crises of the twentieth century. As a historian, he wrote, with considerable fidelity, about the thoughts and emotions of men in the past, especially in the eighteenth century. As a thinker, he recorded the problems of his own society because they were his problems. Thus his writings document both the past and the present and often serve to show both the continuities and discontinuities between the eighteenth and twentieth centuries. His own life reveals in large measure the problems encountered by the eighteenth-century "natural-rights" liberal faith in the twentieth century.

Critics have often complained that Americans still live in the eighteenth century; and in view of the findings of Marx and Freud and countless behavioral scientists, it would seem that only a willful ignorance could account for this innocence, this persistence in the habits of liberal democracy. Yet Becker was neither ignorant nor innocent. Critics might say, as they did in the Depression, that he was ignorant of the "true direction" of history, and that he refused to acknowledge the scientific, predictive values of dialectical materialism. On the other hand, they might repeat the charge that he chose deliberately to ignore the insights of conservative religion into human nature, as these insights are expressed in the dogma of Original Sin. The liberal in the twentieth century has repeatedly, and sometimes deservedly, been subjected to such criticisms from both the extreme left and the extreme right. He has often been unable to turn the other cheek because the other cheek was also being slapped by one of the two extremes. In a world such as this, Becker's appeal will always be to a minority of men who share his horror of fanaticism and oversimplification, who are aware of the inevitable distortions of thought that come from the class struggle or the imperfections within man, but who still endeavor to think well.

One might disagree with Becker on innumerable points, which would not have offended him, and yet find him one of the most attractive if minor figures of our age. Socrates is beloved by men who reject his image of the cave with its distinction between reality and appearance; Montaigne is appreciated even by those who refuse to believe, as he did, that life is largely a spectator sport. Becker was no Socrates or Montaigne, but he had, usually for the better, many of their qualities. It may be of some comfort to the humanist that Socrates and Montaigne have endured longer than their opposites in the favor of posterity; and if posterity is so humane and philosophical in its preferences, there may be hope for Becker as well. Indeed, there may be hope for all men of good will, regardless of their convictions.

In the field of history, Becker's humane beliefs were reflected in his efforts to prevent the de-humanization of history, which might some day rank among our gravest errors. We in the West have, temporarily at least, shown signs of resisting the tyranny of an impersonal economic interpretation of history, but we have often done so at the price of embracing unattractive alternatives. In defiance of "the economic interpretation," we have lent a willing ear to those who believe that history is a rope of sand, that all events are equally contingent, and even that the principal determining factor in history is "chance." Or else we have listened, overlong, to those who speak despairingly of the insoluble predicaments of man, of the inexorable rule that makes all men the victims of the crises and tensions of their milieu, and of the guilt that stains every man so that, for all intents and purposes, it is useless to distinguish between the criminal and his pursuers. Finally, the claim has been set forth, in the name of "technical history," that the professional historian cannot deal with the most profound human experiences or with the needs of his own time and place; according to this line of reasoning, the best historian might be a man without convictions, or an intellectual eunuch.

It was the genius or talent of Becker that he could appreciate many of these points of view and utilize their insights before rejecting their claims to totality. He employed the economic interpretation when, in his opinion, events warranted it. He could properly understand the rôle that either "chance" or "the climate of opinion" plays in human decisions and interactions. He was able to see that man is imperfect and that no statesman or citizen could emerge from a holocaust such as World War One without some responsibility for its horror. Also, as he showed on a few occasions, he could write better "technical history" than some of its more ardent champions, although he was keenly aware of its limitations and its frequent failures to achieve the "objectivity" it valued above all else. Like every man, Becker lacked omniscience and made occasional errors, but his work is sufficiently distinguished to present the scholar with the paradox of how a "relativist" such as Becker could attain more "objectivity" in his studies than many who may have had a "sounder" theory of knowledge.

Becker's temperament was overwhelmingly rationalistic, but he was well aware of the subtleties, the ironies, and the contradictions that the historical process reveals. As a result of this awareness, he believed that historical inquiry should have a blunting effect upon dogmatism or fanaticism. While he often regarded historical thinking as "an inferior form of thought,"[67] he generally believed that it is an indispensable element in any rational or moral life. With his teacher Turner, he has recalled our attention to the fact that the questions of historical scholarship are as big as life. Scholarship without insight or sympathy, and without literary qualities, he thought, could only offend those whom it ought to enlighten.

Becker may have been guilty of eclecticism, although there are worse crimes. Indeed, his eclecticism may account in part for the variety of his achievements and his eminence among historians. Already it is possible to chart the probable course of his reputation among thoughtful historians and to venture a few predictions. He seems sure to be remembered along with Henry Adams and Charles A. Beard for his abiding concern with the direction of history, even if his questions appear more impressive than his answers. Within the ranks

[67] Becker quoted by Robert R. Palmer, "Thoughts on *The Heavenly City*," *Carl Becker's Heavenly City Revisited*, 133.

of socially oriented historians, he will be remembered as one of the more subtle and self-conscious students of Turner's and Robinson's; his oscillations between involvement and detachment will be of perennial interest to those who find consistency dull. Where the writing of political history is concerned, he will be remembered, if at all, as a promising disciple, at the beginning of his career, of Turner and Osgood, before he turned his attention to intellectual history. In intellectual history he will rank very near the top, and he will outshine all of his teachers and most of his contemporaries in that field. Although he could not write narrative history as Francis Parkman had and seemed largely indifferent to that kind of history, it will be understood that this was a limitation he shared with most of his teachers and contemporaries. If, however, any American has written more understandingly of the dilemmas or ironies of history, it could only be Henry Adams. While Becker contributed little or nothing to hypotheses about the movement of social bodies in the way that Adams or Turner did, he has had no rival as yet among historians in his grasp of the psychology and thinking of historical figures, or of the psychology of belief, or of the translation of belief into action.

Becker's historiography, with its phases of "pragmatism" and especially of "relativism," will be seen as an extension of the "presentism" of several of his teachers; probably it will emerge as being richer in texture and more consistent than that of his friend Beard, who usually outshone him in his writings on politics and the historical process. Becker's pragmatic theory that intelligence is interwoven with purpose and desire will probably be seen as having led him, as he himself later sensed at least in part, to faulty or misleading conclusions concerning the relativity of historical knowledge. The question of the relationships among history, science, and philosophy will, however, long remain a stimulating one, partly because of the propositions Becker put forth. Error is sometimes more exciting than truth, and the truth of the correspondence theory of knowledge is, admittedly, a very lack-lustre affair in comparison with the brilliance that Becker displayed in his questioning of it. Error may often serve as a stimulant to the creation or discovery of newer truths, and if Becker erred in several significant respects no one should ever forget his part in destroying the absurd idea that "facts speak for themselves." Error, like truth, is comparative; the history of thought often shows not so much the progressive realization of truth as it does the elimination of faulty or premature solutions to philosophical or historical problems. Here

Becker's attacks upon those who denied the importance of the philosophy of history were invaluable.

Becker, as has often been pointed out, was not an original thinker in any striking way, but he was an elegant one, whose elegance came from an abiding concern with the lucid expression of ideas arrived at by honest reasoning. Probably he will stand among the better essayists of our time, and as one of the most accomplished writers of nonfiction in America. One may regret that he was not more deeply passionate in his feelings, but one ought not to judge him by any standards that deny the dignity of thought. He was more virtuous than vital, more philosophical than prophetic, but understanding is not always an inferior form of activity. He will endure for many years as a somewhat paradoxical example of his own Jeffersonian verity "that in the long run all values, both for the individual and for society, are inseparable from the love of truth, and from the disinterested search for it."[68]

[68] "What Is Still Living in the Political Thought of Thomas Jefferson?," *Detachment and the Writing of History*, 240.

Bibliography

1. Manuscript Collections in the Regional History Archives, Cornell University, Ithaca, New York

The Carl Lotus Becker Papers.
The George Lincoln Burr Papers.
The Charles Hull Papers

2. Books, Articles, and Reviews by Carl Becker

America's War Aims and Peace Program (Washington: Committee on Public Information, War Information Series, November, 1918).

The American Frontier, Review of Frederick Jackson Turner, *The Frontier in American History, The Nation,* CXI: 538 (November 10, 1920).

Assessing the Blame for the World War, *Current History,* XX: 455-457 (June, 1924).

The Beginnings of the American People (New York, 1915).

Benét's Sympathetic Understanding, *Mark Twain Quarterly,* VII: 13 (1943-44).

Benjamin Franklin (Ithaca, New York, 1946).

Benjamin Franklin, *Dictionary of American Biography,* VI (New York, 1931).

Benjamin Franklin, *Encyclopedia of the Social Sciences,* VI (New York, 1931).

Books That Changed Our Minds, *New Republic,* XCVII: 135 (December 7, 1938).

Cavour and the Map of Italy, Review of William Roscoe Thayer, *The Life and Times of Cavour, The Dial,* LI: 389-392 (November 16, 1911).

A Chronicle of Facts, Review of John Spencer Bassett, *Our War With Germany, New Republic,* XXV: 382-383 (February 23, 1921).

Cornell University: Founders and the Founding (Ithaca, New York, 1943).

The Declaration of Independence, A Study in the History of Political Ideas (New York, 1956 edition).

Detachment and the Writing of History, *Atlantic Monthly,* CVI: 524-536 (October, 1910).

Detachment and the Writing of History: Essays and Letters of Carl L. Becker, ed., Phil L. Snyder (Ithaca, New York, 1958).

Europe Through the Eyes of the Middle East, *New Europe,* XV: 98-104 (May 13, 1920).

The Eve of the Revolution (New Haven, Connecticut, 1918).

231

Everyman His Own Historian: Essays on History and Politics (New York, 1935).

Freedom and Responsibility in the American Way of Life (New York, 1955 edition).

German Attempts to Divide Belgium (Boston: World Peace Foundation, Vol. I, No. 6, August, 1918).

German Historians and the Great War, Review of Antoine Guilland, *Modern Germany and her Historians*, and Heinrich von Treitschke, *History of Germany in the Nineteenth Century*, *The Dial*, LX: 160-164 (February 17, 1916).

Government of Dependent Territory, *Annals of the American Academy of Political and Social Sciences*, XVI: 404-420 (November, 1900).

Growth of Revolutionary Parties and Methods in New York Province, 1765-1774, *American Historical Review*, VII: 56-76 (October, 1901).

The Heavenly City of the Eighteenth Century Philosophers (New Haven, Connecticut, 1932).

Henry Adams, *Encyclopedia of the Social Sciences*, I (New York, 1930).

The History of Political Parties in the Province of New York: 1760-1776 (Madison, Wisconsin, 1909).

Horace Walpole's Memoirs of the Reign of George III, *American Historical Review*, XVI: 255-272, 496-507 (January, April, 1911).

"How to Keep Out of War," *The Nation*, CXLVI: 378 (April 2, 1938).

How New Will the Better World Be? (New York, 1944).

How New Will the Better World Be?, *Yale Review*, XXXII: 417-439 (March, 1943).

In Support of the Constitution, *The Nation*, CXL: 13-14 (January 2, 1935).

An Interview with the Muse of History, Review of G. M. Trevelyan, *Clio, a Muse and Other Essays*, *The Dial*, LVI: 336-338 (April 16, 1914).

Journey to the Left, Review of George Soule, *The Future of Liberty*, *Saturday Review of Literature*, XV: 6 (November 28, 1936).

La Belle France, Review of William Stearns Davis, *A History of France*, *New Republic*, XXIII: 207-208 (July 14, 1920).

The League of Nations, Review of twenty books about the League, *The Nation*, CIX: 225-228 (August 16, 1919).

Letter from Danton to Marie Antoinette, *American Historical Review*, XXVII: 24-46 (October, 1921).

A letter to the editor of *The Nation*, CXXXVII: 510-511 (November 1, 1933).

A Little More Grape, Captain Bragg, *The Nation*, CX: 260-261 (February 28, 1920).

Making Democracy Safe in the World, *Yale Review*, XXXI: 433-453 (March, 1942).

Modern Democracy (New Haven, Connecticut, 1941).

Modern England, Review of T. M. Healy, *Stolen Waters*; Sir Frederick Maurice, F. Maurice, ed., Gilbert Slater, *The Making of Modern England*; Ernest Taylor, *The Taylor Papers*; Ernest Alfred Vizetelly, *Republican France 1870-1912*, *The Nation*, XCVI: 641-643 (April 24, 1913).

Modern History, the Rise of a Democratic, Scientific, and Industrialized Civilization (New York, 1931).

The Monroe Doctrine and the War, *Minnesota Historical Society Bulletin*, II: 61-68 (May, 1917).

Napoleon—After One Hundred Years, *The Nation*, CXII: 646 (May 4, 1921).

New Liberties for Old (New Haven, Connecticut, 1941).

Nominations in Colonial New York, *American Historical Review*, VI: 260-275 (January, 1901).

Obituary for Othon Guerlac, *Necrology of the Cornell Faculty*, 1934.

Obituary for Preserved Smith, *American Historical Review*, XLVI: 1016-1017 (July, 1941).

On Being a Professor, *Unpopular Review*, VII: 342-361 (April, 1917).

Progress, *Encyclopedia of the Social Sciences*, XII (New York, 1934).

Progress and Power (Palo Alto, California, 1936).

A reply to Oswald Garrison Villard, Sir Edward Grey, *The Nation*, CXXVII: 316-317 (September 20, 1933).

Report on the Twenty-sixth Annual Meeting of the American Historical Association at Indianapolis, *The Nation*, XCII: 57-58 (January 19, 1911).

Review of Charles Francis Adams, *An Autobiography*, *Political Science Quarterly*, XXXI: 611-612 (December, 1916).

Review of Henry Adams, *The Degradation of the Democratic Dogma*, *American Historical Review*, XXV: 480-482 (April, 1920).

Review of Ray Stannard Baker, *Woodrow Wilson and World Settlement*, *The Nation*, CXVI: 186-188 (February 14, 1923).

Review of James Curtis Ballagh, ed., *The Letters of Richard Henry Lee*, *The Nation*, XCIX: 691 (December 10, 1914).

Review of Harry Elmer Barnes, *The New History and the Social Studies*, *Saturday Review of Literature*, II: 38 (August 15, 1925).

Review of Charles Beard, *Cross Currents in Europe Today*, *The Nation*, CXV: 552-553 (November 22, 1922).

Review of Charles and Mary Beard, *The Rise of American Civilization*, *The Nation*, CXX: 559-560 (May 18, 1927).

Review of J. B. Black, *The Art of History: A Study of Four Great Historians of the Eighteenth Century*, *American Historical Review*, XXXII: 295-296 (January, 1927).

Review of James H. Blount, *The American Occupation of the Philippines, 1898-1912*, *The Nation*, XCV: 309-310 (October 3, 1912).

Review of J. B. Bury, *The Idea of Progress*, *American Historical Review*, XXXVIII: 304-306 (January, 1933).

Review of Herbert Butterfield, *The Whig Interpretation of History*, *Journal of Modern History*, IV: 278-279 (June, 1932).

Review of Houston Stewart Chamberlain, *The Foundations of the Nineteenth Century*, *The Dial*, L: 387-391 (May 16, 1911).

Review of Edward Channing, *A History of the United States, I*, *The Nation*, XXCI: 40 (July 13, 1905).

Review of Edward Channing, *A History of the United States, II*, *The Nation*, XXCVII: 440-441 (November 5, 1908).

Review of Edward Channing, *A History of the United States, III*, *The Nation*, XCV: 482-483 (November 21, 1912).

Review of Cleveland B. Chase, *The Young Voltaire*, *American Historical Review*, XXXII: 608-610 (April, 1927).

Review of Gilbert Chinard, *Jefferson et les Idélogues*, *American Historical Review*, XXXI: 585-586 (April, 1926).

Review of Madelaine Clemenceau-Jacquemaire, *Vie de Madame Roland*, *American Historical Review*, XXXV: 854 (July, 1930).

Review of Benedetto Croce, *History: Its Theory and Practise*, *New Republic*, XXX: 174-176 (April 5, 1922).

Review of William E. Dodd, *The Life of Nathaniel Macon*, *The Nation*, LXXVIII: 878 (May 12, 1904).

Review of H. E. Egerton, *The Causes and Character of the American Revolution*, *American Historical Review*, XXIX: 344-345 (January, 1924).

Review of Edward Eyre, ed., *European Civilization: Its Origin and Development*, *American Historical Review*, XLIV: 346-348 (January, 1939).

Review of Bernard Fay, *L'Esprit Revolutionnaire*, *American Historical Review*, XXX: 810-812 (July, 1925).

Review of José Ortega y Gasset, *Toward a Philosophy of History*, *Yale Review*, XXX: 815-817 (June, 1941).

Review of G. P. Gooch, *History and Historians of the Nineteenth Century*, *The Nation*, XCVII: 208-210 (September 4, 1913).

Review of J. F. C. Hearnshaw, ed., *The Social and Political Ideas of Some Great French Thinkers of the Age of Reason*, *Journal of Modern History*, III: 116-118 (March, 1931).

Review of Lucius Henry Holt and Alexander Wheeler Chilton, *A Brief History of Europe*, *New Republic*, XXII: 322 (May 5, 1920).

Review of Ellsworth Huntington, *The Character of Races*, *American Historical Review*, XXX: 571 (April, 1925).

Review of Howard Mumford Jones, *America and French Culture, 1750-1848*, *American Historical Review*, XXXIII: 883-885 (July, 1928).

Review of L. Cecil Jones, *The Interpretation of History*, *The Dial*, LIX: 146-148 (September 2, 1915).

Review of Henry Cabot Lodge, *The Story of the Revolution*, *The Nation*, LXXVII: 366-367 (November 9, 1903).

Review of Maurice Mandelbaum, *The Problem of Historical Knowledge*, *Philosophical Review*, XLIX: 361-364 (April, 1940).

Review of Fulmer Mood, *Development of Frederick Jackson Turner as a Historical Thinker*, *American Historical Review*, XLIV: 263-265 (January, 1944).

Review of Ernest C. Mossner, *Bishop Butler and the Age of Reason*, *American Historical Review*, XLIII: 116-118 (October, 1938).

Review of Charles Oman, *On the Writing of History*, *American Historical Review*, XLV: 591-593 (April, 1940).

Review of Coleman Phillipson, *Alsace-Lorraine: Past, Present, and Future*, *The Nation*, CVIII: 328-329 (March 1, 1919).

Review of James Harvey Robinson, *The Human Comedy*, *The Nation*, CXLIV: 48-50 (January 9, 1937).

Review of James Harvey Robinson, *The Mind in the Making*, *New Republic*, XXX: 174-176 (April 5, 1922).

Review of James Harvey Robinson, *The New History*, *The Dial*, LIII: 19-21 (July 1, 1912).

Review of Gaetano Salvemini, *Historian and Scientist: an Essay on the Nature of History and the Social Sciences, American Historical Review,* XLV: 591-593 (April, 1940).

Review of William L. Shirer, *Berlin Diary, 1934-1941, Yale Review,* XXXI: 173-176 (September, 1941).

Review of Henry Osborn Taylor, *A Historian's Creed, American Historical Review,* XLV: 591-593 (April, 1940).

Review of Frederick J. Teggart, *The Processes of History, American Historical Review,* XXIV: 266-268 (January, 1919).

Review of H. G. Wells, *The Outline of History, American Historical Review,* XXXII: 350-351 (January, 1927).

Review of A. N. Whitehead, *Adventures in Ideas, American Historical Review,* XXXIX: 87-89 (October, 1933).

Review of Norwood Young, *The Life of Frederick the Great, New Republic,* XX: 329-331 (November 12, 1919).

Samuel Adams, *Encyclopedia of the Social Sciences,* I (New York, 1930).

Samuel Adams, *Dictionary of American Biography,* I (New York, 1928).

Some Aspects of the Influence of Social Problems and Ideas upon the Study and Writing of History, American Sociological Society, *Publications,* VII: 73-107 (June, 1913).

Carl Becker and Frederick Duncalf, *Story of Civilization* (New York, 1940).

Tender and Tough Minded Historians, Review of H. H. Powers, *America Among the Powers, The Dial,* LXV: 106-109 (August 15, 1918).

Thomas Hutchinson, *Dictionary of American Biography,* IX (New York, 1932).

Tribute to Frank Egbert Bryant, *Frank Egbert Bryant 1877-1910* (Lawrence, Kansas, March, 1911).

The Unit Rule in National Nominating Conventions, *American Historical Review,* V: 64-82 (October, 1899).

The United States: An Experiment in Democracy (New York, 1920).

A Usable Past, Review of William E. Barton, *The Life of Abraham Lincoln, New Republic,* XLIV: 207-208 (October 14, 1925).

Value of the University to the State, *The University Press Bulletin,* I, Lawrence, Kansas, No. 36 (December 3, 1910).

What Are Historical Facts?, *The Western Political Quarterly,* VIII: 327-340 (September, 1955).

What Is Historiography?, *American Historical Review,* XLIV: 20-28 (October, 1938).

What Is Still Living in the Political Philosophy of Thomas Jefferson? *Proceedings of the American Philosophical Society,* XCVII: 201-210 (1944).

The Will of the People, *Yale Review,* XXXIV: 385-404 (January 30, 1940).

The Writer in Soviet Russia, Review of Max Eastman, *Artists in Uniform, The Nation,* CXXXVIII: 624-625 (May 30, 1934).

3. Books, Articles, and Reviews about Carl Becker

Letter from Henry Adams to J. F. Jameson about Becker published in *American Historical Review,* L: 675-676 (April, 1945).

James Truslow Adams, Review of Carl Becker, *The Declaration of Independence, New Republic*, XXXII: 338 (November 22, 1922).

Sir Norman Angell, Review of Carl Becker, *How New Will the Better World Be?, Saturday Review of Literature*, XXVII: 8-9 (March 18, 1944).

Moses J. Aronson, Review of Carl Becker, *New Liberties for Old, Journal of Social Philosophy*, VII: 93 (October, 1941).

Baltimore Sun, November 22, 1935.

Harry Elmer Barnes, *A History of Historical Writing* (Norman, Oklahoma, 1937).

Charles A. Beard, Review of *The Heavenly City, American Historical Review*, XXXVIII: 590-591 (April, 1933).

——, Review of *The United States: An Experiment in Democracy*, and of Paul L. Haworth, *The United States in Our Time, The Nation*, CXI: 416-417 (October 13, 1920).

J. B. Brebner, Review of *Freedom and Responsibility, Yale Review*, XXXIV: 555-558 (March, 1946).

Adrian Coates, Review of *The Heavenly City, Philosophy*, VIII: 495-496 (October, 1933).

Merle Curti, Review of *Everyman His Own Historian, American Historical Review*, XLI: 116-118 (October, 1935).

William E. Dodd, Review of *Everyman His Own Historian, Journal of Modern History*, VII: 465-466 (December, 1935).

Max Farrand, Review of *The United States: An Experiment in Democracy, Mississippi Valley Historical Review*, VIII: 407-409 (March, 1921).

Guy Stanton Ford, Carl Lotus Becker, *American Philosophical Society Year Book*, 1945.

——, Review of *New Liberties for Old, Mississippi Valley Historical Review*, XXVIII: 623 (March, 1942).

Leo Gershoy, Introduction to *Progress and Power* (New York, 1949).

——, Invitation to Learning, A Discussion of Carl Becker's *The Declaration of Independence* on the Columbia Broadcasting System, February 22, 1948.

——, Review of *Modern Democracy, Yale Review*, XXX: 839-841 (June, 1941).

——, Zagorin's Interpretation of Becker: Some Observations, *American Historical Review*, LXII: 12-17 (October, 1956).

Louis Gottschalk, Carl Becker: Skeptic or Humanist, *Journal of Modern History*, XVIII: 160-162 (June, 1946).

Louis M. Hacker, Historian of Revolutions, *New Republic*, XXCV: 260-261 (January 8, 1936).

C. G. Haines, Review of *The United States: An Experiment in Democracy, American Political Science Review*, XV: 616-617 (November, 1921).

Samuel William Halperin, Review of *Modern Europe, American Journal of Sociology*, XXXVII: 689 (January, 1932).

Walter H. Hamilton, Review of *The Eve of the Revolution, The Dial*, LXVI: 137 (February 8, 1919).

Marjorie S. Harris, Review of *The Heavenly City, Journal of Philosophy*, XXX: 190-193 (March 16, 1933).

Robert C. Hartnett, Review of *How New Will the Better World Be?*, *Thought*, XIX: 495 (September, 1944).

David Hawke, Carl Becker, Master's thesis (University of Wisconsin, Madison, Wisconsin, 1950).

Homer Hockett, Review of *Everyman His Own Historian, Mississippi Valley Historical Review*, XXII: 332-333 (September, 1935).

Ithaca Journal, November 27, 1935.

Leland Hamilton Jenks, Review of *Everyman His Own Historian, American Sociological Review*, I: 160-161 (February, 1936).

Isaac Joslin, Review of *The Beginnings of the American People, Mississippi Valley Historical Review*, II: 276-277 (September, 1915).

Paul Kiniery, Review of *New Liberties for Old, Thought*, XVII: 381-382 (June, 1942).

Hans Kohn, Review of *How New Will the Better World Be?*, *New York Times Book Review*, March 19, 1944.

Joseph Wood Krutch, The Doctrine of Recurrence, Review of Carl Becker, *The Heavenly City of the Eighteenth Century Philosophers*, *New York Herald Tribune Books*, December 18, 1932.

Harold J. Laski, American Scholarship, Review of Carl Becker, *New Liberties for Old, New Statesman and Nation*, XXIII: 244-245 (April 11, 1942).

Max Lerner, Review of *The Heavenly City, Yale Law Journal*, XLII: 1143 (May, 1933).

William MacDonald, Review of *The Beginnings of the American People, American Historical Review*, XXI: 352 (January, 1916).

Andrew C. McLaughlin, Review of *The United States: An Experiment in Democracy, American Historical Review*, XXVI: 338 (January, 1921).

Charles E. Merriam, Review of *How New Will the Better World Be?*, *American Political Science Review*, XXXVIII: 556-557 (June, 1944).

Moorhouse F. X. Millar, Review of *Modern Democracy, Thought*, XVI: 409-411 (September, 1941).

Lewis Mumford, Review of *Progress and Power, American Journal of Sociology*, XLII: 429 (November, 1936).

Reinhold Niebuhr, Review of *New Liberties for Old, The Nation*, CLIII: 430-431 (November 1, 1941).

———, Review of *Modern Democracy, The Nation*, CLII: 441 (April 12, 1941).

David Noble, Carl Becker: Science, Relativism, and the Dilemma of Diderot, *Ethics*, LXVII: 233-248 (July, 1957).

Obituary of Carl Becker, *American Historical Review*, L: 885 (July, 1945).

Frederick Ogg, Review of *The Declaration of Independence, Yale Review*, XLIII: 600-604 (April, 1924).

Stanley Pargellis, Review of *Everyman His Own Historian, Yale Review*, XXV: 213-214 (September, 1935).

Thomas P. Peardon, Review of *Freedom and Responsibility in the American Way of Life, American Political Science Review*, XL: 138-139 (February, 1946).

Ralph Barton Perry, Review of *Modern Democracy, Virginia Quarterly Review*, XVII: 440-446 (Summer, 1941).

————, Review of *New Liberties for Old, Yale Review*, XXXI: 408-411 (December, 1941).

"P. G.," Review of *Modern Europe, New Republic*, XVII: 351-352 (October, 1931).

Raymond O. Rockwood, ed., *Carl Becker's Heavenly City Revisited* (Ithaca, New York, 1958).

George H. Sabine, Preface to *Freedom and Responsibility in the American Way of Life* (New York, 1955).

A. M. Schlesinger, Review of *The Declaration of Independence, Mississippi Valley Historical Review*, IX: 334 (March, 1923).

Samuel Sillen, Review of *Modern Democracy, New Masses*, XXXIX: 22-24 (May 6, 1941).

Charlotte Watkins Smith, *Carl Becker, On History and the Climate of Opinion* (Ithaca, New York, 1956).

Phil L. Snyder, Carl L. Becker and the Great War: A Crisis for a Humane Intelligence, *The Western Political Quarterly*, IX: 1-10 (March, 1956).

Cushing Strout, *The Pragmatic Revolt in American History: Carl Becker and Charles Beard* (New Haven, 1958).

William Roscoe Thayer, Review of *The Eve of the Revolution, Yale Review*, VIII: 652 (April, 1919).

C. H. Van Tyne, Review of *The Eve of the Revolution, American Historical Review*, XXIV: 734 (July, 1919).

Joseph S. Ullian, Becker and His *Heavenly City*, unpublished paper written at Harvard University, 1953.

Unsigned Review of *The Eve of the Revolution, Catholic World*, CIX: 405-406 (June, 1919).

Unsigned Review of *The Heavenly City of the Eighteenth Century Philosophers, America*, XLVIII: 365 (January 14, 1933).

Unsigned Review of *Modern Europe, New Republic*, LXVIII: 107 (September 9, 1931).

Unsigned Review of *The United States: An Experiment in Democracy, The Outlook*, CXXVI: 334 (October 20, 1920).

Eliseo Vivas, Review of *Everyman His Own Historian, The Nation*, CXL: 487-488 (April 24, 1935).

Wilson O. Wallis, Progress and Power, *Journal of Social Philosophy*, II: 338-346 (July, 1937).

Washington Herald, November 21, 1935.

Elizabeth A. Weber, Review of *New Liberties for Old, American Political Science Review*, XXXVI: 596-597 (June, 1942).

Edmund Wilson, Review of *How New Will the Better World Be?, New Yorker*, XX: 68-74 (April 15, 1944).

Robert Gale Woolbert, Review of *How New Will the Better World Be?, Foreign Affairs*, XXII: 655 (July, 1944).

Perez Zagorin, Carl Becker on History, Professor Becker's Two Histories: A Skeptical Fallacy, *American Historical Review*, LXII: 1-12 (October, 1956).

4. Other Sources

John Dalberg Lord Acton, German Schools of History, *Historical Essays and Studies* (London, 1907).

————, *Lectures on Modern History* (London, 1952).

Henry Adams, *Mont-Saint-Michel and Chartres* (New York, 1904).

————, The Tendency of History, American Historical Association, *Annual Report, 1894*, 17-23.

Herbert Baxter Adams, Special Methods of Historical Study, *Johns Hopkins University Studies in Historical and Political Science*, II (Baltimore, Maryland, 1884).

Charles McLean Andrews, These Forty Years, *American Historical Review*, XXX: 225-250 (January, 1925).

Noel Annan, *Leslie Stephen, His Thought and Character in Relation to His Time* (Cambridge, Massachusetts, 1952).

O. K. Armstrong, Treason in the Textbooks, *American Legion Magazine*, XXIX: 8-9, 51, 70-72 (September, 1940).

Roland H. Bainton, *George Lincoln Burr: His Life and Works* (Ithaca, New York, 1943).

Harry Elmer Barnes, Assessing the Blame for the World War, *Current History*, XX: 171-195 (May, 1924).

————, *The Genesis of the World War* (New York, 1926).

————, *A History of Historical Writing* (Norman, Oklahoma, 1937).

————, James Harvey Robinson, *American Masters of Social Science* (New York, 1927).

Charles A. Beard, *An Economic Interpretation of the Constitution* (New York, 1913).

————, *President Roosevelt and the Coming of the War, 1941: A Study in Appearances and Realities* (New Haven, Connecticut, 1948).

————, That Noble Dream, *American Historical Review*, XLI: 74-87 (October, 1935).

————, *The Office of Justice of the Peace in England in Its Origin and Development* (New York, 1904).

————, The Frontier in American History, *New Republic*, XCIX: 148 (June 14, 1939).

————, Review of Frederick Jackson Turner, *The Frontier in American History*, *New Republic*, XXV: 349-350 (February 16, 1921).

————, *Public Policy and the General Welfare* (New York, 1941).

————, Preface to Brooks Adams, *The Law of Civilization and Decay* (New York, 1943).

————, Review of Arnold Toynbee, *A Study of History*, *American Historical Review*, XL: 307-309 (January, 1935); XLV: 593-594 (April, 1940).

————, Written History as an Act of Faith, *American Historical Review*, XXXIX: 219-231 (January, 1934).

Ralph Bourne, Twilight of Idols, *Untimely Papers* (New York, 1919).

F. H. Bradley, *The Presuppositions of Critical History* (London, 1874).

————, *The Principles of Logic*, I (London, 1932).

Carl Bridenbaugh, *Cities in Revolt: Urban Life in America, 1743-1776* (New York, 1955).

Robert E. Brown, *Charles A. Beard and the Constitution* (Princeton, New Jersey, 1956).

John W. Burgess, *Political Science and Comparative Constitutional Law* (Boston, 1893).

———, Political Science and History, *Annual Report of the American Historical Association for the Year 1896*, I (Washington, D. C., 1897).

———, *Recent Changes in American Constitutional Theory* (New York, 1923).

———, Preface to *The Middle Period 1817-1858* (New York, 1897).

———, *Reminiscences of an American Scholar* (New York, 1934).

Everett Carter, *Howells and the Age of Realism* (Philadelphia, 1954).

Harold Dean Carter, *Henry Adams and His Friends* (New York, 1947).

Edward P. Cheyney, Law in History, *American Historical Review*, XXIX: 191-202 (January, 1924).

Chicago-Record Tribune, October 16, 1901.

R. G. Collingwood, *The Idea of History* (Oxford, 1946).

Henry Steele Commager, *The American Mind* (New Haven, Connecticut, 1954).

Benedetto Croce, *Logic as the Science of the Pure Concept* (London, 1917).

———, *Theory and History of Historiography* (London, 1921).

Merle Curti, Frederick Jackson Turner, 1861-1932, *Probing Our Past* (New York, 1955).

Merle Curti and Vernon Carstensen, *The University of Wisconsin*, I (Madison, Wisconsin, 1949).

John Dewey, *Freedom and Culture* (New York, 1939).

———, *Individualism Old and New* (New York, 1930).

———, *Logic: the Theory of Inquiry* (New York, 1938).

———, No Matter What Happens — Stay Out, *Common Sense*, VIII: 11 (March, 1939).

William E. Dodd, *Ambassador Dodd's Diary, 1933-1938*, William E. Dodd, Jr. and Martha Dodd, eds., (New York, 1941).

———, Karl Lamprecht and Kulturgeschichte, *Popular Science Monthly*, LXIII: 418-424 (September, 1903).

———, *Woodrow Wilson and His Work* (New York, 1920).

Irwin Edman, *Philosopher's Holiday* (New York, 1938).

Richard T. Ely, *Ground Under Our Feet* (New York, 1938).

John Rutherford Everett, *Religion in Economics* (New York, 1946).

Dixon Ryan Fox, *Herbert Levi Osgood, An American Scholar* (New York, 1924).

Leo Gershoy, *The French Revolution and Napoleon* (New York, 1933).

Edward Gibbon, *Memoirs of My Life and Writing* (London, 1891).

Louis Gottschalk, *Understanding History* (New York, 1950).

———, *The Era of the French Revolution* (New York, 1929).

———, *Jean Paul Marat, A Study in Radicalism* (New York, 1927).

Albert Bushnell Hart, A Dissent from the Conclusions of Professor Barnes, a Contribution to a Symposium Assessing the Blame for the World War, *Current History*, XX: 455 (June, 1924).

History of Blackhawk County, Iowa and Its People, John G. Hartman, Supervising Ed. (Chicago, 1915).

Charles Homer Haskins, *The Renaissance of the Twelfth Century* (Cambridge, Massachusetts, 1927).

———, *The Rise of Universities* (New York, 1923).

Luther V. Hendricks, *James Harvey Robinson* (New York, 1946).

Frank H. Hodder, The Genesis of the Kansas-Nebraska Act, State Historical Society of Wisconsin, *Proceedings,* 1912 (Madison, Wisconsin).

———, The Railroad Background of the Kansas-Nebraska Act, *Mississippi Valley Historical Review,* XII: 3-22 (June, 1925).

Richard Hofstadter, *The Age of Reform, From Bryan to F. D. R.* (New York, 1955).

———, *The American Political Tradition* (New York, 1955).

E. H. Holland, Tribute to Frank Heywood Hodder, *The Graduate Magazine* of the University of Kansas, XXXIV: 3 (January, 1936).

William Dean Howells, *Criticism and Fiction* (New York, 1891).

———, *The Rise of Silas Lapham* (Boston, 1886).

Ralph Gordon Hoxie (and others), *A History of the Faculty of Political Science, Columbia University* (New York, 1955).

Charles Hull, ed., *The Economic Writings of Sir William Petty* (Cambridge, England, 1889).

Henry James, *Selected Novels of Henry James* (New York, 1954).

William James, *Essays in Pragmatism* (New York, 1955).

J. F. Jameson, *The American Revolution Considered as a Social Movement* (New York, 1926).

Henry Johnson, *The Other Side of Main Street* (New York, 1943).

Sidney Kaplan, Social Engineers as Saviors: Effects of World War I on Some American Liberals, *Journal of the History of Ideas,* XVII: 347-369 (June, 1956).

Hans Kohn, *German History: Some New German Views* (Boston, 1954).

James C. Malin, Frank Heywood Hodder, 1860-1935, *Kansas Historical Quarterly,* V: 115-121 (May, 1936).

———, *Essays in Historiography* (Lawrence, Kansas, 1946).

———, *The Nebraska Question, 1852-1854* (Lawrence, Kansas, 1953).

Maurice Mandelbaum, *The Problem of Historical Knowledge* (New York, 1938).

Marjorie Medary, The History of Cornell College, *The Palimpsest,* XXXIV, 145-152 (April, 1953).

Charles Merriam, John W. Burgess, *Dictionary of American Biography,* XXI: 132-134.

Fulmer Mood, The Development of Frederick Jackson Turner as an Historical Thinker, *Publications* of The Colonial Society of Massachusetts (December, 1939).

G. E. Moore, William James' Pragmatism, *Philosophical Studies* (New York, 1922).

Edmund S. Morgan, *The Birth of the Republic* (Chicago, 1956).

Reinhold Niebuhr, *The Nature and Destiny of Man* (New York, 1941, 1943).

Herman Clarence Nixon, Precursors of Turner in the Interpretation of the American Frontier, *South Atlantic Quarterly,* XXVIII: 83-89 (January, 1929).

E. J. Oliver, *Coventry Patmore* (New York, 1956).

Vilfredo Pareto, *The Mind and Society,* I, *Non-Logical Conduct* (New York, 1935).

Vernon L. Parrington, *Main Currents in American Thought,* I (New York, 1927).

————, *The Beginnings of Critical Realism in America* (New York, 1930).

Lucien Price, *The Dialogues of A. N. Whitehead* (Boston, 1954).

Sir Herbert Read, *English Prose Style* (New York, 1955).

David Riesman, *Individualism Reconsidered* (Glencoe, Illinois, 1954).

James Harvey Robinson, History, *Columbia University Lectures on Science, Philosophy and Art, 1907-1908* (New York, 1908).

————, *The Mind in the Making* (New York, 1912).

————, The Newer Ways of Historians, *American Historical Review*, XXXV: 245-255 (January, 1930).

James Harvey Robinson and Charles A. Beard, *The Development of Modern Europe* (New York, 1907).

Elliott Roosevelt, *As He Saw It* (New York, 1946).

Wilhelm Roscher, *Principles of Political Economy*, I (Chicago, 1878).

Bertrand Russell, *A History of Western Philosophy* (New York, 1945).

————, *Philosophical Essays* (London, 1910).

George Sabine, *A History of Political Theory* (New York, 1950).

Edward Norman Saveth, *American Historians and European Immigrants* (New York, 1948).

A. M. Schlesinger, *The Colonial Merchants and the American Revolution* (New York, 1918).

William Holmes Stephenson, *The South Lives in History, Southern Historians and Their Legacy* (Baton Rouge, Louisiana, 1955).

Cushing Strout, The Twentieth Century Enlightenment, *American Political Science Review*, XLIX: 321-339 (June, 1955).

George Sokolsky, *Liberty Magazine*, XVII: 41-42 (May, 1940).

Frederick Jackson Turner, Social Forces in American History, *American Historical Review*, XVI: 217-233 (January, 1911).

————, *The Early Writings of Frederick Jackson Turner* with an Introduction by Fulmer Mood (Madison, Wisconsin, 1938).

————, *The Significance of Sections in American History* (New York, 1932).

Peter Viereck, *Shame and Glory of the Intellectuals* (Boston, 1953).

H. G. Wells, *What Is Coming? A European Forecast* (New York, 1951).

Morton G. White, *Social Thought in America, The Revolt Against Formalism* (New York, 1949).

William Appleman Williams, A Note on Charles Austin Beard's Search for a General Theory of Causation, *American Historical Review*, LXII: 59-80 (October, 1956).

Index

243